THE STRENGTH IN US ALL

SARA HENDERSON

MACMILLAN
AUSTRALIA

First published in Macmillan in 1994 by Pan Macmillan Publishers Australia
a division of Pan Macmillan Australia Pty Limited
63–71 Balfour Street, Chippendale, Sydney

Reprinted 1994 (twice)

National Library of Australia
cataloguing-in-publication data:

Henderson, Sara, 1936–
The strength in us all.
ISBN 0 7329 0783 7.

1. Henderson, Sara, 1936– . 2. Women ranchers—Australia—Biography. 3. Women in business—Australia—Biography.
I. Title.
636.0092

Typeset in 12/13 pt Bembo by Midland Typesetters

Printed and bound in Australia by
McPherson's Printing Group

CONTENTS

Acknowledgements vii

Preface ix

CHAPTER 1 *October* 1991 1

CHAPTER 2 *November* 1991—*December* 1991 19

CHAPTER 3 *January* 1992 47

CHAPTER 4 *February* 1992—*March* 1992 55

CHAPTER 5 *April* 1992 82

CHAPTER 6 *May* 1992 93

CHAPTER 7 *June* 1992—*July* 1992 115

CHAPTER 8 *August* 1992 145

CHAPTER 9 *September* 1992—*October* 1992 207

CHAPTER 10 *November* 1992 215

CHAPTER 11 *December* 1992 251

CHAPTER 12 *January* 1993 263

CHAPTER 13 *February* 1993—*March* 1993 271

CHAPTER 14 *April* 1993—*May* 1993 281

CHAPTER 15 *June* 1993 287

CHAPTER 16 *July* 1993 300

Epilogue 356

This book is dedicated to
LOVE …
in every form.

ACKNOWLEDGEMENTS

Once again I owe my survival to a wonderful family, be it ever so small—but slowly growing, also to true friends. And now since the publication of *From Strength to Strength*, to thousands of caring and genuine people who have come into my life by letter, phone, fax and in person. Without all of you this book would not have been possible. Your continual support, encouragement and strength have made it possible for me to survive.

The number of new friends the book has brought into my life is staggering. I am so fortunate—all the great things happening in my life, and all brought about by other human beings.

You are all, one could say, my extended family.

How does one define 'family'? Maybe as a group caring for, and interested in the welfare of, those they love. If this could be a definition, then a family's boundaries are infinite, in so much as, for as long as you live, you are extending your family, in all directions, every day of your life.

No matter what horrendous crime you read about or despicable human behaviour you hear about, they can invariably be traced back to a tragedy or family breakdown. Often the complete lack of a family life is to blame.

A FAMILY IS THE BASIC FOUNDATION OF THE WORLD. And to have a peaceful and harmonious planet, we must start right back at the foundations. We must make our immediate family strong and then radiate out and develop an extended family. Even one person and a pet, is a family and something to build on.

My extended family, I hope I can say, now includes all of the readers of *From Strength to Strength*, and all the people who have helped make both books possible.

A very special thanks again to Pan Macmillan and everyone connected with the publishing and selling of my books.

And a very, very special thanks to Marlee and Franz for working nonstop running the station while I was working, writing and travelling to conferences and on book tours. It could not have been possible if they had not carried my work load.

To one and all I say thank you … and reach out and extend your family.

PREFACE

Well, here it is, book number two. I never thought there would be another ... I never thought there would be a first!

I am still coming to terms with the fact that I wrote *From Strength to Strength* and that people have taken it to their hearts and it is so popular. I am even told of ten-month waiting lists at local libraries and only a four-day period in which to read the book.

I read the manuscript so many times between October 1991 and February 1992 that by the time it was ready for printing, I was sick of the sight of it. It wasn't until six months after publication that I actually sat down and read the finished product, which was quite different from the stack of loose pages that I had worked with for so many months, with its corrections, insertions and arrows pointing in every direction. When I put the book down I felt a small glow of pride, deep down, brought on by the knowledge that the book had been accepted with open arms.

And the message now is that you want me to write more. When my publisher suggested I write a sequel, my first reaction was, 'But so little time has passed!'. However, when I started to take stock of what had happened in my life since I put down my pen after *From Strength to Strength* and realised all the stories I had forgotten, I was amazed. My life seems to have become even more hectic—if that's possible—since I found I had a bestseller on my hands!

1992 was, to put it bluntly, one bloody hell of a year. Not as eloquently put as the Queen's *annus horribilis*, but when you're reading the following pages, I am sure you'll be quick to agree.

All the problems you read about in *From Strength to Strength* didn't just disappear when I won the Qantas/Bulletin Business Woman of the Year. No, the problems just kept on coming, and Marlee and I just had to cope as best we could.

But it was incredibly difficult and there were times when I really didn't think I would survive. It was my sixth year as 'captain of the ship' and I was showing distinct signs of fraying around the edges. All the endless hard work, long hours and continuous pressure were taking their toll. I had not had a break or a holiday for so long I could not remember the last time I had relaxed.

However, I could see a faint glimmer of light at the end of the tunnel and I just kept staggering on towards it. Throughout my journey down that tunnel I felt as if I were in a bowling alley, constantly dodging bowling balls that were being thrown at me, a good percentage of which scored direct hits.

By the middle of the year I was sure I was finished, I was so down physically, financially and emotionally that I could see no possible way to survive.

But then the letters started to arrive.

People from all over Australia and New Zealand sent, and are still sending, heart-warming letters that were so genuine and so touching, they could be from old friends. Almost all the letters told of personal struggles, heartbreak with children and court cases, and triumph over tragedy.

With all your problems and struggles to survive, you still took the time to write and pat us on the back and tell us what a wonderful job we were doing and to keep up the good work. Such genuine care, love and concern came to us through your words that it was humbling. So many people put faith in what we were struggling to achieve that there was no way Marlee and I could throw in the towel and quit, as tempted as we were.

And so, as the hundreds upon hundreds of letters came to me at Bullo, my strength and determination slowly returned and once more I started striding towards the light.

In a way, this book is a kind of thank you for all your wonderful letters, faxes, phone calls and visits. To thank you all for giving me the courage not to quit, and the strength to get through a very bad year. You asked me hundreds of questions about what was happening to us now, and so here are the answers.

For some reason *From Strength to Strength* stirred the true human spirit and evoked a whole range of human emotions. People ask my advice on how to survive, how to keep going and where to get the strength from to carry on. I'm not sure I have all the answers, but I hope this book helps you to see that the strength you need is right there inside you. I hope it helps you to keep on 'keeping on'. To keep fighting for the success, love and happiness in life that you deserve.

Sara Henderson, 1994

All the strength you need to achieve anything is within *you*.

Don't wait for a light to appear at the end of the tunnel, stride down there … and light the bloody thing yourself!

CHAPTER 1

October 1991

And the winner is … It was the 29th October 1991 and I was back again in the Regent Ballroom in Sydney. In a few seconds the 1992 Business Woman of the Year would be announced and my year would be at an end.

The excitement of the day was still there, but my nerves were in a lot better shape than at my own presentation the year before. Then, I was in a complete daze, with people carefully guiding me in the right direction; and the most terrifying aspect of that day was making my first speech. But this year I could relax and enjoy, and take in all the happenings.

The ballroom was packed, as usual. The event is by invitation only, and each year the invitations are never enough. You can glance around the room and tick off an endless list of famous names.

Mrs Hawke presented the award for the second year and again Helen Daley had all the proceedings running smoothly. Faces and names that were a blur to me the year before all came together and I spent a very enjoyable afternoon being a part of another great day—even though this time I wasn't the star attraction.

October 1991

When the luncheon finished and the photos of me with the new BWOY were taken, a group of us withdrew to the lounge and caught up on each others' lives over the past twelve months. We then wound up with dinner.

However, as thrilling as the day had been, the truly exciting event for me was the following day. The nerves I experienced on my award day were now back with me, in force! Because the next day I was to hand over my manuscript.

As the night wore on, the nerves increased, and there was very little sleeping done. After fitful dozing most of the night, my eyes refused to close, so at 4 a.m. I gave up the fight, and, reclining in a monstrous eight-foot-wide bed, in a beautiful air-conditioned suite at the Regent Hotel, I clasped my hands behind my head, stared at the light reflections on the ceiling, and thought back over the month. What a hectic, chaotic, non-stop panic it was. 'But what a finish!' I said to myself as I lay there in luxury …

The beginning of October we were still mustering, or I should say Marlee and the rest of the team were still mustering. I was writing full time, racing to meet the hand-over date for the manuscript.

The invitation for the 1992 Business Woman of the Year award was staring at me from the letter holder on my desk as I worked. The plan was I would fly to Sydney for the luncheon on the 29th and then hand over my manuscript to the publishers the next day. I was into a writing routine, a set amount of pages each day. These handwritten pages would be promptly whisked away by Carole, a wonderful Canadian, who put her life on hold to type my lifestory. Carole was responsible for the publisher receiving a well set out, neatly typed manuscript. If it had been up to me, I shudder to think what they would have had to work with.

Marlee had bought a word processor a few days after I signed the contract to write the book.

'It's wonderful, Mum,' she said. 'The salesman showed me. You can correct everything on the screen, and when it's the way you want it, just press a button and it prints a copy and stores it all on that little disk. And it's easy to operate!'

Famous last words! After flipping through the 300 pages of instructions—who writes those things?—I still didn't know how to feed in the paper. However, I persevered, and was finally having a wonderful time moving words and phrases all over the screen, when satisfied with the complete page, I did as instructed: stored. Even with my limited knowledge, I was really starting to like this modern marvel ... then Uncle Dick turned off the generator to check the oil in the engine and I lost everything.

I quietly covered the word processor and went back to my trusty old typewriter. Well, not straight away; I wrote my first copy in longhand. As hard as I try, for some reason I cannot type my first thoughts straight onto a keyboard. When I sit down in front of that keyboard and try to get started, nothing happens. So, as time consuming as it is, my first thoughts go down in pencil.

It was while scribbling away that I silently hoped a good typist would just happen to wander by—and my prayers were answered when Carole arrived. Carole was very proficient with a word processor; Carole was very proficient, period. My stack of handwritten pages disappeared at such a rate I had to start writing at 3 a.m. each morning to keep a reasonable distance ahead.

By October I was writing the ending, and going through the final corrections for the first half of the book, and all this was disappearing into the remarkable machine.

Carole's plan was to store the whole manuscript and print out the finished product during the last few days. This unnerved me no end, watching all my hard work disappearing, so she assured me, onto a small disk. Remembering Uncle Dick's oil-changing habits, and thinking just of the generator breakdowns that occurred so regularly at the 'Bullo River Electricity Company', I made one request:

'Print out daily.'

Carole said it wasn't necessary—everything was safely stored, the machine was completely 'fail-safe'.

I persisted.

'Humour me. Print out daily.'

Along with not trusting my all to a machine, I think mostly I wanted to see the pile of printed pages growing each day, to prove to myself that I *was* actually writing a book. I needed to see the evidence. Whatever the reason, it was fortunate I insisted.

So my days would start with me correcting the final draft and writing the end of my story, in pencil. At about 8 a.m. I would hand all this over to Carole and we would go over the corrections for the final draft, with her questioning various Australian expressions and some of my 4 a.m. hieroglyphics. Some of those took me a few minutes to decipher.

She would then start typing and I would move on to any station work that was urgent, or write if I had a clear day.

But one day at the beginning of the month I knew I wouldn't get much work done. In fact, there would not be much work done by anyone, because some Hercules transport planes were coming to Bullo to do touchdown, take-off practice on our airstrip.

Bullo has been a practice strip for many, many years for the big Hercules. Charlie, of course, had offered the strip for use at any time, and because of its clear approaches and isolation, the offer was readily accepted. So the big planes made regular visits to Bullo for training sessions with the new pilots. This was their second visit this year; the previous visit was on the 15th June, which was very fitting because it was the anniversary of Charlie's death.

The Hercules making night touchdowns are a breath-taking sight. To put it into words, simply … in the Outback darkness, with the stars as a backdrop they look like flying Christmas trees.

It certainly was a spectacular event to mark that anniversary, and I know Charlie would have approved.

Most of our staff had never seen a plane of this size up

close, and they were naturally all very excited. Most of them were new to station work, so *everything* was new and exciting. We did, however, have two dyed in the wool, fair dinkum stockmen, who, because all the new hands looked to them in cattle work, felt they should appear as if a Hercules landing on the strip was commonplace, and certainly nothing to get worked up about. But when the giant planes landed, there they were, out with cameras working overtime.

When the planes taxied towards the group lined up along the fence, all mouths just fell open and cameras were momentarily forgotten. As the planes got closer and closer, and bigger and bigger, our two stockmen forgot their cool, and started to stumble backwards, fell over in their haste to retreat, and were heard to exclaim, as they lay sprawled in the big planes' path: 'Holy shit!'

There followed a conducted tour inside and out, and over. Cameras ran hot, taking photos of people waving from the hatch on top of the plane. Two jeeps were unloaded, along with the ground crew. The crew's job included laying out the landing lights and constantly patrolling the airstrip paddock to make sure none of the cattle decided at the wrong time to jump the fence and wander onto the strip for a munch of grass.

However, one particular cow was at that moment on one of her night sorties. A very frustrated signal officer finally came to Marlee and said he was having great difficulty keeping this cow off the strip. Whenever he tried to shoo her away she kept charging him. Marlee went to his rescue; it was one of our older poddy calves (orphaned calves which are hand-fed and raised until they are big enough to survive on grass. They are called 'poddy' calves because without their mother's milk they develop a big tummy, or a 'pod', for the first six months or so.) When Marlee called her name, Buckshot walked over to her and let Marlee put a rope around her neck to lead her quietly back to the garden. The feed being much better there than the airstrip, Buckshot munched happily on the grass for the rest of the evening, while we happily watched the aeronautical display.

The big planes would touchdown, roll for a hundred yards or so, then the pilot would gun the engines for take-off, do a lazy bank, circle and approach the strip again. Standing at the far end of the airstrip, we watch, captivated, as the Hercules appears out of the darkness. A massive bank of lights grows bigger and bigger; the hum of the engine, which is surprisingly quiet on approach, increases in volume as the plane races towards you on touchdown. There are amazing patterns created in the dust as it swirls up from the propeller turbulence and dances in the lights, only to be swept away a split second later, and replaced by the next creation from the spin of the blades. At this stage, that is all you can see: giant lights and swirling dust patterns racing towards you at frightening speed. Then a deafening roar as this huge black shape blots out the sky. The roar continues as the plane climbs gracefully in a lazy bank; then, as it levels out to fly the leg down the airstrip, the pilot eases on the throttle. The lights disappear as the plane is on the leg, down the strip. After a few minutes it turns a few miles out and once more the giant lights signal its approach on another touchdown run.

Even if you don't love aeroplanes, it is still an overwhelming experience.

They finished about ten, loaded the landing lights, jeeps, and ground crew, circled the homestead, and flew past in formation. They waggled their wings and we watched the flying Christmas trees slowly fade into the darkness of the night.

Next day it was back to the normal work routine.

1991 was what I called our 'water year'—the year we sank five new bores (wells). We hired a very competent drilling company out of Alice Springs, who did the job in record time. Or it seemed record time, compared with the drilling we'd had done the year before. That was a nightmare experience of continuous breakdowns: old drill rig, old machinery, old trucks; even their fridge broke down. At one stage the crew disappeared, without a word of explanation, and were gone over a week. Finally, after having arrived months late in the first place, and after weeks of breakdowns and delays, they disappeared for good, without finishing the job.

So we brought in the second drillers, and what a difference! They were a pleasure to watch. A beautiful hydraulic modern rig, spick-and-span, not a thing out of place, and what an efficient crew ... although danger lurks everywhere, even with the most efficient of crews.

The last hole was to be drilled only three miles from the homestead, so Marlee insisted I come to watch this marvellous rig in operation. All the other bores had been easy, drilling mostly through dirt and clay, and the holes had been shallow, striking water at one hundred feet. This one had to be difficult. The drill hit a barrier of sand and rock, making the drilling process slow because of the changing of the bits. They finally broke through with a bit that looked like two porcupines rolling together.

When the water started up the pipe it started to get very wet and muddy around the work area, so Marlee and I moved back about twenty feet and sat on the grass, out of harm's way—or so we thought! A great whoosh of water and everything else came up the pipe with such force it hit the yoke just above ground level, did a ninety-degree turn, and shot out in our direction.

'Look out!' was shouted at us from everywhere, but luckily the noise coming up the pipe had already alerted us, giving us those precious few seconds to move. And move we did! However, a few stones still managed to catch Marlee on the side of the face, cutting her cheek ... enough to realise what could have happened if we had both caught the full blast.

The crew congratulated us on our speed, and we said it must have been all those years of practice, dodging wild bulls in the yards. Any way you look at it, it was a lucky escape!

We drilled more bores than we intended, or could afford, but with our 48-mile rough road over rocky mountains we had to utilise that marvellous team while we had it.

We equipped two bores but had to cap the other three. They will have to wait until we can afford the machinery.

It was fortunate that we'd put in the bores because 1991 turned out to be the worst Wet Season in the station's rainfall records for twenty-eight years. The surface water dried up so quickly that before long we were pumping water out of the bores into creek beds and billabongs, so the cattle didn't have to walk long distances between their feed and water.

We did do other improvements during the year, but by far the best, and a mega giant step towards a proper operation, was the new two-inch water pipeline to Nutwood Paddock. All two and a half miles of it. Nutwood is one of the most used watering points on the station, and has been a nightmare situation for as long as I can remember.

There was a line to Nutwood, which was laid about fifteen years earlier and should have lasted a lifetime. But like all things done on the station back then, it was handled in the 'anything will do to get it working' fashion. According to Uncle Dick the instructions from the manufacturers on how to lay poly pipe were: the pipe had to be buried deep; no lumps of dirt or rocks to be used as cover material; pipe to be laid at cool time of day; markers to be put at joins; and pipe never to be dragged over rough ground.

Again according to Uncle Dick, the pipe had in fact been laid in a twelve-inch ditch, in the heat of the day, so that when the poly cooled it shrank and pulled out of the joins. It was covered with dirt, rocks, cow dung, pieces of wire, you name it. The biggest problem, however, was not having markers at the joins. This caused endless hours of digging around in giant pools of mud, just trying to find the pipe in order to locate and fix the broken join. But the one that really upset Dick was that the pipe had been dragged over rough ground, which resulted in deep gouges along it. Eventually pressure build-up would cause the pipe to split along these weak points. All these faults became evident to Dick during his fifteen years of constant maintenance on the line—repairing the split sections, the holes rubbed by rocks, and rejoining the parted joins. During the years Charles was running the station the only connection I had with this endless problem was that Dick would regularly hand me orders for more pipe joiners and rolls of more pipe. And whenever I needed the handyman, he was always in Nutwood fixing the pipeline.

When I took over the running of the station this was just one of an endless list of problems I had to face. Knowing I had too much on my plate Dick just kept ordering joiners and pipe, while he kept a constant watch to make sure the cattle always got a drink. They had grown up with this very inadequate watering system and were very well mannered and patient. You could see them sitting under the trees, in the shade, waiting for one group to finish drinking, then quietly the next group would stand and walk over for their drink. During the hot weather, when they needed to drink at least three times a day, they would even have nightshifts.

But as our herd increased in number and the rainy season each year became worse, waterwise, the problem could no longer be contained. Nutwood Creek was drying up, so pumping water was the only solution. Dick finally came to me and said the water problem had him beat. He was pumping twenty-four hours a day and still couldn't deliver enough water for the cattle to drink—and we were in the cool months. From September on, when the temperature started to climb they would need double the quantity. The problem had to be solved. And now. What was needed was a bigger storage tank, to fill overnight for a reserve for the heavy drinking sessions during the day.

Many storage possibilities were discussed, but we finally agreed on a half-million-gallon turkey nest. Dirt was about the only thing our corrosive water couldn't eat through.

I had better pause here and explain a 'turkey nest,' just in case you think it's for a bird. It is built out of dirt, is circular, and ends up looking like a very large turkey's nest; but it holds water. It really is an above-the-ground dam, but can be built out in the middle of a flat paddock, just as long as the soil is right. Sandy soil, for instance, is no good; swampy areas, where water sits for long periods after rain, are usually fine. A bulldozer or scraper is used to build the nest. The size of the circle depends on how much storage is required. Dirt is laid, layer by layer, and is compacted by the weight of the machine constantly driving over it. The base of the wall is around forty-five feet wide, tapering to about fifteen feet wide at the top. The height of our wall is about fourteen feet. We thought the whole operation was *massive*, and were proudly showing our great step forward in development to our stock inspector, Bluey Lewis, when he told us the next-door property had a five-million-gallon one.

'It's so big, the tide goes out,' he said casually.

Nevertheless, we were very excited with our newest acquisition, and Dick installed new pipe junctions so the water could flow into the turkey nest at night and not into the old storage tank.

Our next problem soon surfaced, however. After pumping day and night for a week there was only a few inches of water in the bottom of the nest.

'The line is just not big enough,' said Dick with a frown, knowing full well that those few words meant the expenditure of many thousands of dollars. You would think running water through a pipe from point 'a' to point 'b' over flat ground would be a relatively easy exercise. Not so, and I was about to find out how wrong that thought was.

Two and a half miles of two-inch poly pipe is not cheap. And although I wanted the installation done properly money had to be top priority and we had to economise wherever possible. Dick knew this without being told, so he said maybe we could get away with laying only half the line, because some of the original one and a half-inch pipeline had been replaced about five years before with two-inch pipe. By what method, he didn't say. Saving any amount of money was acceptable to me, so I ordered the pipe and an endless amount of joiners and a booster pump to push the water down the line faster. When the one and a half-inch line was dug up, it turned out to have a join every few feet!

Dick stood looking at it, shaking his head. 'The stupid bastards dragged the pipe.' He wasn't looking at all the joins, he was pointing to parts of the pipe with scoring along it. 'These parts didn't split, but about every other part did.'

The new pipe was laid strictly according to instructions. To lay the old line needed many hands, picks and shovels, and weeks and weeks of digging. The trench for the new line needed only Marlee and the grader. A tilted blade did two two and a half mile neat cuts, at the correct depth, and the whole job was done in an afternoon. The new line had a permanent marker at each join and followed the road, not cross country like the old line. Cross country certainly had its problems. I remember one of the stockmen standing at the door saying he couldn't repair the break in the Nutwood line because a big bull buffalo was wallowing in the mud pool around the break and was refusing to be budged.

Dick installed the booster pump and we were ready to go. There he was, at the Nutwood end, waiting for 'big mobs' of water to flow. Marlee and I were back at the bore site. Dick was talking to us on the two-way radios in the Toyotas.

Marlee started the pump. I stayed well away—vividly remembering my last encounter with a pump, all of twenty-six years ago. I had no desire to renew my acquaintance. We waited; nothing. Dick's disappointment came over the radio, mumbling to himself in very descriptive language, forgetting we were listening. We were all in deep thought over the 'noflow' problem when an almighty crack came from behind me.

'What the ★#!★ was that!?' came over the radio. I turned to see poly pipe rising out of the ground like the Loch Ness monster! It flipped down in a whip-cracking action, the whiplash from this action travelling right to where the pipe entered the booster pump. If the pump hadn't been bolted down it would have been airborne, and it weighed around 200 pounds plus! When the pump held its ground, after much shaking and rattling, the shockwave continued on down the pipe and finished up blasting out into the big squatter tank, where the pipe was attached to a fitting in the side. The crack we heard was the pressure blasting into the tank and finally exploding in an enormous fountain. Which drenched everyone and everything in the area. What was it with pumps and me? I didn't have long to ponder this phenomenon because the next shockwave hit and exploded once more. Dick was screaming something into the radio, but at our end it sounded like the *1812 Overture* and the 4th July all rolled into one, with each oom-pah-pah stroke of the pump. Marlee quickly turned it off and the poly pipes once again became lifeless. Until the silence was shattered by Dick screaming over the radio: 'Turn off the bloody pump!'

He drove back up the line. It had held. The tank had not fared as well; there were a few fractures around the fitting but it certainly couldn't have taken more. Dick rigged a temporary line over the top of the tank and secured it with baling wire. I told him about the pipes rising out of the ground and the exploding fountains of water and he looked at me patiently. So I told him to turn on the pump to watch. Poly pipes rose up from the ground all around him, like a scene from *Fantasia*. The temporary pipe over the top of the tank whipped through the wire in seconds, and was dancing and spraying everywhere.

'Resistance,' was all Dick said, standing there thoroughly drenched, after he had turned the pump off. 'The water is hitting a blockage, and the pressure builds up and rebounds back up the line.'

'What's it hitting?'

'Dunno.'

Next time around we wired the pipe at five points around

the top of the tank, before it disappeared into the depths. This time around I was standing on a ladder; my job was to push against the pipe to stop it working free of the tiedowns. Dick was adjusting the pressure chamber, hoping to reduce the whip, and Marlee was standing on the pipe, between the pump and the tank. We tried again ... as the pipe worked free of each tiedown the whip increased. It was down to two wires, the ladder was gone and I was swinging to and fro with each oom-pah-pah. Next second I was sitting on the ground with Marlee and the pipe was doing its thing again—watering everything in sight!

Well, it took all day to solve the problem. The day, and a good part of the night, was spent driving up and down the line, joining and rejoining the pipe where it had blown. What a blessing the markers were!

I lost count of how many times that line was joined, but finally, by torchlight and headlights, the pump was working, on a very low setting, with the pipes at the tank vibrating slightly. The waterflow had hardly improved, but we had to put our investigation on hold while water was pumped to the cattle, who, bless their hearts, had waited patiently and watched us through all this, and were still lined up at 3 a.m. to have their sunset drink.

The problem was right under our noses, or right at our feet to be more precise. We were deep in thought and staring at the old pipeline lying there in all its assorted lengths and sizes and amazing variations on joining methods (some included inner-tube rubber and fencing wire). It amazed me that any water had got through at all. I began to think: if this half had all these weird and wonderful 'make do' repairs, so must the other half. It did! When the rest of the pipe was dug up, it was just as bad. There was so much resistance on the line, it's a wonder the pressure build-up didn't knock the tank right off its stand.

Another mile and a quarter of pipe was ordered and put in place. Now we really *did* have a two-inch line all the way to Nutwood.

October 1991

The big moment had arrived. Dick was back down in Nutwood, at the end of the pipe. Marlee started the pump. I stood back at a fair distance, waiting for all hell to break loose.

Nothing. Everything hummed quietly.

'Are you sure it's pumping?' I asked Marlee.

'Feel the pipe.'

I put my hand on the Nutwood line and could feel the pulse of the pump pushing the water down the line.

Suddenly Dick's voice came over the two-way. 'Better get down here, we have a problem.'

We drove in silence. What now?

We saw the problem as we approached, but it was a problem that made us all smile. The water was coming out of the pipe with such force it was shooting right over the tank, missing it completely. This was solved quickly and the water finally gushed forth into the tank, filling it rapidly.

'I would venture to say we have increased the flow,' Dick said, jubilant.

Finally, after all those terrible years, we now had a good water supply to Nutwood. But we weren't getting off that easily. We went from not enough water to too much! The next morning the cattle were swimming around in a small inland sea. Most were sloshing around in mud. Our poor cows … in twenty-four hours they'd gone from waiting most of the day for a drink from 10 gallons of water to swimming in thousands of gallons.

Within a few days, however, the paddock dried out. Dick changed the line over to the still-empty turkey nest and it slowly filled a few thousand gallons a night. We installed new drinking troughs and pulled down the old water tank, which was a converted old grain silo.

So, after many nightmare years of water shortage and water panic, the old watering point at Nutwood was gone, forever! Replaced by a half-million-gallon turkey nest, and a hand-fashioned delivery pipeline. But best of all, the cattle didn't have to line up for hours for a drink. They were really funny with the new set-up, and approached with caution. They stayed way back in the shade of the trees for quite a while to survey the scene. The bulls came forward first and did a good deal of sniffing. The cows and calves watched from behind the tree-line protection. You could just imagine the calves saying, 'Mummy, I want a drink.' And the cows replying, 'Just wait till your father checks this out!'

Although somewhat bewildered by their palatial drinking arrangement, they soon adjusted and treat it all now as old hat.

We had had rain in September and heavy storms kept gathering at regular intervals. Although the rain was light, it did look like we were in for an early wet, so I ordered the first load of our Wet Season fuel (diesel fuel to last us six months during the time our road is cut off by the rising rivers), and it arrived around the 20th October.

I was writing non-stop by this point and each day the pile of typed pages slowly grew as the pressure to finish on time increased. Carole again pointed out the time wasted printing out each day. I insisted, and she patiently tapped her foot each afternoon as the machine clicked away, printing out the day's work.

One week to go and the writing, correcting and reading all came together into one finished manuscript. I put down the pencil with a sigh. Finished! I thought. What will I do all day now?

What an amateur! I didn't have a clue that I wouldn't draw a calm breath for the next twelve months. But this was all in front of me; at that point I was naive enough to think that my job ended with the handing over of my manuscript. Boy, was I in for a shock.

I was leaving for Sydney on Sunday 27th, so I wanted to finish on the Thursday, leaving Friday free to sit quietly and read it all through for the last time, and keeping Saturday in reserve for the unexpected.

Carole said she would print out a second copy from the

disk, to keep in a safe place at the station. She had heard of an original manuscript being lost without any copies. She would keep a spare copy just in case I lost it, or the publishers did. I said, 'Okay', though I had my hands on the original and it wasn't going anywhere! I think Carole just wanted to show me that the book really *was* on that little disk. I had made it clear I didn't believe so.

So at about 3 p.m. on Thursday Carole pressed the key marked 'Print' and we waited for the printer to churn out the last twenty pages of manuscript she had typed into the machine that day.

Nothing happened.

There was a lot of mumbling and key-pressing for the next five minutes. Carole was very upset. 'It won't print out!' was all she said.

We called the repair man, and after an hour or so of being told over the phone to check this, check that, the result was he had no idea why the machine was behaving in this manner. It would have to come into the workshop.

So Carole had to retype the last twenty pages again, printing each page as she went. This only put us slightly behind schedule; but the real bombshell hit the next day.

After many more phonecalls Carole came to me visibly shaken. It appeared that the machine not only would not store, but now it had managed to wipe the entire book from the disk. The disk was blank! That meant the only presentable copy for the publishers was my insisted upon, daily print-out copy. We still had the first typed draft of course, but it was too riddled with corrections and a far cry from the finished manuscript because all the corrections over the months had been done on the word processor.

Carole was very upset. As for me, I never let the one and only copy out of my sight. It was my constant companion, I even took it to bed!

And even now, lying in bed at the Regent, thinking about this, and what would have happened if we hadn't printed out daily, still made my stomach lurch.

I looked at the clock—8 a.m. Finally it was time to shower and dress for my appointment.

I sat down in the publisher's office and was introduced to all the people who would be working on my book. We were all very formal, as most people are on the first meeting. But it soon became evident they were all waiting for the manuscript—the big moment had arrived. So, with shaking hands, a very happy but nervous me handed over the only copy of the manuscript. James, my publisher, had obviously heard the same story as Carole about the lost manuscript, because he turned to one of the staff and said, 'Please run off two copies now.'

Many strange feelings coursed through me at the moment the manuscript left my hands. There was disbelief—I had never before been able to persevere long enough to write a two-page letter, yet here I was handing over a 400-page manuscript! That it was about my life caused another emotion—was it enough of my life to make an interesting story? Was it *too much*? However, the overpowering emotion was one of dread—would anyone find it interesting? Would it even *sell*? The thrill of writing the book had taken full possession of my mind during the time I was writing, so there'd been no room for any thoughts of doubt. But now that I had finished, these thoughts of doubt seemed to be my only thoughts—apart from thinking constantly of all the changes I still wanted to make.

Though I suppose uppermost in my mind at that moment was: would it even be published? If the publishers didn't like it, the whole thing would stop there. What a turmoil my mind and stomach were in! I desperately wanted to know what they thought, but knew it would be some weeks before I'd hear anything.

I left the office in a daze and took a cab back to the city. I wandered around the shops, buying gifts for Marlee and Danielle. Finally, I went back to the hotel.

There were several messages from Marlee, all saying the same thing: 'Call me!'

I did.

'Well?' was the first thing she said.

'We'll know in a few weeks.'

'What? What do you mean, "a few weeks"?' She continued, 'Aren't the publishers reading it now? *Why* aren't they reading it now?'

I patiently explained that my manuscript was not the only one the publishers were handling. They read stacks of manuscripts a day.

'Well, tell them to stop wasting their time. Just read yours!' she said indignantly.

'Marlee, maybe your judgement could be just a little biased, considering I am your mother. Contrary to what you believe, this is not the only manuscript in the world.'

She still had her say about what they should be doing, but finally I convinced her that we would just have to be patient and wait the few weeks. Difficult as it was.

I flew back to the station on the 31st. For the first few days I wandered around the house aimlessly. I would wake at 3 a.m. to jot down something to put in the book, only to realise I had finished it.

I finally settled back to 'life after writing a book', and the station work began to occupy my day again.

CHAPTER 2

November 1991–
December 1991

It was definitely spring. Love was in the air and Cupid was working overtime at Bullo. Carole, for the most part of October, had walked around with stars in her eyes. The cause was a certain dashing Irishman named Dermot. Dermot was working on Bullo for the cattle season. At first I was sure being lovestruck was the reason the manuscript had disappeared from the disk. As October progressed Carole became more and more starry eyed, and a few times when Dermot came into the office to speak to her during the day she needed quite a while before she was normal enough to carry on working.

But Dermot's effect on Carole, or Carole herself, were not to blame for the wayward manuscript. When the machine was checked in the workshop, it seems a big black bug had walked into the disk slot in the side of the machine and kept walking, and finally was all mashed up in the disk drive or vice versa. The repair man said it was a first; but first or not it still meant a lost manuscript and a new disk drive.

Apart from this hiccough Dermot and Carole did have a very cute but difficult courtship. It was a bit like 'love in a goldfish bowl'. The cute part was the ingeniousness of their dating. They would both dress up for their date, and Dermot, in white shirt, tie and suit, would call and knock on Carole's door. He would sometimes take her a bunch of wild flowers and chocolates ... or a block of chocolate. Occasionally a normal block wasn't even available and it would have to be cooking chocolate. He would then escort her to the living room area, away from the rest of the mob sitting in the kitchen area. They would sit and have cocktails and snacks, listen to soft music and watch the sun set.

Earlier in the day Carole would have prepared a special dinner for two, and with candlelight and background music, they would now pretend they were in a restaurant. Carole would dash out to the kitchen every now and then to bring in the next course. Dermot would serve the wine, then they would sit down and continue the evening. Sometimes they would dance cheek to cheek to some romantic music. Of course all the while the rest of the staff would make cat calls from the kitchen and walk past and wave at them at regular intervals. That was the difficult part. But despite the minor intrusions, they would have a lovely evening, and as the weeks went pleasantly by, their love grew. They left Bullo near the end of the season and were married in Canada in 1992.

The next helicopter muster went ahead as scheduled and we had our hands full with the work of handling a yard of cattle. We had the sale cattle drafted out of the mob in a few days and were waiting for the road-train transport to arrive. The trucking company sent in a driver not experienced on station roads and, naturally, he came to grief on one of our jump-ups (a steep incline up a mountainside). This jump-up was not only a steep climb but also a tight curve, a very tight semicircle. The driver didn't swing wide enough and ran out of road, the result being the second trailer ran out of road and ended up hanging over the edge. The prime-mover and the first of the double-decker trailers were on the road, with most of the second trailer out in midair.

The driver held the rig with the brakes, and he quickly followed up with big piles of rocks behind each set of wheels. He was thirty miles from the homestead and twenty miles in from the highway, about halfway in our front drive. He called his base on his truck radio and explained his position, or predicament. They phoned us and explained what had happened, and it was then up to us to solve the problem.

Marlee drove the grader out the thirty miles to pull the trailer back on the road. First she pulled the prime-mover and trailer further up the jump-up, hoping the second trailer would swing back towards the road and the back wheels could get some traction, but it wasn't working out that way. The second trailer started to swing out further into midair, so she had to stop or the coupling gear in between the two trailers would have started to twist, making towing impossible and also costing a lot of money to repair. The driver told her just to keep pulling and said the trailer would eventually swing back, but Marlee said, 'In what condition?' and added that she didn't think the owner would be pleased. The driver decided it might be best if they tried Marlee's plan. So they chained the hanging trailer to the grader, unhooked the prime mover and first trailer and towed them up and over the jump-up. They then came back to the homestead in the truck, and then Marlee 'walked' the bulldozer to the site. This took six hours.

Her plan was to build a dirt ramp up the side of the cliff, at a 90° angle to the road, in the middle of the curve, alongside of the trailer hanging over the edge. It took many hours and many tons of dirt. When the ramp was finished she walked the dozer up until it was level with the back of the airborne trailer and directed the truck driver to attach the chains to the axle of the trailer, then to the dozer blade. Marlee lifted the blade high in the air and slowly walked the dozer up the ramp. The back of the trailer slowly swung around until it was hanging over the road, behind the grader, instead of at a ninety-degree angle, out in space. Marlee slowly let the blade down and lowered the trailer safely onto the road. The coupling gear on the trailer wasn't even damaged, so the last trailer finally joined the rest of the rig and arrived safely at the yards. The cattle were loaded and, just to be on the safe side, Marlee followed the truck to the end of our road. She wanted to make sure the driver didn't get into any more strife because he now had our cattle on board.

A week of branding and attending to the various requirements of the animals in the yards followed. I don't like the branding part of the work. I think my favourite time is when the calves that are too young to wean are let out of the yard, and are then 'mated' up again with their mothers. It's just like Mum picking up the children from school. As each little calf goes out the 'bush' gate (the bush gate is the gate that lets the animal back out into the paddock, or free), the calf is barring all the time. All the cows are waiting around the calf pen, calling and sniffing and licking their calves through the rails. The older cows know the routine and casually munch on the grass further out in the paddock. They know their calf's call and when it comes racing out the gate, screaming, 'Mum! Where are you, Mum! I'm starving! Haven't had any milk for days—just water and hay. And, boy, do you know what they do to you in there? Have you ever been in there? Mum?', the old cow will just lift her head, let out a long, powerful m-o-o-o, and say, 'Over here, dear.'

The inexperienced young mothers are just as bad as the calves. The entire time their babies are in the calf pen they pace up and down the fence, frantic, mooing all the time, licking and sniffing their calves through the rails, panicking every time a calf makes a slight noise. If they do move away from the fence for a drink or to graze, they come thundering back as soon as any calf sneezes. They rush up to each baby as it's let out the gate and sniff it all over, to make certain it's not theirs. When the right calf finally does come out, they have trouble recognising it as their own, having sniffed three or four hundred calves before it. The calf then has to chase the udder around in circles saying, 'It's me, Mum. Can I have a drink? I'm famished!' The young mum keeps sniffing and the baby keeps pleading: 'It's me!', until finally Mum stops panicking and recognises her baby and lets it have a drink of milk.

Carole and Dermot were still very much lovestruck when Cupid appeared again. This time I was very, very happy, because he found Marlee's heart. For the first time in years, I saw the smile come back into her eyes!

She was working down at the main yard site, near the homestead, unloading the portable panels from the truck with the front-end loader. She jumped down from the cabin, a fair jump of about three feet, landed on a rock hidden in the loose dirt and turned her ankle. Hopping back to the house, she was halfway across the flat when Franz, who was also on his way back to the house, came up behind her. He swept her into his arms and carried her the rest of the way. I was in the kitchen cooking when he walked through the back door with Marlee in his arms. Thinking she was seriously injured, my heart immediately hit the floor. Then I saw the smile on her face and I knew it wasn't serious.

Franz carefully lowered her into a chair and Marlee thanked him formally. He accepted formally and went about his business. I looked at her ankle. It did not appear broken; however, it was very swollen and I could see it was a bad sprain.

'Well, I'll call the doctor, but I know he'll tell you to put your foot up and rest it for a while,' I said.

Marlee: 'Can't do that. We still have the rest of the cattle to load.'

Me: 'I don't know how you're going to get around.'

'I will carry her.' Franz was back again, standing there, looking down at Marlee, smiling.

It was when she looked up to say 'Thank you' that I saw her eyes were smiling. Franz immediately sparked my interest. He had only been with us a few weeks and I'd been so busy I had hardly spoken to him. I decided then that I would find out more.

My constant prayer was for Marlee to find happiness again. She had been a very sad human being since we lost her Charlie, hard working and pleasant when in company, but lacking in that zest for life that was so much Marlee. No matter how she tried to hide her sadness, one look into her eyes and I could physically feel her pain.

Yet suddenly here I was seeing the twinkle creeping back into those lovely sad eyes and the corners of her mouth lift in that little extra curl when she now smiled. My prayers it seemed had been answered and I immediately filed another: 'Please God, let her have found another wonderful man.'

Marlee and Franz continued to be polite to each other and Marlee didn't say anything to me. But I was sure of the train of events that would unfold sooner or later so I patiently waited for Cupid's arrow to take effect.

I was sitting in the office, catching up on the urgent paperwork, as usual. I really do hate office work, so I leave it to the last desperate ditch and then attack full on, until the super urgent emergencies are dealt with. Then I leave the rest of the work until it gets bad again and start the routine all over again. I know it sounds silly, but it is the only way I can cope with office work.

It was the first week of November and I was attacking a pile of urgent papers when the fax machine started clicking and whirring. I skated my office chair over to the receiving tray, glumly thinking 'more bloody work', picked up the single sheet of paper and was greeted with a

> *Dear Sara,*
> *Very late last night I finished your manuscript. It is wonderful! And I can't congratulate you enough. It needs a bit of work here and there (I am leaving those comments to the editor) but all manuscripts need that. Not all*

manuscripts however have the enthralling, compelling and utterly readable qualities of yours. We are excited and proud to be publishing this book and take it from me—you've got a bestseller on your hands.
Kindest regards,
James

P.S. The ending was superb.

I sat there with tears streaming down my face. I had to keep brushing them away so I could read and reread the fax. I was so happy—and relieved. They liked it …

Marlee came into the office and saw me crying.

'What's the matter?' she asked with deep concern, ready to do battle with whoever had reduced me to this state. 'Tell me who did this to you!' She put her arms around me.

'No, no, everything is all right,' I managed to say, and I handed her the fax.

Her face lit up as she danced around the room, singing, 'I told you so! I told you so! Didn't I tell you? Didn't I? Oh, think of all the things we can buy—an air-conditioned D-10 bulldozer, with remote television to work the rippers, you know you can't see your rippers on the D-10s and … Oh, yes a new Toyota. We can retire Matilda! [Marlee's brave and true, but very old, utility, which just keeps on going, somehow] Oh, and …'

'Just a minute, the book isn't even published yet, then the people have to like it, and, more importantly, buy it. We're a long way from anything positive yet, so just keep your long shopping list in your back pocket. One step at a time.'

'I'm telling you this book is going to sell. It's going to be very popular, I just know it. And when it does all the things I told you it would do, right from that first day we talked with James in the hotel in Sydney, I'm going to say "I told you so", again.'

But despite this terribly exciting event in our lives, we still had to get on with the work. There was no cracking open of the champagne—we still had cattle in the yards and as far as I was concerned it was too early to be celebrating.

The trucks from the trucking company were late again and we were waiting for the office to call to say the truck was stuck somewhere along our road. But they had problems other than our road, namely too many cattle to move and not enough trucks to do it. We ended up with the same driver again. This time he got past the round jump-up but managed to get bogged in a creek crossing and just about every other place imaginable, all the way to the yards. Marlee had to go to his rescue again, with the grader, and tow him out of each bog. She was still on crutches and apart from driving the grader could only give orders ... well, she is good at that.

Having got him to the yards they loaded the cattle and Marlee followed him back in the grader, while one of the stockmen went with the driver in our truck. The grader was slower than the trucks and by the time Marlee reached the crossing over the Bullo River the driver had the road-train hopelessly bogged in the middle of the river. The road crossing the river is gravel about twelve inches thick in a river bed of pebbles and more gravel, nobody, but nobody gets bogged on the river crossing. But our favourite driver did! He had the prime mover at an angle to the road and buried to the axles. Where you come up out of the riverbed the road cuts into a twenty-foot-high riverbank. To pull him back onto the road, so the truck could be pulled up the cutaway, Marlee had to tow at an angle with a very long chain. He had dug the truck in so far that the only way the grader could move it, and for the truck to get traction, was to jerk the wheels out of the massive hole he had dug, in a rocking action. This was repeated many times, until finally he shouted, 'One more big pull should do it!'

Marlee backed down once more, right up to the radiator of the truck—giving as much run-up as possible—and revved up the cat engine, to give the grader 'pulling' power. The chain ran out after the grader and snapped taut as all the slack was taken up. The grader motor roared along with the big truck engine as they struggled in unison to move the rig out of its bog. The truck started slowly to lift, the driver gunned his engine and the grader kept the tension on the chain. The truck was out of the hole and Marlee continued to pull to get the following trailers through the mess but the driver stopped. Suddenly the window behind her shattered into a thousand pieces, and the towing chain whipped past her ear with only centimetres to spare, cracked like a whip end and crumbled heavily, a link at a time, onto the seat beside her. The grader made a giant lurch forward, as it was released of its load. Marlee stumbled forward, crutches going in different directions, and ended up in a heap on the floor holding her ankle.

The poor chain had taken a pounding during the towing exercise—the driver had been zigging when he should have been zagging, constantly jerking and snapping the chain taut. Although very heavy, it had much too much weight on it and one too many jerks! It was very dangerous to have the chain at that length, but there was no choice, considering the depth of the bog, and the position of the truck.

So although it was over in seconds Marlee had narrowly escaped instant death. If the grader had been on a straight pull, the chain would have exploded into the cabin and killed her. She followed the truck out to the highway and got back to the homestead at 3 a.m., finally able to rest her injured ankle.

For the next load of cattle we requested another driver, said we didn't mind if we waited another few days! We asked for a driver with 'off road' experience and were rewarded with an exceptional one. He came in the road without a hitch, right to the yards, around all the manmade bogs. He said the other driver flatly refused to drive over our road again—having his trailer hanging over a cliff and a tow chain nearly causing a fatality had unnerved him. That was okay by us. But once more the legend of Bullo River's dangerous road was alive and well, and in technicolor, in all the pubs for a few hundred miles.

Once more the yards were empty and silent.

Even though all our helicopter musters were over, we still had to do our yearly bullcatching. Our targets were not the breeding bulls but the old 'scrubbers', or wild bulls. Most of these old rogues get away in the helicopter musters, and the only way to catch them is one at a time. This is necessary to bring the herd under control. When breeding, only one bull is needed for about thirty cows—this ratio varies, of course, with climate, feed and breed. So with the male and female births fairly even each year, a herd ends up with too many males. In a controlled herd these males are castrated when young and become steers. But when you bring a wild herd under control, there are no castrated steers, only very old, wild, inferior breeding bulls and they must be removed from the herd. Our herd is in transition and so we still have some of these 'old scrubbers' walking around. Each year the young females go into the breeding herd and the male calves are castrated; they then become our sale cattle. This is the controlled part of the herd. To bring the herds in the North under control all the 'scrubber' bulls had to be caught or shot. Most of the big properties just shot these animals to bring their numbers down and then introduced good breeding bulls. Being a small property, we needed every penny we could make to survive, so we catch the bulls and sell them to the meatworks. Bull meat is now in much demand for smallgoods, as it has a stronger flavour than steer meat.

Back in the old days, we caught the bulls on horseback. You'd gallop along at full speed, chasing the bull, and then you'd jump off the horse at a full gallop, grab the bull's tail and throw him. In the early 1980s the horse was replaced by a vehicle and bullcatching became merely very dangerous, instead of *insanely* dangerous, which was what jumping off a horse at a full gallop could only be described as. Charlie employed contract bullcatchers to catch our surplus 'scrubbers', and it was during this time that Marlee learned the technique. Marlee had asked her father many times if we could do our own bullcatching instead of paying the contractor sixty per cent of the income. But he would never agree. It just wasn't worth the risk.

However, in 1987 I gave in and we bought a four-wheel drive, short wheelbase Toyota. We stripped it down, fitted it with roll bars and reinforcing bars and lined the under chassis with armour plate. And with all the knowledge she had gained watching the contractors, Marlee was after the scrubbers with a vengeance!

We call the bullcatcher the 'green machine' because it was making us money; and it continued to do so for the next six years. Each year it brought in between $30,000 to $50,000. Apart from the stockmarket, the $8000 spent on the bullcatcher was by far the best investment I have ever made. Naturally there were expenses, plus a back-up truck and stockmen, and of course the healthy station supply of bulls helped. But having all the elements in place has meant the 'green machine' has proven to be a great money spinner.

So when Marlee's ankle was strong enough, she was off bullcatching—until the rains arrived and made the road unpassable for the road-trains, and I would worry for the same amount of time, until she put the bullcatcher in the shed, to rest for the rainy season.

As dangerous as bullcatching is, and it is very dangerous, there have still been some funny situations. One time Marlee was out catching on the salt flats by the Victoria River. The salt flats are very large and stretch for many miles, and being flat and smooth with no trees are an excellent area to chase bulls. But they are no good if it's wet. Marlee had just chased five bulls out into the middle of the flats when a thunder storm struck and the area was drenched in a few minutes. Then the storm moved rapidly up the valley.

During the storm the bulls just stood still, but the fun and games started when Marlee wanted to catch them. Every time she got the bull in position to bump him over, she would hit the brakes and the bullcatcher would go skating by. The rain had made the surface like a skating rink. In fact the bulls found her performance so entertaining, that instead of running away they all stood and watched. And although it took many hours of frustrating skating, all her spectators ended up back at the homestead yard, well and truly caught. 'That will teach you to stand and laugh at me' she told them as she closed the gate on their freedom. They all looked back at her with the same expression they had on their faces as they watched her skate this way and that. It seemed to say, 'Ah yeh, but you still looked a right twit, skating around out there on the salt flat!'

Marlee drove back to the house still smarting.

Very heavy rains in late November finally started the creeks and rivers flowing and officially announced the beginning of the 1991/1992 Wet Season. The last of the stockmen helping with the bullcatching left and we were down to only family. Normally the rains signalled the end of the mustering season and that meant it was 'slow down' time, until after New Year at least. But not so for us, this year. We were so excited about our small crop of hay the year before that this year we planned to plant three times the sorghum, and we were about to embark on a new business venture: cubed hay.

We were lucky in 1990—despite not having much knowledge of what we were doing, we still had a fairly successful sorghum crop. So we went into the new planting with great enthusiasm. But we were soon to learn it is a harsh world, the world of farming.

One thing I've learned from my short time trying to be a farmer is that our farmers have to be the bravest, most optimistic people in the world. To go back to the land year after year, after what nature throws at them and the world economy does to their income, takes a special kind of person. I take my hat off to them.

The ploughing was endless; it continued over the horizon, forever. Week after week the tractors turned virgin soil into ploughed fields. After what seemed like an eternity, the land was ready for planting. We now had to wait for the rain. There had been a few storms in November, and December was getting regular rain, but it all had been light, not the good soaking needed to plant seed. Luckily the rains were enough to keep the dust to a minimum, making ploughing not too unpleasant. But as December progressed the rainfall record was only half that of the year before.

It did have one small advantage, however. With only a bit of shovel work here and there, we were able to drive out the road and go to Darwin for Christmas shopping. Marlee and I raced around Darwin buying gifts and food. Uncle Dick would ask me to buy his present for Marlee and ask Marlee to buy my present from him. And added to this, Danielle would request I buy her present for Uncle Dick! Shopping tended to be very confusing. I ended up buying everyone's presents for each other and then realised I hadn't bought any gifts from me.

Christmas Day was dry and hot. So much so that it was really too hot to eat a baked dinner in the middle of the day. So we delayed eating until late afternoon. About four in the afternoon there was a wonderful storm, which cooled everything down and made dinner much more enjoyable. However, the intensity of the storm worried me a bit—it was fast-moving and violent, with frequent thunder and lightning and heavy rain lasting only a few minutes. Usually, if the storms at the beginning of the season are violent, it seems to set the pattern for the whole season.

But the worst heatwave or the most powerful storms on the planet would not delay the opening of presents on Christmas morning. Marlee is enthusiastic about almost everything in life, but nothing compares to her enthusiasm for present-opening on Christmas Day.

When the girls were little, Christmas was always so much work for me, and that, on top of my usual load, meant I always found myself behind with never enough time for all the things that needed to be done. I would be wrapping the presents at six o'clock in the morning, with three eager little girls excitedly waiting outside my bedroom door poised to rush each present to the tree as soon as it was ready. One year when I was feeling sick and was very much behind, Marlee just couldn't contain herself any longer. She offered to help wrap the presents with her eyes closed. That way, she said, she wouldn't be able to see them!

Her enthusiasm or desire to see her gifts had not diminished over the years and this particular Christmas she was extra, extra bubbly—the reason being that Franz had returned to join us. It was now obvious they felt very strongly about each other.

So here she was, rousing me out of a deep sleep at 6 a.m. so we could start opening the presents.

'When you get Uncle Dick up here,' I mumbled sleepily. That dampened her spirits considerably. If she found it hard to wake me, she'd find it near impossible to wake Uncle Dick. Especially after Christmas Eve.

As usual on Christmas Eve we decorated the tree, the cassette player playing Christmas carols in the background. We had ham and mustard sandwiches and fruit cake, and champagne, instead of the traditional egg-nog. Uncle Dick had as much beer as he could get his hands on, about two mouthfuls of a ham sandwich; followed by more beer chasers.

As the alcohol flowed, so had the stories of past Christmases. Uncle Dick had brought up to the house with him some old Christmas photos and was showing these to Franz as he related some of his many anecdotes. The stories and the beer had continued well into the night. So I was very confident it would be a few more hours before Uncle Dick surfaced and was feeling sufficiently recovered to come to the house and be 'jolly old Santa'.

As I lay there in bed I went back over some of my memories ...

One Christmas on Bullo the children went out alone to chop down their first tree. At the time they were teaching the horses to tow things on long ropes behind them. The first test, it seemed, was to be a Christmas tree. This particular horse wasn't at all pleased with the state of affairs, and when he was finally attached to the tree on long ropes, he showed his displeasure by bolting. By the time the girls had the situation under control, the tree was minus most of its foliage and looked very bedraggled. So they set off again to get another tree and took turns carrying the tree back home.

Charlie loved Christmas, as much as the children. But even more than the presents, he loved the food and egg-nog; especially the egg-nog.

Our most famous, or should I say infamous, Christmas story was naturally about Charlie. It was in the 1970s, Christmas Eve, the light was fading, the sky was darkening, and all eyes on Bullo were looking into the sky, towards Darwin. Charlie was late! The children wanted to see their father, but more importantly they were very interested in the cargo of presents and Christmas goodies they knew would be on the plane. Heaven! Unlimited chocolates and lollies for two whole days. Something they dreamed of all year.

Mummy of course was worrying about the turkey, ham, fruit cake, plum pudding, and everything else needed to produce the Christmas dinner everyone on the station was so looking forward to.

The weather was turning ugly and it was fast approaching last light; in a few minutes it would be too dark to land, according to DCA regulations. Charlie always put the landing lights on when he was a long way out, so we could see him. It was this bright light that the children's eyes were searching for in the darkening sky.

Last light came and went in silence, and it broke my heart to see the looks on those little upturned faces.

'Come along, I'm sure Daddy will get here first thing in the morning,' I said trying to sound cheerful while thinking of the 101 things—food preparation, cooking, gift wrapping etc—that would be expected of me the moment the plane did land. And here I was, actually praying for this rather than consider the alternative: the possibility that he had crashed somewhere.

I started telling the girls what we could do that night, so we could have an early start on Christmas Day, when we heard the distinctive sound of the Beaver's radial engine droning through the dark sky.

We all rushed outside and there was the twinkling light heading up the valley, very low, searching for the airstrip or the lights of the homestead. We all darted around looking for torches. This was a regular routine rather than a 'one off' exercise; Charlie was not known as 'last light Charlie' for nothing! We were very well trained on the landing procedure after dark, so having each found a torch, we ran onto the airstrip and stood in our designated positions, resting the torches on our heads.

The Beaver roared over us at about forty feet, went to the end of the strip and turned and lined up on the four torches forming a small square in the middle of the airstrip. These were Charlie's instructions exactly—by having the four lights in this position opposite the house he knew how much runway there was each side of the lights.

The Beaver is a short take-off and landing aircraft, so length wasn't a big problem. But he had to land fairly close to us so he could judge the distance to the ground. It was so dark by now that he had no hope of judging by eyesight, and with no moon the depth perception was zero.

He touched down, with quite a bump, but under the circumstances you would have to say it was a remarkable landing. We didn't have time to praise it though, he touched down so close to us we had to run off the strip to avoid being run over as he whooshed by. The girls were elated. 'Daddy was home!' Not to mention the boxes of wonderful food, chocolates and lollies, and the presents!

Charles stepped out of the plane like the conquering hero, sat down and directed the unloading of the precious cargo. There would be squeals of delight when he told one child she would have to close her eyes while her sister unloaded her special present! Ready now to start his Christmas Eve celebrations, he asked for an egg-nog. But was shocked when I told him there wasn't any—that he had only just arrived with all the ingredients needed to make it. He said he thought that was a legitimate enough reason, and was content to go on directing with the aid of a cold beer until we unloaded all his surprises, and the egg-nog was forthcoming.

However, Charlie's surprises were not over yet, not by a long way. I was up most of the night, unpacking food, making stuffing for the turkey, making more egg-nog, icing fruit cakes, making special cream custard for the plum pudding, wrapping many, many presents and generally doing those 1001 things most mothers do for Christmas. My problem being I didn't have the weeks of lead-up to Christmas Day. I had one night.

I finally fell into bed about 1 a.m., still with loads of work not done, most presents still to wrap, and no sooner had my eyes closed it seemed it was time to get up. At 6 a.m. three little girls were standing over me, peering into my sleepy eyes, wanting me to start the day.

It was again the usual scene: the girls waiting for each gift to be wrapped and handed to them out the door, then after a shake and rattle it was rushed to the tree. I went from gift wrapping to the kitchen. I was so rushed I didn't even remember to tune into our early morning radio session. I was up to my elbows in stuffing, surrounded by a turkey and a few chickens, and stopping to fill Charlie's egg-nog glass regularly as each little girl brought it into the kitchen for a refill.

I finally had the turkey in the oven cooking slowly and most of the vegetables ready when I was dragged into the living room by the children. They had worked hard and had everyone seated, Daddy's glass was full and Uncle Dick was ready to hand out the presents but Daddy wouldn't start until Mummy was there. I gratefully sagged into a chair that had been saved especially for me, thankful for the only rest I would get for the rest of the day.

Only a few presents had been unwrapped when a plane engine was heard. The plane swooped low over the strip then circled and landed. I waited, hoping Charles hadn't invited a planeload of people to Christmas lunch and forgotten to tell me. He said he hadn't, or didn't remember. We had no idea who it could be, so we all waited.

Charles went out to meet the plane. We watched as four men walked back across the lawn with a very sheepish-looking Charles.

He had forgotten to cancel his sar-watch, which means he didn't call flight service and say he had landed safely and to close his flight. So according to them he was still in the air somewhere. As this was not possible, fuel-wise, they would have had to assume he had crashed somewhere. Before they raise the alarm and mount a search party they always call the place of destination, but because I didn't call in at our radio time they were unable to confirm the plane had landed. So they had to fly here to check! Of course Charlie couldn't call in and say he was on the ground at Bullo when he was still twenty minutes out from the station at 'last light', the legal landing time. He told me later that he had planned to call in first thing on Christmas morning, but forgot. Charlie's favourite pastime. This would have been perfectly all right, because they couldn't start a search until daylight. He could have told them he had radio trouble and the whole affair would have been solved there and then. But … he forgot.

So now we had four very grumpy DCA officers on our hands. Actually, grumpy wasn't a strong enough word to describe them. All had left their families at home on Christmas Day, and they were not impressed. Charlie, loving an impossible challenge, took the situation into his own hands, and started them off with an egg-nog, grilled ham and eggs. He insisted they sit down to all this, which of course I had to cook. But knowing full well that Charles could lose his pilot's licence over this, for once I didn't mind.

While I was busy in the kitchen cooking, Charlie looked after the egg-nog. And when I had breakfast for four laid out in the kitchen, Charlie had four DCA officers laid out in the living room! He didn't tell them egg-nog was alcoholic. And the way I made it, it was lethal! My recipe included a couple of pints of heavy cream, a couple of pints of full cream milk, four-dozen eggs, half a bottle of rum, half a bottle of scotch, and half a bottle of French cognac ... oh yes, and nutmeg to taste. The original recipe was even stronger, but long ago I toned it down and never told Charles. Even sparingly, whatever way you looked at it, it was a potent drop, to be sipped slowly over a long period of time. Moderation was never part of Charlie's vocabulary, and so it was that Christmas morning. It was, 'Merry Christmas, bottoms up', and the visitors followed suit. They had finished two egg-nogs by the time they sat down to breakfast; by the time they had finished the formal investigations and filled out the stack of required forms they'd consumed a good few more.

It soon became evident to the merry group that something was amiss. They were supposed to be grumpy, annoyed for having to spend their Christmas on a wild goose chase, and should have been severely reprimanding the renegade pilot. Yet here they were, laughing and joking and having a whale of a time, with no thoughts of leaving.

It was the pilot, when walking out to the plane to radio in, yet again, to say they were delayed, who realised he wasn't walking in the normal fashion. When he returned and asked Charles if the egg-nog was alcoholic, he was cheerfully answered with, 'Oh, yes.'

They now faced a dilemma. Who would fly home? They were all under the influence of liquor, so by their own rules they were grounded. Of course Charles was sitting with a very smug expression on his face, but I could read it clearly. He had manoeuvred events to precisely this point; he had turned a very difficult situation right around and now his adjudicators were in the hot seat, unable to judge him. I had to hand it to him; he was a devious one.

Charles offered to fly them home, said a few drinks never seemed to affect his flying. The offer and remark were met with stony silence.

Over the next few hours they consumed a record amount of coffee and food. They joined us for lunch; the effect of the egg-nog was wearing off, so they were very grumpy again, but mainly because Charles had conned them so completely. They would only drink water and coffee they made themselves, because Charles had added a shot of rum to the coffee they were drinking to sober up! His only reply to their horrified looks after tasting the laced coffee was: 'But I always drink coffee that way.'

By supervising their own recovery they decided it was safe to take-off by mid afternoon. That way they wouldn't be breaking all the rules in the book—only some, slightly. And Charlie solemnly declared he would never breathe a word. So the unsaid agreement was they would consider Charlie's form '225' (bad-behaviour report) a genuine mistake and no action would be taken. Nevertheless, even in their weakened position, they severely reprimanded Charlie. He was told in no uncertain terms that if he stepped out of line again, they would throw the book at him. And with that, they made, as much as was possible, a dignified departure.

The children, who had waited virtually all day to open their presents, could now go ahead. Charlie sat, egg-nog in hand, and smiled over the rest of the day's festivities, totally pleased with himself.

I would have to say the very worst Christmas in my whole life had to be our first Christmas on Bullo. When we first arrived, way back in the early 1960s, it was near the end of the year. The stockmen were still mustering; the staff included our manager, John Nicolson, and a cook-cum-saddler.

The cook was an interesting character, quite gentlemanly really, and strongly reminded me of my mum's descriptions of the 'remittance men' who stayed in their hotels in New South Wales in the 1930s and 1940s. A remittance man was from England and received regular payments from his family to stay away.

He was a heavy drinker, as most men in the Outback seem to be. So the meals were quite curious. Stews consisted of lots of water, whole onions—with skins intact—whole potatoes—with a lot more than the skin still there—big lumps of ghastly dried salt beef and big mobs of dried vegetables. These vegetables defy description: the peas could double for bullets if you ran out of ammo, and never softened, even after days of boiling, and the beans, carrots and parsnips just disintegrate into a tasteless pulp. Throughout the week, this terrible concoction was added to daily.

I had no interest in cooking, never have and never will, but after witnessing the standards of hygiene and the culinary talent of the Bullo River cook, I told Charles that if he wanted to live to a ripe old age, maybe I should cook. Or, I added hastily, maybe I could supervise the kitchen. After all, I had years of supervising experience under my belt, if not cooking.

John quickly advised against it, telling Charlie that if I entered the kitchen, other than as a guest, there would be a general strike. This was still the Outback, circa 1960, and a woman in the kitchen bossing the men around would cause no end of trouble. The final convincing statement was, if I went into the hallowed domain to cook, even for the family, the cook would up and leave and I would have to then cook for all the stockcamp. It would therefore be best for everyone if I just stayed in the background and acted like a visitor.

For my part, I certainly had no desire to take over that hole of horror they seemed to think was a kitchen, and it was true I wasn't much of a cook in a good kitchen ... In that nightmare of a substitute I probably wouldn't have succeeded in boiling water.

Not wanting to demand centre stage with the men watching, and fall flat on my face, I had to suffer in silence. I was still in shock anyway from leaving a beautiful home in the Philippines, with servants in every room and a chef in the kitchen. Having landed in this totally alien place was a complete trial in itself. Just watching the children, and keeping them out of danger, and teaching them, and surviving the heat, took most of my day. The thought of having to cook for the stockcamp in that awful place brought out hives just thinking about it.

So the children and I ate lots of dry bread, jam, boiled potatoes—when the mail plane brought them—custard and sloppy jelly and lots of dried fruit. Charles, the true believer, would have hefty servings of whatever it was in the big pot, although he would always cover it with half a bottle of tomato sauce.

As our first Christmas approached I asked Charles if maybe I could cook Christmas dinner instead of the cook. Just the one meal, I added quickly. He consulted with John ... the answer came back negative. There was a wonderful array of goodies coming in on the mail plane a few days before Christmas and our cook-cum-saddler-cum-stockman wanted to show off his supposed culinary skills. I dreaded the moment.

For the next few weeks the children and I counted off the days to the mail plane's arrival. I had ordered many presents and Christmas goodies and decorations and my sister and Mum had put together boxes of everything for us. The plane was bringing it all. At last I felt the first stirrings of excitement since being dumped into that strange new life.

The rain started about six days before Christmas Day. One morning I woke to discover the sun wasn't shining—the sky was dark, grey and low. It immediately reminded me of a tropical low, the likes of the weather in Manila; and that's just what it was like. It sat over the North for many weeks and we had non-stop rain.

About three days before the mail plane was due we knew

we could kiss goodbye to our Christmas dinner and all the wonderful presents sent by our families. In those days our mail plane was a DC-3, on the milk run from Darwin to Perth. During the Wet Season, I was about to learn, it only landed on tarmac or sealed strips; for half of December, and all of January and February, it hardly landed on any dirt strips for fear of bogging. Bogging on a station strip would keep the plane out of action for months until the wet was over.

So Christmas looked bleak. And we were a very glum family. We would have no fresh food, no presents, no extra goodies. It was back to the terrible concoction in the big pot. Just the thought made me sick to the stomach. If we had had a plane in those days, Charlie could have flown off into the wild blue yonder and returned with Christmas—as he did in all the years to follow. But we didn't.

After a day or so of moping, I told the children we would make our own gifts. Being only three and five as they were, Mummy did most of the making. We gathered lots of wild flowers and stuffed them into empty half-gallon wine flagons and smaller rum bottles, which we then dotted around every available corner of the tin shed and caravan. We made paper daisy chains out of old magazines and newspapers and coloured them with crayons. Nothing was safe from becoming a Christmas decoration. We even painted small nuts with the children's waterpaints and stuck on cut-out pictures with flour and water paste. And we made a small Christmas tree out of lots of branches from a gum tree. This the girls arranged in the centre of the tin shed, and they draped streamers and daisy chains around the walls and from bottle to bottle of wild flowers. As I pause now to describe this scene, words fail me. Charlie sat and presided over the proceedings with a glass of hot rum mixed with orange cordial in one hand, a cigar in the other, and a big smile on his face, looking for all the world like he was in the snow-covered house where he was born, enjoying all the comforts of home that he considered were his right. He had this very unusual talent of ignoring anything that didn't meet his standards.

Much was made of the presents, handmade by the children; there were many sing-a-long Christmas carols and the enthusiasm of the little girls made a bright spot in a rather sparse and disappointing Christmas Eve and Christmas Day.

Our 'cook' was also doing his bit. Christmas lunch was to be a big surprise, and he had been performing daily. But he didn't fool me. I knew there was absolutely nothing in that kitchen or pantry that even remotely resembled good food or a Christmas dinner!

I had suggested maybe lunch could be served later in the day when it was not so unbearably hot. This was rejected by the 'kitchen cabinet'. Apparently their Christmas celebrations started *after* lunch, when they all went off into the bush, sat down under a tree and got smashed on hot rum or cheap wine. Having been in the Outback for just on four months at that stage, I could completely understand this need to regularly exit from the harsh life via alcohol in order to survive. Although I never succumbed to this method, I can truly empathise with it.

So, as decided by the powers that be, we sat down to lunch on the stroke of twelve noon, in temperatures of 110 degrees Fahrenheit. I'll go into some detail here to set the scene clearly ...

The kitchen had a dirty-looking wood stove, covered in grease and soot, standing in one corner. This threw out heat of about 150 degrees. Next to it was a normal stainless steel sink, suspended in midair—or so it seemed—on the wall. The tap also was suspended at the end of a long pipe. When you turned on the tap the water pressure made the tap and pipe flap up and down. If you didn't hold the tap down while you filled the jug or saucepan, you ended up drenched from head to toe. Next to the sink was a wall with a long but shaky shelf, a feeble attempt by me to improve the overall appearance of the kitchen. Since my arrival I had managed this change and one other—I had insisted that the kitchen be fly-screened. So the next wall was all screen. The storeroom made up most of the next wall, and then there was a bit of a zig-zag and the last little space was also screened. The walls were unpainted tin, black with soot and grime. The ceiling was only rafters and the tin roof was draped in sooty cobwebs. The only furniture in the area was a table and a variety of steel chairs. Boxes, for sitting on, set off the rest of the decor perfectly. Mum, bless her heart, had packed in my survival suitcase a bright, new, seersucker tablecloth. It was the only thing that reminded me of civilisation. There it lay, in the midst of alien surroundings.

All the stockmen had washed and spruced themselves up and combed their hair, which was board-stiff, on account of being washed in hard water and soap. There were two ways of wearing the hair—either straight up in the air or straight out from the head, like a ledge. For my part, I had the little girls dressed in the lovely dresses they wore on their arrival, and had not so much as looked at since that day. Up to now they had only ever been seen splashing under the hose in their swimsuits or playing mud pies and covered in mud. But today they looked a picture, a very hot and sweating picture, but still a picture to behold in that harsh setting.

We sat down. The cook had thoughtfully placed two square biscuit tins on two of the chairs for the girls, so they could reach the table. I was ceremoniously led to the only other chair and then all the men found various things to sit on. Finally we were all seated to await that special Christmas lunch. Since I hadn't smelt any mysterious or delicious smells wafting from the kitchen during the morning, or any day for that matter, and my eyes had so far not seen the evidence of the preparation of any food, I was at a loss as to what gourmet's delight we were about to experience.

Charlie was doing his bit by telling us a mixture of funny and delightful stories of Christmas in Maryland, of snow and frozen ponds. How in the days when he was a boy the Negro help would cut the frozen pond into blocks of ice and store the blocks in straw in an underground cellar, and how the ice would last all through the summer and cool the endless gin and tonics that were consumed in the hot weather. While he answered the children's 101 questions about snow and frozen ponds, the cook started to place the meal on the table. First to arrive were two tin plates, stacked with mashed potatoes. This was not the fresh variety, I might add; this terrible stuff came in four-gallon drums in flake form and could double for washing powder if need be. Next, as Charlie was describing all the wonderful food that was stored in the cellar over the winter in Maryland, the cook placed another two plates on the table. These were piled high with boiled, dried vegetables, and were what we had been eating for months, when our fresh supply of onions, potatoes and cabbage ran out. Could this be it? I thought miserably. No, I reassured myself. Surely not. The best is yet to come. He then lowered the last tin plate onto the table with great ceremony. The special surprise.

I stared in horror for a full ten seconds, then let out a terrible moaning wail, fled from the kitchen in tears and locked myself in the caravan.

For the children's sake I had tried very hard to put on a cheerful front, and had worked hard at making the day something special. But you can only go so far before you can pretend no longer. And sitting in that drab, ugly kitchen, in temperatures of a blast furnace, had me to the limit of my endurance. The tin plates of powdered potatoes and dried vegetables had me struggling to control my emotions; but when the cook placed a tin plate with a grey-coloured, boiled bullock's heart, sliding around in grey water, on the table, as Christmas dinner, something inside me snapped.

Charles was very sympathetic, and managed to calm me down with a promise that we would celebrate Christmas Day when all the boxes of goodies finally arrived with the mail plane. And that is what we did. The tropical low moved away and the sun dried out the airstrip and around mid January the mail plane managed one landing before the next low settled over most of the North and cut us off again. The stockmen went out on the plane to Wyndham. The big rain had officially started the Wet Season and tradition was that they all went to town and sat in the pub and yarned about the season just finished, until the wet was over. So that left us with the cook and John the manager. Because of my reaction to his *pièce de résistance*, and the departure of the stockcamp, our 'remittance man'-cum-cook told John he would not stay the wet to cook and repair saddles, and with that he tipped his hat and departed on the plane also. If his saddle work was anything like his cooking, we weren't losing much, I thought. John took a few bottles of rum and his swag, and said he was going to check fences and would be gone for a week.

We were alone, finally. We had a family Christmas dinner at night, when it was cool. It rained most of the day as I struggled with the wood stove, but by sunset, with the girls and Charles all pitching in, we sat down to the first real food we had seen in months. And we thoroughly enjoyed every mouthful.

That Christmas seemed to set a precedent, and from then on we were always running late on celebrations. They could be celebrated weeks, sometimes months, after their true date. The children didn't celebrate their birthdays on time until they were well into their teens. We did manage Christmas on time, but New Year suffered badly.

I smiled as these memories came flooding back, and laughed as I thought of the others Uncle Dick had related well into the night. Yes, it would be many hours before he would surface, I thought to myself.

Nevertheless, Marlee insisted I get out of bed. She told me Franz had gone down to Dick's house to drive him back. I wondered what sort of state he'd be in.

I showered and dressed and walked out into our living room to start another Christmas Day on Bullo. We sat down and a very seedy Uncle Dick handed out the gifts, as he has done for so many Christmases.

Christmas celebrations only briefly interrupt full-time

farming, and once the festivities were over, we went straight back to work.

Everyone was so tired on New Year's Eve that it was hard to stay awake at dinner. We decided to go to bed and get up just before midnight in time to celebrate. I didn't even hear the alarm and slept in the new year.

My New Year's resolution ... be awake to welcome in the beginning of 1993!

CHAPTER 3

January
1992

Rain was almost daily. Having waited and waited for the ground to be moist enough for seeds, it was now getting too wet. Then, after a week of hot sun and high winds, it would all turn to dust again.

Although the storms were frequent and extremely violent, the rain was still very light. Tremendous wind storms with dry lightning would strike regularly. We would sit and watch thick dustclouds from the newly ploughed paddocks go rolling by the homestead and Marlee would say, 'There goes Bullrush Paddock.' When another storm hit the next day from the opposite direction and more clouds of dust rolled by, she would say, 'Here comes Bullrush.'

The storms were very disturbing, they would come from any direction and increase in their intensity. By January our storms are usually settled into a pattern. They come from one direction, and being so far into the season there's wind for a while, which then settles down to steady or torrential rain. These particular storms would start with sudden torrential rain, the rains would stop and then strong winds and heavy rain would strike from another direction. However, the most disturbing aspect of the storms was the sudden and enormous whooshes of wind that just seemed to come out of nowhere. We had, in total, about seven of these violent storms by the second week in January and it did seem that this type of storm had settled in for the season, which was a little disquieting to say the least.

I was safely inside my office working when another of these storms struck. It was about 5 p.m. Everyone else was out in the fields planting and ploughing. The rain started suddenly, without warning, and it was torrential. I heard the French doors in the living room bang as the wind hit them. I ran to close them. Our storms usually came from the back of the house and over the years we have had a few doors blown off their hinges. The wind was so strong I couldn't close the doors at the same time—that is, with one hand on each door to bring them together. I had to put my shoulder behind one door and hold it while I pushed both bolts top and bottom into position. There are eight doors across the back of the living room so I had quite a task ahead of me. The wind was whistling and screaming under the doors and through the rafters in the ceiling. It was very eerie, quite unlike any storm I had yet experienced in the Outback. However, it did remind me of one I had encountered while at sea ... I shrugged off these morbid thoughts and started to worry about Marlee and Franz out there somewhere in all this ferocity. I'd closed the doors in the living room, and moved into Marlee's bedroom, where there were another six which Marlee nearly always left open. She had closed them this time, but the storm had blown two open and rain was driving into the room. I struggled to close them. By now the wind had increased in intensity and when I got the doors in position I realised the bolts were missing. I looked around the room for a heavy weight to put against the door. I found the trunk. But I had to let go of the doors to move it. The rain blasted into the room again. It was so heavy now I couldn't see more than a few feet outside. It was too heavy even to see the back gate thirty feet away.

I dragged the trunk over to the doors, trying desperately

to hold them closed while pulling it. With my back against the doors, concentrating on dragging the trunk closer, I was finding it near impossible to remain upright as a sudden gust of wind and torrent of water would catch the doors and throw me across the trunk. It was coming into the room with such force now that I could have been standing out in the middle of a field instead of a room. The trunk almost in position, I started to struggle with one door as blinding rain hit me with terrible force. My thoughts went again to Marlee. I reached for the other door, through the driving rain, struggling all the while to keep the first door in place while stretching to the other, when suddenly the rain was all sucked out of the room and the door came hurtling towards me with such force it threw me outside. I sat, stunned, in that eerie vacuum for a few seconds, then the rain hit me again and I rushed inside before the next gust of wind could blow the doors off. I started to struggle with the trunk again when the noise started; it was just loud enough to hear above the noise of the rain, but it was so spine chilling I stopped in my tracks. I had my back up against the doors and both hands on the trunk. The noise reached a crescendo, sounding like a siren, and the next thing I remember was the deafening screeching and tearing of metal, which drowned out all other sounds, even my screaming. I looked up and watched as the ceiling of the room rose up in the middle, like a circus tent. It paused in this position for a few seconds and the terrible screeching stopped. The only part of me that moved was my mouth, which had dropped wide open. The rest of me was frozen in my tracks for the one last tug of the trunk.

The wind suddenly abated and the roof and ceiling came crashing back down, not exactly in position, but still holding together, although leaking very freely now. The wind had stopped completely and the eerie vacuum was back and I was a statue of fear, poised in a state of shock. The wind and rain returned almost as quickly as they had subsided, the wind hit the doors and knocked me right over the trunk.

Cursing under my breath I was picking myself up again when the rain was once more sucked out the doors, and the doors slammed with a terrible woosh. Call it instinct, call it reflexes, but when that silence returned I didn't wait for the next step. I took a headlong dive under the bed. The screeching of metal and the splintering of wood deafened me as destruction was unleashed in that room. The roof again rose up in the air, but this time it just flipped back like a lid and suddenly there I was, under the bed, peering up at a menacing sky. Wind was roaring through the doors and rain was pouring in the hole where the roof used to be. The next gust of wind picked up the poor, old, battered roof, twisted it around a few times and dumped the remains back into the room.

The roof had covered a room twenty-five feet by twenty-three feet, with the main support beam across the room being two four-by-two timbers bolted together. This beam was snapped in two places, like a matchstick. And both pieces were lying where, seconds before, I had stood.

I crawled out when the wind let up for a few seconds. The torrential rain was back. My first thought was to save Marlee's belongings; I was already feeling the effects of my lucky escape. I found it very difficult to get out from under the bed because it was low to the ground. My back was hurting and I was shaking visibly. My heart was pounding so hard I could hear it in my ears. Funny the thoughts that go through your mind at times of sheer terror. I clearly remember thinking, 'Good thing you have a strong heart, Sara.'

But my next thought was one of alarm. A strange noise finally identified itself to my shocked brain: the crackling of raw electricity. Electric wires ripped from the ceilings and walls were dangling from rafters and lying on the floor. Water was everywhere and the wind was blowing and bouncing the wires around the room like wild animated beings. My first thought was ... what if the wind dropped, leaving all the wires lying in the water ... I vaulted onto the bed.

The wind gusts were hitting regularly now, rearranging the debris and flinging wires all around the room. All thoughts of saving Marlee's things went out of my head. I was struggling to save myself! I had to get out of the room without being electrocuted. I was trapped in one corner, cut off from the door by hanging live wires that were dancing in water, so I wasn't going to risk stepping on the floor.

The bed was in one corner of the room and there was a set of French doors right next to it. By stretching to my limit I could lean against the wall and manage to open the bolt on the top of the doors. This was a fair manoeuvre, but getting back to the bed without falling on the floor was excruciating, my stomach and back muscles were screaming. I blessed Marlee for not bolting the bottom bolt, which was secured into a metal sheath in the floor and was under water.

I collapsed back onto the sodden bed with the rain pouring down and broken electrical wires dancing all around me, and cried. It took a few minutes to get over the sobbing hysteria stage. Things had calmed a bit by now, but I knew I couldn't just sit there—the first thing I had to do was turn off the electricity. I stood up and jumped out the doors and onto the verandah in a mighty leap. I landed in a heap, but at least I was out of the room. I ran around the front of the house to the living room, which was out of the brunt of the wind. I stopped short when I ran into the room, the breath knocked out of me momentarily as I surveyed the destruction. The entire dining room area of about thirty-five feet by forty feet had lost its roof. The dining table and chairs were sitting in a lake of water, water was pouring over the lounge area, whose roof was still moderately intact, and waterfalling onto the hi-fi. And more electric wires were doing a tango around the room. I had to turn off the electricity!

Fear does strange things to your body. My breathing remained out of step for quite a while; but more frightening was my eyesight—it was very hazy around the perimeter, as if I was looking down a pipe, and then it would fade and return, like turning a dimmer switch round. When I reached the power control box I couldn't read the labels. My eyes were almost back to normal, but I needed my glasses to read the printing under each box. I rushed into the office, which was the part of the house still intact, and grabbed my glasses. They didn't help; the control box was high on the wall and I couldn't get my head back far enough to read through the lower part of the bifocal lenses. I finally felt along the rows of switches and flipped each one in the opposite direction. When all the crackling and hissing of live electric wires stopped, I sagged to the floor and had a good cry. The dogs, who had been watching my mad ravings and actions, silently gathered around me and licked my tears. I don't know how long I sat there, but Marlee's voice jolted me out of my daze.

'Mummy! Oh, dear God, Mummy!' came to me from different parts of the house as she searched each room for me. The screams became more urgent as she couldn't find me. I kept answering her, but she didn't stop calling and couldn't hear me over her own shouting. We eventually collided in the office and hugged each other.

The Wet Season of 1991/92 had the lowest rainfall recorded on Bullo in the twenty-eight years since records began, and it nearly all fell during the time our roof was missing! I spent days on end sweeping water out of the parts of the house that still had a roof. The rain would just pour in and then flow into the dry areas.

Uncle Dick isolated the power in the roofless sections and restored power to the roofed section of the house. We moved all the water-damaged furniture out of the rain, not that any of it could ever be used again. The dining table top looked all right, but just kept expanding daily, until about one week later it disintegrated, leaving only the frame and legs. It was a mammoth job drying clothes and rugs.

I know there is hardly ever a kind word for insurance companies, so I must record that our insurance company was wonderful. We had only a matter of days to get materials for a new roof in our road before the river came up and stopped all possible transport until April. I explained the situation and was told to photograph the damage. If they couldn't get an assessor down in the next few days, we could clean up and get on with the job of putting our roof back. They did fly down the next day, inspected the damage, agreed to our plan of replacing the roof and made the money available for the materials the moment I presented them with the invoices. All in a matter of days. The bank also comes in for a bit of credit. I told them the plan and they allowed me to go further over the already over-overdraft!

So Marlee and Franz drove all night to Darwin, arrived at dawn, loaded the truck with steel, roofing iron, and all the other materials needed to replace the roof and drove straight through the night to the station. And not a moment too soon—the water was seeping in the doors of the truck as they crossed the river.

Not only did it rain all the time the roof was off, but we nearly lost half of the new roof as well! A sudden squall came up out of nowhere, in the middle of the afternoon, when there hadn't been a cloud in the sky, and as soon as the tin was put in position, ready for the tek screws, *wham*! A few holding screws were able to be screwed into each sheet of tin before the brunt of the storm struck. We all stood in the living room and watched loose tin slap and bang, up and down with the wind. Luckily the storm came from the front of the house and the higher roof shielded the lower, still temporary, roof. And the lightly tacked tin stayed in place. If the storm had come from the back of the house, we would've lost another roof all over again.

The day the last sheet of iron was put into place, the sun came out. Well, that might not have been exactly the case, but it did seem that way.

Even though it seemed to rain all January, the total rainfall was one third of the normal rainfall for the month. February proved to be worse, less than half the normal. By the time we were into March we knew it was going to be a bad year for our animals and the new crops.

THE STRENGTH IN US ALL

January 1992

Losing the roof, sorting out and crying over damaged and lost treasures, and replacing the roof, was exhausting and took up most of January. I consoled myself with the saying, 'Bad start, good finish!', and thought, 'Well if the start is any indication, it should be one hell of a year!'

CHAPTER 4

February 1992–*March* 1992

Rain was our main concern. With hundreds of acres of young plants just breaking through the earth, we needed lots of follow-up rain. Weather maps were viewed eagerly on TV each day, as we hoped and waited for a tropical low to develop. We had only had two and a third inches of rain up to the twentieth. The year before, the rain records showed in twenty days the rainfall was ten inches, and that was only normal rainfall. We were very worried about the crops.

On the 21st February I had to fly to Perth. I was speaking at three IBM conferences. One a week. The conferences were for three different divisions, so that meant different audiences each week. I was very excited and of course very nervous.

I left Marlee in charge, with Franz to keep her company. I was sure they wouldn't even notice I had gone, they were too busy gazing into each other's eyes.

When I arrived at the hotel in Perth there was a letter at reception from IBM, welcoming me to their conference, and asking me to be at rehearsal at 10 a.m. the next day. Rehearsals? Up till now I'd usually given only dinner or luncheon speeches, where I would just step up to the podium, smile and start telling stories. I'd never been to a rehearsal!

But, unbeknown to me, I was about to enter the big league of conference presentations, with a firm that was the exemplar in the field. It was like being a part of a big stage production for a Broadway show. I did have a slight idea that this would be different from my other engagements, because the company in charge of the presentation had sent a photographer to Bullo months before, to capture the scenes of the Outback. At the time I found myself climbing mountains, posing casually on overhanging rocks, and doing many weird and wonderful things I never normally do in everyday life.

At the first rehearsal I saw the results of all that hard rock-climbing months before, on an eighty-foot-wide screen by forty-foot high. The photos were breathtaking and sitting there watching the run-through gave even me goosepimples, and I knew the country.

Along with this fabulous backdrop I was to be accompanied by a small orchestra and the lead singer from the stage musical *Chess*, which was playing in Melbourne at the time. Plus there was a choir to back him up. All this would be the finale. There were to be more scenes of Bullo, shot from a helicopter, and these would be on the screen while singer, orchestra and choir built up to the final shot of a blood-red sunset with a bright orange sun slipping behind black mountains and in silhouette a giant bottle tree, its leafless branches cutting through the shaftings of light of the setting sun. It was moving, spectacular stuff, worthy of a Broadway show. I thought it was great as it was, and didn't see the need for me to speak, but unfortunately the others didn't see it in the same light, so I had to start rehearsals.

I found this harder than I could have imagined. Up to now I had spoken only to audiences I could see. This was a completely new world. A couple of guys with headphones, mouthpieces and battery packs hanging off their hips positioned me on stage, while talking to invisible people at the back of the cavernous theatre. Satisfied I was where they wanted me, one said, 'Lights!', and I was blinded by countless massive searchlights beaming down on me. Another row of lights popped on along the edge of the stage and a few more shot at me from the wings. I was definitely 'centre stage and in the spotlight'. I thought I'd been nervous up to this point, but that was nothing. My nerves now went into overdrive. 'What have you gotten yourself into, Sara?' I thought to myself, as I looked around at the brilliant lights and out into the void.

From talking to myself I started having conversations with voices from the black hole, and so my rehearsal continued. It was very strange not being able to see the audience—I like to see people's faces, I find it relaxing to look into eyes and smiles. It calms my nerves. Standing there on that massive stage looking out into a black nothingness had me quite ill at ease. To add to all this new pressure, I had developed a throat infection and was in danger of losing my voice—if the antibiotics the doctor had me on didn't start working immediately. His instructions had been to rest and not to speak! Instructions that came in handy when I found out how many rehearsals they wanted me to attend. But for the most part I went along with it. Speaking to an empty theatre was difficult—I'm not a performer, I just talk to people, tell a story. So I felt a right gig standing up there for hours, going over and over the same thing. I would get an overwhelming desire to say, 'Yoo-hoo! Anyone out there?!'

But apart from my beginner's view of the whole operation, it really was a remarkable presentation. I did get more nervous, if that was possible, when I found out everyone except me was a professional performer. One chap asked me how long I'd been on the circuit.

'Circuit?' I asked with a puzzled expression.

'Yes, the IBM circuit.'

'Well, I didn't know there *was* a circuit. This is the first time I've spoken for IBM. I'm usually running an Outback cattle station with my daughter.'

He went on to tell me he had been part of the musical side of the entertainment for IBM for ten years. Full-time job, just for the IBM conferences.

My nerves were on the increase. Apart from liking to see the faces of the audience I also change my speech around as I speak. And sometimes if I feel the audience shows more of an interest in something in particular I'll continue that subject further. But I couldn't do that this time either, because the photos flashing up on the screen behind me were in sequence and were timed to change at specific times to coincide with the speech. So if I went off rambling on one of my stories I would run the risk of having photos of wild bulls chasing people around the cattle yards while I was talking about dancing or something far removed.

I had to stick to the script. This was on a television screen—an autocue—down in front of me and between the stage and the big black hole. And it terrified me no end. I was having nightmares of the screen going blank and me not being able to remember what I was talking about and what was next. I would wake up in bed in an air-conditioned room with perspiration pouring off me.

Something else that would bring me out in a cold sweat just thinking about it was my entrance. None of this just walking on business; they had me driving on in a bull-catcher. Now, this shouldn't really have caused a problem, given the times I had got in and out of a bullcatcher. But those times were in jeans and sneakers. This time it was a tight skirt and high heels!

So it was off to buy an outfit with a full skirt. The three outfits I had with me all had straight skirts, and unless IBM wanted a chorus line beginning when I tried to get out of the bullcatcher in a straight skirt, I needed another outfit.

I slowly became used to staring into the black hole and giving an animated speech. I even mastered getting out of the bullcatcher in high heels without falling flat on my face. The throat was husky, but was holding out, and I was coming to terms with the autocue monster that told me what to say. That was mostly due to meeting the lovely person controlling it. Once I got to know Sue I relaxed, slightly, because I knew I was in good hands. She told me I didn't have to stick religiously to the script, and that if I changed it slightly she would just stop the text and when I finished digressing I could come back to where I left off. She would be monitoring what I was saying, and would just start the script rolling again once I was back on track. This cheered me greatly, as I was having nightmares about the autocue rolling merrily along and me at double time trying to catch up! But there wasn't too much room for wandering, not with the pictures whirring and clicking away behind me.

So with all these problems far from adequately under control, the big day arrived! My voice was still with me, as were the nerves. I watched a fantastic introduction from the wings, took a deep breath, climbed into the bullcatcher and there I was, centre stage, in those blinding lights. But now the black hole was full of people, and they were clapping.

My only thought at that time was, 'Get out of this bullcatcher, Sara, without falling flat on your face.' I did, but dropped a ball of tissues centre stage. While waiting in the wings my hands had been so sweaty with nerves that I was using the tissues to wipe them dry. I had left the tissues on the bullcatcher's seat, but my skirt swept them onto the floor.

What to do? Ignore the little white ball and walk over to the podium? With thousands of watts of lights shining on me, the ball of tissues could not have gone unnoticed. But I couldn't stand there all day, so I thought, 'What the hell?', and bent down and picked them up. There was a ripple of laughter from the audience and it went well from there. Even the husky voice passed muster. I was the last speaker before lunch, and before ending the morning session, it was announced they would close with more scenes from Bullo

River Station. Once the speech was over, the nerves disappeared, and I was escorted to a seat in the front row, in the black hole. Now on the other side of the blinding lights a whole new world opened up and the theatre was a sea of people. I sat back to enjoy the rest of the show.

The lights faded and two more curtains opened on each side of the main stage. A small orchestra was on one side and a choir on the other. The lead singer from *Chess* came on the centre stage and sang 'This is her country' out of the musical, while aerial scenes of Bullo's mountains, lake, gorges, and vast grasslands filled the whole stage on that massive screen. Just watching the screen in rehearsal gave me goosepimples, but this moving performance brought tears to my eyes.

The closing scene of the blood-red sunset slowly faded as a crescendo of music and a powerful voice soared to the last forceful note of a beautiful song left the darkened theatre spellbound. Even after the lights came on and the vivid sunset had faded into a black screen it was some time before the murmur of hundreds of people took over the room. It certainly was an A1 performance, and I was very proud to be part of it.

If you stay around after your speech you'll soon know if you reached your audience's heart and imagination. I was stopped many times on the way out of the theatre, and the remarks were flattering and genuine. It is a very nice feeling to know that you have entertained so many people and that they walked away having enjoyed the performance totally. I think the most flattering compliment I received came from the general manager of the theatre. He came up to me and said, 'I could listen to you all day! That was a great speech!' And considering he listens to people speaking day after day at endless conferences, I thought that was pretty good.

Having made it through the first day I relaxed a little. One down, two to go. My next speech was a week away—same day, same speech and backdrop, different audience. So I had a week to spare, well, not really; more rehearsals were required. I couldn't fly back to the station between speeches as the travelling was three days and the bad weather could prevent a small plane from landing at the station. So I stayed in Perth for more rehearsals, and rest. This was fortunate because my throat was quite sore by the end of the first conference and the first few days' rest were helpful.

I was in constant touch with Marlee, and she kept me up on the happenings. The army was carrying out their 'Big Wet' exercise. It was a smaller version of Kangaroo '89, an earlier exercise at Bullo only this time they planned to hold the mock invasion in the rainy season.

Now you have to live in the Outback to appreciate what you are up against in the wet. People in the Outback live with the rain as part of their everyday lives, just more of the trials of living where we live. Over the years we have faced all the problems the army was about to confront, and have become pretty good at getting out of impossible situations just through trial and error and more error and solutions. My girls can look at an area of ground or the colour of certain grass and say, 'Don't drive there, you'll get bogged,' or, 'Don't set up camp there—if it rains, that creek is a flash flood creek and it'll wash your whole camp downstream in one big tidal wave.' This isn't a divine gift they've been blessed with; it's purely the knowledge gained from these things actually happening to them over the years! Experience, I find, is an exceptional teacher.

To see the real North in the rainy season is when you go off the sealed roads. And it is then that you really need the experience. Ground that looks perfectly normal, but a horse can sink up to its flanks in seconds if it steps there. Dirt roads that turn to sticky goo, and to travel just a few hundred yards can take hours, if you are lucky. Mostly you sit there for days until it becomes hard enough for traction. If you try to move too soon the dirt sticks to the wheels in layers and coats the entire wheel in a three-inch thick retread of mud, then you lose all traction and the vehicle slides and skids everywhere, and usually into the ditch. You can move at a snail's pace by scraping all the mud from the four tyres at each turn of the wheels, and then doing one more turn. Then the process is repeated over again. It wouldn't do to be under attack.

But the army has to have this experience, among others, to evaluate the problems they would encounter if they ever had to defend Australia in the wet. They'd been coming into the station for months, gathering as much data as they could. So over the months we had had visits from the 'goodies' and the 'baddies' and the umpires and observers.

We had been briefed on baddies pretending to be goodies; goodies under cover, looking for baddies pretending to be goodies; neutral umpires looking for both. We'd been told how we should act if the baddies caught us …

'We will not be captured. We will just shoot all the "baddies"!' Marlee had said, with a very serious expression on her face.

An alarmed briefing officer had quickly tried to assure her they were all actually goodies, not baddies, and that she didn't have to shoot anyone. He went on to tell us that if the baddies threatened to torture us we should not be scared; they wouldn't do it; but that we should still not reveal information about any goodies that had been there, or their movements. Confused? Good, so were we!

I was missing all this fun, but Marlee kept me up to date on all the happenings when she called. One night she had me in fits of laughter telling me about the attack on the homestead by the baddies. They carried out a night attack and surprised everyone. It was a very well-executed ambush, but like all well-laid plans there was one thing they hadn't accounted for. A Yugoslav named Max.

Max is another of the Bullo characters. He has been coming to the station over many years for a month at a time to work on the house. But about five years ago he was involved in a terrible bar brawl and his skull was caved in. He now has a steel plate in it. Before the plate, he was a little vague. Now he's extremely so. As much as he wants to, he cannot work as he once did, and over the years he's spending more time on the station as a place to live.

His English is very hard to understand, and in turn he has great difficulty understanding the language. He is very old-world European, and this causes more problems. For example, if you are younger than Max, he will not take instructions from you. His attitude towards female staff has to be regularly criticised by me. When I'm around he is sickeningly sweet to the girls working in the kitchen; when I'm out of earshot it's a different matter. He'll walk into the kitchen and say, 'Hey, you girl. Get my meal!' and he never finds it unusual when the girl thumps it down in front of him so hard that the food is elevated.

I would tell the girls to bounce him, but they said it was just easier to feed him and send him on his way. One of the girls said, 'He made me so mad one day that I emptied nearly half a salt container over his lunch. But he just shovelled it non-stop into his mouth, saying all the time, "Good tucker, good tucker. You girl, good cook. I like you!"' She went on to say, 'It was then I realised he didn't know he was being rude and that it was just a way of life he was accustomed to and he wouldn't change no matter how much you explained that what he was doing was unacceptable.'

Of course, that was another problem—Max only understood what he *wanted* to understand. If he didn't like what you were telling him he would promptly say, 'I no understand.'

When we got him out of the hospital after his head injury, the doctor explained the operation carefully and said that Max would now be quite muddled in his thinking, and if under stress could lose the plot altogether. I had news for the doctor: he was like that *before* the operation. But these past years Max *is* deteriorating. It's now almost impossible to get anything across to him, and it's a complete waste of time to give him any instructions or to try to explain something to him.

A perfect example of explaining something to Max is the following story:

He came in one day for lunch, late again. The girls in the kitchen wanted to go out to the cattle yards to watch the helicopters mustering, so asked me if I could please give Max lunch. I agreed and off they went. I was heating his meal in the microwave, and he was sitting looking at some photos that had been left on the table. He picked up one of Marlee when she was a baby.

'Nice baby. Who this?' he said.

I replied, 'Mine. That is Marlee, when she was little.'

A blank expression covered his face. 'N-a-a-r-r. That's not yours!'

'Yes! My daughter, Marlee!'

'When you have this?' he asked, pointing to the photo.

'Twenty-five years ago.'

'N-a-a-a-r-r-r! I never see you with …' and his hands traced an outline of a large tummy.

'You weren't around twenty-five years ago,' I said patiently.

'I was here last year!' he said, indignant now.

'No, that's Marlee. *Marlee*! She is big now!' I was fast losing patience. He seemed to pay more attention when you shouted.

'O-o-o-o-h-h,' he said wisely. 'This her baby?'

What's the use? I thought. 'Yes, yes,' I said, hoping to end it. No such luck!

He was thinking heavily as he stuffed food into his mouth. Then out came the next pearl.

'When she have this?' he asked, stuffing food and talking at the same time. 'She got no husband.' Then narrowing his eyes in intense suspicion: 'And where you keep the baby now, ay?'

My initial reaction was to tell him to forget it, or more precisely to shut up, but I knew I couldn't, or we would be hearing the story, as told by Max, that we had 'done away with a baby'! So I took a deep breath and shouted, 'My baby!! Big girl!! Marlee!! My daughter!!'

After this screaming outburst he understood my patience

was at an end, so he said, 'Y-y-ya-a-a, that's all right, that's all right,' put the photo down and left.

I was by now quite exhausted, and not wanting a repeat performance, in the future, quickly put the photo away.

The next morning he came to me. 'Where that baby?' he said.

Oh no, not again, I thought. 'Look Max, forget the baby. B-a-b-y g-o-n-e a-w-a-y!' I spoke as slowly and clearly as I could.

'No, I know that baby. That your daughter. Big girl now, your daughter.' This he explained to me carefully, as if I was the one in doubt. Then he walked out the door, very pleased that he had cleared up that little problem for me. I sagged gratefully into the chair.

So now a poor, unsuspecting baddie had stumbled upon Max sleeping like a babe during the raid on the homestead. Max sleeps in his own room in the staff quarters, about 300 yards from the house. No one had explained the 'mock war' to him. No one wanted to!

'You are my prisoner. Hands up!' the poor, unsuspecting baddie ordered.

But of course he had to get Max awake first! Max's usual nighttime cocktail is an assortment of pills. Pills for the plate in his head, pills for the pain in his side, pills for the pain in his stomach, and sleeping pills to put him to sleep because all the other pains keep him awake. He washes down all these pills with four cans of beer. Hardly surprising that it's difficult to rouse him out of a deep sleep. The poor old baddie had none of this prior knowledge, however, and it took him a good fifteen minutes of shaking before he could even get a mumble.

'You're my prisoner!'

'What you say? What you talk about? Who you? Go 'way.'

'Wake up. This is war. You're my prisoner!' said the baddie, really into the swing of things now.

Max's brain finally started to function as this terrible fact swept into his very groggy brain. 'War?' He was on his knees in a flash, clinging to the baddie's legs. 'Don't shoot! Don't shoot! I tell you everything!' He was screaming now. 'I you friend. You ask, I tell all! Don't shoot, I know everything!'

Max was told he wouldn't be shot and the soldier patiently explained the situation, which of course went completely over Max's head. But our soldier didn't know what he was dealing with ... yet. He said he just wanted to ask Max a few questions about the place and the people there. When he asked how many people were in the main homestead, Max went through every person he had met on the station over the years. The baddie, when telling the tale later, said he realised he was dealing with a character when Max listed more than twenty names and didn't show any signs of stopping. He said that regularly during the interrogation Max would collapse on the floor and cling to his leg, begging him not to shoot. And said he would turn us all over to the enemy if they didn't shoot him! When questioned on fuel, he told of every fuel truck into the station for ten years. Guns? We had enough to arm an army. Food? Rooms of it! The poor enemy came crawling up the flat towards this amazing building, out in the middle of nowhere, manned with thirty-five people and an arsenal of guns that could blow his troops off the face of the Earth and a food and fuel supply to last a prolonged siege!

Later, when Marlee explained about Max, there was much laughter over the arrest. Then apparently the baddie became serious and said he had told Max not to leave his room. When he left him, he was on his knees praying. Everyone drew straws to see who would go down and explain the situation to Max!

So during the week Marlee kept me entertained daily with the normal antics that happened on the station.

The second conference was just as well received as the first. The second audience was mostly from Asia and I did worry that my Outback world would be so totally foreign to anything they knew that it might be hard for them to comprehend anything about our lifestyle. Living all your life in Singapore would make Bullo seem like another planet. But I was wrong, and the applause was even louder than at the first conference.

I felt like a veteran stage performer by the third conference, and, although still nervous, I was starting to look less than completely lost.

But I said I was a 'veteran performer' for another reason. My lawyer called me in Perth and told me the judges on the appeal court had reversed the decision. We had now lost our court case! I was stunned. If you have read *From Strength to Strength* you would know all about the court case. If not, here's a short rundown: Charlie's cousin sued me a few months after Charlie's death for late delivery on a contract of cattle. The contract ran until 1988, and he was suing me for being late on delivery in 1986! It should never have gone to court but it did! We finally won. He appealed. And now I was listening to words I could not believe: 'You lost the appeal'!

The old adage, 'the show must go on!' now had even greater relevance. Probable ruin was hanging over my head, and the fear of this was devastating. But the tight knot in my stomach because of the total unfairness of the whole case, and the pathetic system called justice we are forced to endure, had bile boiling in my throat! Nevertheless, I had to go on and speak at the third conference with a smile on my face.

I returned to Bullo the next day, to try to work out how to pay out a couple of hundred thousand dollars in the next few months and survive. I arrived home for the last few days of the mock war, although I was too wrapped up in my own problems to be interested in the army's; but I was certainly in the mood for war. And the mock war was about to include me.

I was on the phone, telling my lawyer, again, what I thought of the legal system, when this goodie came racing through the door of my office shouting, 'We're under attack! Where can I hide?'

I asked the lawyer to hold, and spoke to the goodie. This was my first morning back; I had no idea what had been happening, but I was soon told that his group had been hiding out on the station for a few days and they were just about to leave when the baddies whooped over the mountain range in a helicopter and launched an attack. He had to get on the phone to call headquarters. And where could he hide?

I gave him the fax phone and told him to get under the desk. I went back to the lawyer. The leader of the goodies was under my feet, talking on the fax phone to headquarters, and I had finally got back on track with the lawyer, and was again patiently listening, when a soldier launched through the door, levelled a gun at me and barked, 'You're my prisoner!'

'Oh, for crying out loud! Get lost!' I shouted, forgetting I was holding the phone.

The goodie under the desk froze in his conversation to headquarters while I abused the enemy over the desk.

'Go away,' I snapped. 'I'm talking to my lawyer. Come back and take me as a prisoner later!'

'Oh, all right,' he said, and backed out the door. 'How long before I come back?'

'Twenty minutes,' I said, and he disappeared.

I closed and locked the door and tried to continue the conversation, but it was impossible with the noise level. The goodies had spread out, and were running in all directions. Guns were firing blanks all over the place. The helicopter was circling the house to block any more goodies dashing for freedom, and someone was pounding on the door, demanding it be opened immediately. I told the lawyer I would call him back later, put the phone down and just buried my face in my arms on the desk and let the chaos drown me.

The pounding on the door stopped and the gunfire faded

as the chase moved across the airstrip to a field near the river. The helicopter was also off chasing someone. Peace was returning.

'Excuse me, can I get out?' I had forgotten the leader still under my desk.

The umpires decided who won the battle and everyone shook hands. The baddies had been declared outright winner, even though the goodie leader had got a message back to headquarters. This was very good, and one member of the team had completely escaped. The leader of the baddies, the chap I told to come back later, mentioned to me that I should not have been housing the enemy.

'What do you mean "the enemy"?' I said. 'They're the goodies. Aren't *you* the enemy?'

'No, we're the goodies!'

'Well you'd better check, because so are they.'

And indeed this was the case. They were a long way from where they should have been but goodies they were. The umpires had assumed the ground goodies were baddies and okayed the attack. Got the picture? Good.

It was all finally sorted out and the two teams of goodies left together to look for the one goodie who'd escaped. It was now assumed he was lost.

This was the last day of the war, so I knew I could call the lawyer the next day without interruption. I hoped.

I was soon to learn that an uninterrupted conversation was not going to get me justice. I thought I had faced some hard times in the past years, without Charlie, but this blow was way below the belt. I was going to have to find another $200,000. Where, I didn't know. The station had just had its worst rainfall on record, even my bank was fighting for survival.

Negative thoughts invaded my mind twenty-four hours a day. 'Give up. Why struggle? Sell! You can buy a lovely house over in the east, on the water, have money in the bank! No more mega problems like running your own water system, electricity system. No weed problems, no feral eradication programs, no BTEC (Brucellosis Tuberculosis Eradication Campaign)! No land erosion problems. Go to dinner when the urge hits you. Go on holidays, dial a pizza!'

In all seriousness, for the first time in our long struggle, the 'give up' thought stayed in my mind longer than it had ever done before. We had worked so hard and so long, and were just getting our nose in front when something like this came along and knocked us flat on our back again.

If it had been some stupid investment I had made then I could accept it. It would have been my own doing and I would accept the consequences. But when it's something beyond your control, you have to fight. As sick as I was at heart I had to start ... I had to find a way to survive ... I had to find $200,000! I had to find a plan. Couldn't ask the bank—at this stage of the recession an Outback property asking for a quarter of a million dollars, on top of already large loans, would put panic into overdrive.

The first thing I needed was time. Time to raise the money. Time to get to April and the start of the new mustering season, to get the cash flow again. I knew not to expect any leniency from Gus Trippe, so I had to find money for the period between February to the end of April.

It was family and friends that pulled us through. Marlee had already put in everything she had, and, bless her heart, Danielle loaned me all her savings! Plus a few good friends heard about the judgement and came through with offers of money. With support and love like this, I couldn't fail.

Months before, my bank, having its own problems, was reviewing all their loans and asked for an update on the property valuation. The one they held was done in 1985 (boom time), and seeing most of the land values had dropped an average of forty per cent, they wanted to review my position. So I was elated when the 1992 (recession time) valuation came back almost double the '85 valuation. It certainly confirmed to the bank that we must have been doing something right and that their investment in us was justified.

By mid March I had my house in order, I hoped, and

with all fingers crossed I started. I told the bank I had lost the appeal, and that I wouldn't go further in the justice system because I hadn't found any justice anyway, so why pay out more money? I said I had things under control (I had been around lawyers too long), and would only come to the bank as the last resort. They were pleased.

I got through, somehow, with a lot of juggling and not a penny to spare for twelve months. But we survived, and that was the main thing. As I write this in 1993, I am still recovering physically from those months of anguish. The torture of months of waiting for the final death knell, which could have come from anywhere, had a devastating effect on my health. February was over and well into March before I could safely say, with a lot of hope, and lots and lots more luck, that maybe, just maybe, Bullo could still be our home.

Boy, and I thought January had been tough!

Very battlescarred I braced myself for the remainder of March. We knew we had more problems looming. The rain was still too light and there wasn't enough for the new plants. The crop was surviving, but the lush, thick look of mid February, which should have still been very evident, was fading to a dull, sparse green.

I arrived back from the IBM conferences on the 12th March, but had to leave again for Sydney on the 18th for another conference. So the few days home were spent washing clothes, catching up on urgent office work, finding money to keep the operation going and writing a speech for the Sydney conference.

At first I thought my fees were quite high, for just an hour's speech, but I soon realised there was a lot more to it than one hour. Each conference has its own theme, so I have to write a speech around it. I type about twenty double-spaced pages and by the time I do some research on the firm, weave the theme and something about the company into my speech, type it and change it, and change it—

most of the time I'm still changing my speech while standing in the wings waiting to go on stage—that one hour can turn into days; and if you add the travelling time it can end up about a week. Still, I can't complain. It is good money.

I was going in three directions at once: washing and ironing, speech-writing and office work, and packing! Marlee came to me and said Franz would have to go to Darwin to extend his visa, so she suggested we drive up to town together. They could do everything required for his visa and then bring supplies back to the station and I could go on to Sydney.

We had anxiously watched a tropical depression that sat off the Western Australian coast for more than a week, and although we had constant cloud cover we only got 1 mm of rain. The sorghum crop needed much more rain than that, and was drying out so fast that Marlee knew baling would have to be started as soon as she returned.

We left for Darwin Sunday 15th, for our short ten-hour drive to the shops. We arrived very late on Sunday night, but were up early for Monday's full program.

It was then off in different directions—Marlee and Franz to immigration and me to R&M (repair and maintenance): facial, leg wax, nails, hair cut and dyed, etc. As the years go by the R&M process gets longer! It used to take a few hours. Now it takes days! Halfway through the first day's maintenance I took a break. I had arranged to meet Marlee and Franz for lunch. I was a few minutes' late and they were already seated. Marlee was wearing her sheepish look; my immediate thought was that she'd gone and bought something very expensive.

I sat down and she said, 'Is it all right if we get married?'

I took a few minutes to recover. I knew they were crazy about each other. All they did all day was look deeply into each other's eyes and smile blissfully! When I did see them, that was. I had been so worried and upset about the court decision that I hadn't been following the progress of their love.

'Well, it *is* a bit sudden,' I said, trying to hide my surprise, 'but of course it's up to you. You're the ones who have to make it work. Though I'm sure you've given it a lot of thought. When were you thinking of?'

'Tomorrow.' That *did* floor me!

'Tomorrow? As in the day after today?' I stammered.

'Well you have to go to Sydney on Wednesday.'

'I'm only in Sydney for two days. That's not very long.'

'It really is immigration. If we don't get married and file Franz's papers by tomorrow night, he'll have to leave the country and might not get back in for two years. So we have to get married tomorrow!'

Very simple. Now why didn't I see that? I wasn't *that* old that I couldn't understand the anguish of young love being separated for two years.

'Mummy, what do you think?' Marlee watched me closely.

'I'm certainly no expert on matters of the heart, but from what I have observed of love and marriage, if it's going to work between two people it doesn't matter if they get married the day they meet or ten years later. The day they marry is just one day in a long journey. The only advantage to waiting is to see if there are any annoying habits you simply can't tolerate or which drive you insane. But I've seen couples wait years before marrying and they still end up in the divorce court; and I have also seen couples marry within weeks of meeting and they too end up divorced. There's really no guideline. It's completely up to you.'

'So it's all right if we get married?' Marlee asked excitedly.

'Well, darling, I think you're old enough to make up your own mind, don't you?' I was flattered that she wanted my approval.

'But I want to know what you think.'

'Okay. I think that if you love each other, and you are happy, and you are faced with a two-year separation, you can only go ahead and get married.'

They sat and smiled through the rest of the meal. My mind was in such confusion, I won't even bother to try to describe it. Marlee jumped up and said they had to go and buy clothes. So off they went, shopping first for Franz's wedding clothes, then for Marlee. I had a few things to arrange, but found myself sitting pondering the events of the past hour. Franz is a wonderful man, and in many ways is like Marlee's Charlie. He is a man of few words, very capable in any job he tackles, easy to be with and interesting to talk to.

All the years since Charlie's death I kept telling Marlee that one day she would meet another man, and would love him as she loved Charlie. But she was so emphatic in her 'no!' that over the last year I had started to believe she was right.

Now that my prayers had been answered, I was at a bit of a loss. I had loved Marlee's Charlie as a son, he was just too good to be true and when we lost him it was the closest I came to breaking.

Still, despite this devotion, I knew I would have no trouble letting Franz into my heart, alongside Charlie. Just one look at Marlee's happiness was enough for me. It just bubbled out of her 24 hours a day. She had come back to life and Franz had brought her there.

As I have said to her many times lately, she has been very lucky to have loved two wonderful men in half a lifetime. I am two-thirds through my life and am still looking for one wonderful man!

I rallied myself from my thoughts. There was lots to be done. A wedding to be arranged in less than a day! I left the restaurant happy in the knowledge that not only would Marlee's Charlie move over and let Franz have a place in my heart; but that my Charlie would even move a little to give him some room too!

Danielle was coming over to visit on the station for a while, and was due to arrive in Darwin Tuesday night. So we called her and told her to get an earlier bus.

'Why?' she asked.

'Because I'm getting married tomorrow and I want you there,' Marlee replied.

Poor Danielle was completely flabbergasted.

Because of all the problems I had been dealing with there hadn't been too many chatty phonecalls between Danielle and me. Also Danielle and Martin had been away a lot, working at mine sites. Martin had landed a big contract pouring concrete at a mine a fair distance from home, so they only came home on the weekends. With them away most of the time and my constant problems, I hadn't mentioned Marlee and Franz's budding romance. Danielle and Martin knew of Franz of course, but nothing else had been said.

So Danielle caught the bus, to get to Darwin in time for Marlee's wedding.

I had a frantic afternoon, spent a good part of it and part of the night on the phone. I suppose you could say it was a *Yellow Pages* wedding. After I left Marlee and Franz I rushed to a florist and ordered a lovely fresh flower garland for her hair and a delicate posy to match. I then headed back to the apartment to do some furious phoning. I didn't call any friends in Darwin, there just wasn't enough time. I decided that Marlee and Franz would have to be satisfied with Danielle and me.

After I ordered the flowers I rushed into an appliance store and bought a small cassette player and some classical tapes that I thought would be nice background music for the ceremony. I found the nicest photographer by phone, and he promised to turn up the next day to photograph the ceremony and take some outside shots after they were married. I ordered a stretch limo for transport, and booked a suite for them at the Beaufort Hotel, for their wedding night. I also planned dinner for the four of us at the restaurant.

I finally sat back and asked myself what had I forgotten. I decided I'd covered everything, and relaxed. But not for long. Marlee and Franz arrived back with parts, food and other requirements for the station. We just had time to meet Danielle's bus. Franz brought back a takeaway dinner and we all sat down and talked and Danielle asked Franz questions and generally gave him the once-over.

Tuesday morning was an early start, and we went off again in all directions, returning to the apartment in time to prepare for the wedding. The flowers arrived and were perfect. Their arrival I think signalled the start of the excitement; up to that point, to me at least, it didn't seem real. There had been so much rush, there wasn't time to get excited. But gazing at those beautiful flowers nestling amongst all that soft pink paper made me realise Marlee was really getting married. My heart was glad. Her long sadness was over. She had worked so hard and alone for so long, and I thought it was only fair that she should now have some happiness. And this was the beginning. I carefully carried the garland into the bedroom. Her suit was just right and when I put the flowers on her hair it was the perfect touch. She loved her posy, it was decorated with pink and white ribbons with delicate little wedding bells at the end of each one. I stood and looked at the picture of sheer happiness. All systems were go and I felt no sense of hesitation. All my instincts said this was right.

'Okay, we're ready,' I said as I ushered our little family group towards the door.

I didn't say anything about the limo and when we got out of the lift Marlee said, 'Oh, we didn't call a cab.' I told her I did, and it was waiting outside. Marlee's mouth fell open when she saw the long white limo, and there were cries of delight as we all reclined into the velvet, air-conditioned interior.

The registry office was delightful, like a small chapel with ample seating. It was tastefully decorated with pot-plants and carpet, and had a very large polished table at the end of a short aisle. I plugged the cassette player into a power point at the back of the room and adjusted the volume for background music. The photographer arrived and it was all systems go.

Marlee cried most of the time; I think she cried from happiness, because of Charlie, because she never believed she would have a second chance at love, and because life at that moment was so full of promise and just too good to believe! I shed a few tears myself, for most of the same reasons. Franz smiled all the time and Danielle did a bit of both.

It was a lovely ceremony and the music was a great touch. Even the photographer commented on how nice it all was.

We went outside afterwards to take more photographs, hopefully without anyone crying. There was an enormous Moreton Bay fig in the courtyard so we assembled in front of it. We were standing there, smiling for the camera, when Lynette Ainsworth, longtime friend, came rushing into the courtyard with a basket of frangipani flowers and threw handful after handful over Marlee and Franz.

'Why didn't you tell me?' she cried as the flowers continued to fly. Apparently Danielle had called her sister Bonnie and Bonnie had called Lynette, who had then dropped everything and rushed over with only minutes to spare.

We explained the situation and thanked her for her thoughtfulness. After introducing her to Franz we all spent some time catching up on each other's lives.

It was then on to the lovebirds' next surprise, the Beaufort Hotel. Danielle had gone there earlier in the day to register and had prepared the room. She'd put champagne and strawberries in the fridge and had put some lovely little lace nothings under the pillow for Marlee.

We led Marlee and Franz to the elevator and took them up to the suite. They were thrilled. I don't think they could have been happier if they'd tried. We toasted their happiness and arranged to meet them for dinner in the restaurant.

The dinner that night was the end to a perfect day. It really *was* a wonderful wedding, and amid all the turmoil a perfect retreat, even if it was only for a few hours. It was like a fairytale. Just looking at Marlee and Franz's happy faces made me feel alive. Seeing them so happy told me the fairytale would last.

On Wednesday I had to fly to Sydney. Marlee and Franz came back to the apartment after they had their special wedding breakfast, so we had a few hours together. Then I was off to the airport. Before I left they thanked me for a wonderful, perfect wedding day. They said they could not have had a better day if there had been months of preparation.

'It was just what we would have wanted—right down to the strawberries in the fridge … Oh, and Franz thanks you very much for the naughty lace things I found under my pillow,' said Marlee, beaming.

Danielle went to stay with Bonnie for the few days I was to be in Sydney and the plan was she would meet me in Darwin on my return trip, and come down to the station with me.

I sagged into the seat on the plane and let out a deep sigh.

'Sara,' I said, 'you just never know what the next day will bring!'

My Sydney conference was more what I was used to. Gone were the spotlights, the technicians with walkie-talkies, people running to and fro with clipboards, directions from a black void telling me to look this way and that and count backwards from ten and walk this way and stand on the 'X' and don't move! It was all gone. I was back in a nice, normal conference room with a few hundred people and I could see their faces and talk to them. Even though the nerves were there, it was so much more relaxing than Perth.

The next day I went to the publishers and met all the people working on my book, including Jeannine Fowler, who would be in charge of the tour, the publicity, and me! It was shaping up to be quite a marathon. The last details of the book were being arranged, the cover looked great and I was promised the first copy in my hand by April. It certainly was an exciting feeling. Of course everyone there knew what to expect and what they were doing, except me. I was just following it all, in a complete daze. Just smiling and nodding my head, while their enthusiasm washed over me. It is a great tonic for the soul to be patted on the back and told you are wonderful, even if you don't understand why, or what is about to take place. Just being told everything down the road is going to be fine heals the soul, and my soul definitely needed a fair bit of TLC! Except for Marlee and Franz's wedding day, the year so far had been miserable hell.

The main reason for my being there, however, was to meet the sales reps. They are a very important link in a long chain of very important links. They have to go out and convince the bookstores why they should put in big orders for lots of books. They were a great bunch of people and very complimentary about my book, and they actually seemed to enjoy selling it. One of the women reps was telling me how she enjoyed relating some of the stories in the book to the booksellers, and how they would become interested and ask questions, when one of the other reps came over.

'Go on, tell the truth. The book is selling itself. The stores are asking for it,' she said.

'Well, that's true,' she replied. 'But I still enjoy telling the stories, and they enjoy listening.'

This was very heady business for me. I still couldn't come to grips with the fact that I had even written a book—I thought that when it was in my hands and I was looking at it, then maybe it would become believable. But until that time I was still struggling with all the wonderful predictions. This was definitely fairyland. I decided not to worry; I had had enough of doing that. So I enjoyed the moment. If the book didn't do what it was supposed to do, then at least I would still have these lovely memories.

I would have loved to have stayed and basked in all the glory and praise, but I had to fly back to Bullo on Saturday. Back to reality. Back to stacks of office work climbing up the walls and a smaller pile of faxes and phonecalls. I had to put this aside for a while to concentrate on organising the payments to Gus Trippe. I had told the lawyer to offer a four-month payment plan, with the first payment of $50,000 on the 31st March, and much to my surprise it had been accepted. So I thought, good, first step in place. I now had the time I needed.

But things are never that straightforward, and I was faxed an incredible fourteen-page agreement to sign, none of which made any sense at all: 'The party of the first agrees with the party of the second … and, according to para 6-(3)-iii of the third clause … where as not so if … para 4g(c)ii not pursuant to the fact …' and on and on, for page after page. I told the lawyer that I didn't understand a word of the whole fourteen pages and that if he thought I would sign such a document after being in court for five years because of one word, he would have to think again. His response was that it was your normal standard guarantee agreement. My response was that I would not sign anything I did not understand; and, anyway, what was the bottom line of all those pages of gobbledygook? Ignoring my vulgar language he informed me the bottom line was, quote, 'I guarantee to pay the said amount'.

If he thought 'gobbledygook' was vulgar, he was now seconds away from hearing some real language.

'The bottom line is, "I promise to pay"! Fourteen pages and that's all it says, *"I promise to pay"*?' I had hundreds of choice words I would've liked to have used but I refrained, and politely said, 'Well, if that is all it says, then that is all I will sign, "I promise to pay the above amount."'

'Oh, you can't do that.'

'Why?'

'You must sign or they might not agree to the four-month payment plan.'

'Okay,' I said. 'The first payment is only a week or so away, stall until I make it.' I didn't have it in hand yet.

I never did sign that agreement and it was very fortunate that I didn't because the second half of the document had me guaranteeing to pay some ludicrous amount for court costs. That was the first page I put a thick black line through, and by the time I had read the whole thing, all the pages had thick black lines through them.

It was now back to the fields of sorghum with the crazy hay baler. Oh, how we will rejoice if ever we can afford to buy a better machine! Every time you said 'hay baler' Uncle Dick's eyes crossed! There had been extensive work done on the monster during the year, and it really did behave extremely well, considering; but it probably spent as much time in the workshop as it did baling hay. The rubber belts that form the bale of hay were really starting to show wear and had to be joined hundreds of times to make it through the season. They only just made it, and it was obvious that new belts would have to be on the budget for the next season's sorghum.

On Monday the 30th a bank cheque for $50,000 was paid by one lawyer to the other lawyer. I was sick to the stomach and angry most of the week leading up to the payment, but on the day of the handover I really had trouble containing myself.

I silently vowed I would have my day. Somehow, some way … I would have my day.

CHAPTER 5

April 1992

We now knew we were in one of the worst droughts the station had had for many years. Darwin recorded the lowest rainfall for fifty years, which was as far back as they had kept records. It was our worst rainfall in thirty years. None of the creeks ran, the river stayed at the same level. We could drive out the road in March without any grader work, just a bit of shovel work. It was terrible.

My next trip away from the station wasn't south this time, but north. I had been invited to attend the CGS (Chief of the General Staff) Land Warfare Conference in Darwin. The army had invited me six months back, in October. The conference ran for five days and this time, being a land-owner representative, I wouldn't have to speak. I was looking forward to it. Apart from it being very interesting, it would be the first conference I had attended in two years as a spectator.

I was packing when Marlee came into the room and said she would have to come to Darwin with me. The doctor had just called to tell her something had shown up on her recent pap smear and he would like to do another check.

My stomach hit the floor. 'What do you mean, "something"?'

'He said it was nothing to worry about. He just wants to make doubly sure.'

My stomach returned to normal, but the worried state remained. 'Well, at least we can have a few quiet days together. That'll be nice,' I said cheerfully.

We drove to Darwin on Sunday and booked into the hotel late Sunday night, as was our usual procedure. We went again in the seven-ton truck so Marlee could take back another load of the endless list of supplies we never seem to stop needing on the station.

Monday I went to the first day of the conference and Marlee went to the doctor. I found the conference very interesting. There were representatives from many different countries: England, USA, Indonesia, Malaysia, Canada and more. There were local, interstate and federal politicians. Also a fair representation of business and industry. Along with the conference, each day included a bit of sightseeing for the 'out of towners'. Near the end of the week there would be trips to the army, navy and airforce installations, and I wanted to see them; but first on my list of priorities was Marlee. I went back to our room to check if she was back.

The moment I saw her face my heart stopped. The doctor had found a small growth on the lip of the cervix—very small, but it could not be left. She was going into hospital on Wednesday for the operation. She told me not to panic; the doctor had assured her the growth was very small, only just forming. The operation would be only a nick to cut it all away. Quite straightforward. They had caught it at the very beginning, fortunately. A straightforward operation, which would not affect her having children. Don't worry.

One thought went through my mind: 'She's talking too much.'

Despite our fears we both continued to treat it as a small, 'not to worry' operation. We were both ignoring the implications.

I attended the conference the next day. I don't remember much of the happenings—most of the day passed in a daze.

The afternoon was more sightseeing, so I excused myself to spend the time with Marlee. Wednesday was Marlee's birthday. I wished her a happy birthday—not that you can feel very happy on your birthday when you are about to go into hospital. We had breakfast together, Marlee had to be at the hospital at eleven and was to be operated on in the afternoon. I said I would attend the conference up to the morning teabreak and then come back to the room to see her to the taxi and be out to the hospital after lunch. I had been invited to sit at the CGS's table for lunch and didn't think I should stand them up at the last minute. I kissed Marlee goodbye and said I would be there straight after lunch.

The rest of the morning and lunch were not enjoyable. I should have just gone to the hospital and sat it out with Marlee, but I'm notorious in the family for cracking up if any of my children are sick or hurt. When the girls were little, whenever one of them had an accident the other two would wash and clean her up before they brought her to me, because if I saw the blood I would just go to pieces. And of course the famous story was when I sat outside the operating theatre for hours when Danielle had her appendix out, anxiously waiting for her to be wheeled out, when she had gone to recovery, recovered, and was back in her room mounting a search for what she knew would be her frantic mother. So I think Marlee thought the longer I kept away, the better.

Thoughts were invading my mind all day and through the lunch and I really had to concentrate on the conversation. I found I would be asked a question, and although I'd be looking at the person my mind refused to take in what they were saying. I was continually asking for the question to be repeated. I excused myself as quickly as I could. I had to get to Marlee.

Finally, in the taxi, I let my mind wander over the past few days. Shock has many faces, different every time. My shock reaction when I lost Charles was total disbelief. I just would not believe that he could die. Weeks after his death

I found myself thinking he would walk in the door. I was numb, had no feelings whatever. When I lost Mum, it was as if a hand reached inside me and tore away part of my heart. I felt wounded, as if by a gunshot. My heart hurt and it took time to heal. When Marlee's Charlie was killed I experienced sheer terror. I felt as if my life was unravelling and I could do nothing to stop it. I was powerless. I needed knock-out pills to black everything out while my mind and body recovered from the panic I was experiencing. This time my mind was combating shock differently, yet again. I was defiantly ignoring it. And I realised strangely enough that Marlee was too. This wasn't a conscious decision—from the moment Marlee told me she had cancer of the cervix I refused to accept it and pushed it out of my mind. I suppose that's why I went on attending the conference. We were both ignoring it, treating it all as a casual matter, even though deep down we both knew it wasn't.

I arrived at the hospital and we sat and talked about nothing really, and waited until it was time for her to leave for the operation. After she left I paced the room and tried to occupy my mind. I stared out of the enormous windows that spanned the width of the room. It was a large room, nicely carpeted, and had a small table and chairs, a very comfortable sofa and a private bathroom. I couldn't help but remember the one and only time I had been in hospital in Darwin way back in 1964. No private hospitals in Darwin in those days. And definitely no private rooms. It was everyone in together, and sometimes you had a lot more than the patients in the ward with you. If an Aboriginal woman was in hospital the whole family would camp on the lawn outside the ward and wait until she went home, and when it rained they would camp in the ward. It was all very casual. Most of the time they would just sit under the tree and shout back and forth to each other and the children would run around in the garden and play.

Back then, the wards were long and narrow. No air-conditioning, only fans. Lino on the floors and floor-to-ceiling louvres. It was so hot the fans just circulated hot air. It was much cooler out under the trees, which was where most of the Aboriginal patients sat with their families, if they weren't too sick. You would constantly hear a nurse calling out, trying to find an erring patient.

But those days have gone. I was now standing in a perfectly temperature-controlled air-conditioned room, looking out at landscaped gardens. No campers—the hospital had its own little motel wing for family members. There was a bistro where you could order food any time of the day, a personal fridge and your own phone. Darwin had come a long way since the 1960s, hospital-wise.

The waiting dragged on. The phone made me jump. It was Franz. Poor Franz, waiting alone back on the station. Marlee had only gone to Darwin for a further check-up, but it hadn't turned out as the doctor had hoped and so she had had to break the terrible news to Franz over the phone. I told him she was still in surgery and that I would call him the moment she was out. I called Danielle. I called Susan, to keep from thinking. But eventually it was back to the pacing.

At last she was wheeled in from recovery. The nurse said the results were good—they had only had to remove a small part and had caught the cancer right in the forming stage. It was very lucky Marlee had had the test when she did. But she wasn't let off that easily. The cutting machine had slipped on the way out leaving Marlee with a few more cuts than required, and they had also had to be stitched. This was why she'd been so long in surgery.

She was very groggy, and as the hours passed I could see this was not the short stay she thought it would be. I called Franz about an hour after she came back from recovery, but she was still so groggy all she could do was mumble and I finally had to tell him she would be much better in the morning. She vomited well into the night. When there was nothing left to vomit, she started dry-retching. She had to keep her eyes closed—if she opened them or took her head off the pillow the vomiting would return.

I sat by the bed and quietly talked to her. Every now and then her hand would feel for mine, give it a squeeze and then she would smile, and the smile said, 'Thank you for being here.'

Around midnight she drifted off into a fitful sleep. The pills the nurse had given her to stop the vomiting and the pain had finally taken effect. I left. The nurse had said it was all right to sleep in the room with Marlee, but I wanted to go back and apologise and bow out of the rest of the conference. I knew where I would be for the next four or five days.

She was a very sore and miserable girl the next morning. She had only slept a few hours after I left and was awake most of the time until dawn. Still sick in the stomach, she couldn't eat. Danielle had sent a basket of flowers containing all Marlee's favourite foods, but they had to sit in the fridge. They were too rich for her even to think about.

Marlee wanted me to attend the rest of the conference and the functions at night, but I wouldn't hear of it. How could I go dancing when she was lying there so sick and miserable? Besides, I told her, I would only eat all that fattening food and put on more weight. And anyway, I would much rather be with her, and that was the truth. This was not a time for her to be alone with her thoughts. This was her first operation and I knew how frightened she was. And when the shock wore off, she still had to come to terms with the fact she had just been operated on for cancer. Although the operation was over, and the doctor had said the cancer had been caught in the very early stages, there were still five years of tests. That alone has a terrible psychological effect on you. As you approach each six-monthly test there is the stress level that builds up and then the agonising wait for the results. We both had to come to terms with this.

We were still managing to maintain this defiant attitude towards this terrible disease. For days on end, sitting in that hospital in silence, just holding Marlee's hand while she slept, I concentrated my eyes on her body and challenged the cancer. Over and over in my mind I screamed at it like a banshee, 'Get out of my daughter's body!'

At times during those first days, when Marlee was so ill she could only open her eyes, smile, squeeze my hand, and close her eyes again, we were as one. I just know she could feel me battling, fighting for her while she was too weak to do battle herself. She could feel my strength pouring into her body, and she would smile her thanks. After a few days she joined me in the fight.

She was walking very carefully and slowly now. Because of the extra stitching she was not only sore inside but extremely sore outside as well. She could only be flat on her back or standing—sitting was just too painful. It was interesting watching her go from flat on her back to standing without her bottom touching any surface, and we did get a few laughs from that. She started to laugh again and eat, and slowly things got back on track again. Franz was holding down the fort at Bullo and was a very lonely and worried new husband. He had to wait until I came home before he could leave for Darwin. We still had the truck in Darwin but because Marlee couldn't even sit down driving a big truck over bumpy roads for ten hours to get home was not on the cards for quite a while.

Marlee's 'short' hospital stay stretched into ten days. I went home on the sixth day and flew into Bullo in a four-seater plane from Kununurra. Franz flew out on the same plane heading for Darwin. Marlee said he appeared at her door with orchids and everything felt better from that day on. During the early morning he would go and arrange the supplies to be loaded on the truck and then he would return to the hospital to spend the rest of the day with Marlee. She said from the day Franz arrived she had most of the nurses attending her every need, every minute of the day. I can understand that. Franz makes most women sit up and take notice. He is definitely not a man who can walk into a room and blend into the background. He's 6 foot, 3 inches tall, with a nicely muscled frame and is so physically fit it's disgusting! He has greeny-brown eyes, golden-auburn hair and a smile that over the years has probably got him anything he wanted! And was continuing to do so at the hospital until Marlee could finally check-out and the long trek home had started.

The drive back to the station was a bit of a nightmare for Marlee. She had to lie down on the seat all the way. By the time Franz had driven carefully to Katherine, he decided that they would stop for the night. Marlee was not faring very well, but of course would not admit it. But she didn't utter a word of protest as he led her gently to the room and a bed she could stretch out on.

The last 48 miles over the Bullo road got a few yelps out of her and I had a very relieved but exhausted patient on my hands as we carefully eased her down from the truck. The doctor's instructions had been, 'Do nothing, except walk slowly around.' She still couldn't sit in a chair, so it had to be lying down or slow walking.

But there was no real recovery time allowed for any of us. A film crew from '60 Minutes' was due to arrive on the station in a few days' time. This had been arranged well before we received the news about Marlee's operation. I had called them the day after the operation to tell them we had a very incapacitated star—so much so that she could not even sit on a horse or drive the bullcatcher. She was only capable of smiling for the next week or so and could they possibly delay the filming for at least a week? By that time she'd be able to walk without looking as if she were in agony. The crew was scheduled to leave for Cambodia the day after they left the station—it was into Darwin overnight then straight on to Cambodia—so the filming had to be now.

I tried to get them to understand that the action parts discussed were going to be very subdued, and I didn't want them disappointed. We did have a rough outline as to what we were going to film, and up till now there had been no doubt in my mind as to who was going to supply all the action. Marlee. I went on to explain that Marlee was only capable, at the moment anyway, of smiling, and even that was done with care. The producer thought they could get around the problem, but I don't think they realised how sick she was.

When she finally did make it home she let go. She fell apart. She had been holding everything inside. The realisation that she had just been operated on for cancer hit her and the floodgates opened. She felt she was letting me down, because this program was part of my book launch. The book came out in the shops a few days after the Sunday program was to go to air. She was devastated that she couldn't do what was needed of her to make a good and interesting film. I told her not to worry about performing and just to hurry up and get better. If the book was no good it wouldn't sell if we made *High Noon*, so not to worry.

Danielle, my little trooper, flew over from Queensland and provided the outside action, and Marlee managed to stand there and smile while instructing one of our guests in the art of milking. But even this took it out of her and she went back to bed soon after. It would have been nice to see her in action with Danielle, because they are both a pleasure to watch. However, despite all the problems behind the scenes it still was a terrific show, but I think that was because we were working with professionals.

I didn't realise the stress I was under until I saw myself on screen, when the program finally came to air in May. It didn't even look like me! Susan called from Queensland after she had watched it and said the same thing: 'It doesn't even look like you. Sara, you'd better slow down, or something's going to give. You cannot keep pushing yourself this way.'

She was right, I was splitting myself too many ways. Dealing with the terror of cancer was the biggest thing on my mind at the time. It's heartbreaking if you have to face this dreadful disease yourself, but to have one of your children under sentence is the worst thing imaginable. The pressure of financial commitments I had to meet over the next year was bad enough—finding $50,000 every thirty days for four months was with me day and night. And then to add Marlee's tragedy ... it wasn't any wonder I didn't look like me. I didn't *feel* like me! I felt like a zombie, and after looking at the show I now knew I looked like one. In hindsight I'm amazed how I did get through—how we all got through. It just goes to show how you really *can* beat the problem if you don't waste time waiting and wondering.

We had three lots of tourists in the next two weeks. Danielle stayed and helped for as long as she could. She was her usual strong self when things seemed the blackest. My other new blessing was Franz. He and Danielle together whipped the outside operation into shape and gave Marlee a chance to recover. Franz's care and concern for Marlee was always visible—each day she grew stronger and happier with his support. But cancer is a frightening enemy. We were constantly doing psychological battle with it and it was draining us.

However, with the bad there always has to be some good, if you look for it. And ours came in the form of a tourist. Fate is a strange thing, as I have said many times. The day before our guest was due to arrive I was wishing her away. We still had the '60 Minutes' team filming, I was stretched beyond my limits, and Marlee was still too sick to care. Franz was working wonders just keeping things operating in the mustering section. To put one last card on this shaky stack would bring down the lot. I did actually try to contact our guest at her hotel, but missed her by hours. I was going to explain the situation and ask if she would rather not come. But too late. She was on her way. I sat and thought, 'What a mess.' Marlee was having nightmares, worrying about not being able to have children, and what if it comes back ... These and other frightening thoughts were constantly in her mind. I saw it every time I looked into her eyes. The last thing we needed right now was tourists.

I told Marlee just to stay in her room and rest. Whatever

happened, happened. Danielle had to go back to Queensland—she had overstayed as it was. Martin had job commitments waiting so she had to be there. Franz had things fully under control, with Marlee telling him what the stockmen were to do and him checking that every instruction was carried out to the letter. So things were moving towards the first muster of the season.

Our guest arrived on time, and what a delightful person she was. Truly sent straight from heaven. I laid all our cards on the table about Marlee's illness, told her we were still in shock and would understand if she wanted to leave, but that she was very welcome to stay—if she wanted to. She did stay, and was a pleasure and delight every moment she was on Bullo. And the hand of fate? She had had the same operation as Marlee, many, many years before. And the cancer had been much more advanced than Marlee's. She told Marlee cheerfully that she had had children and had not had one hint of trouble in all the years since. Marlee talked to her for days, about everything, including their mutual love of horses. She was such a bright and enthusiastic distraction in our life, much needed at that time, and to think I nearly stopped her from coming …

Time alone will tell if Marlee is in the clear, but if nothing else, this experience has helped me conquer the fear that invades your own body when you hear that someone you love dearly has CANCER. To this day I ignore it, refuse to accept that it exists. In my mind I have banished it from our life and from Marlee's body, and I will accept no other result.

I know Marlee is handling it well; she has far more steely resolve than I and has probably challenged cancer to a duel with swords. So if a determined subconscious is the secret to killing cancer, then it has gone from my Marlee, and is now licking its battle wounds in some dark and sinister cave.

Lunch lingered on well into the afternoon and we answered so many questions—all interesting—about the operation of such a big cattle station. I sat back and watched with delight as Marlee took over answer time. It was lovely to see the fire back in her spirit. Boots, our station stallion, was the other star of the day. He spent the afternoon putting his head through one or other of the open French doors and nuzzling various people, in the hope of being fed. He would gently rest his chin on a shoulder and wait for a morsel. If he was not given something immediately he would try to take the food any way he could. But when everyone recovered from the shock of a horse sharing lunch with them, he was fed continuously.

I also had the first inkling of the life of an author. We had tried to get books to the station in time for the luncheon. The company had wanted to give each couple a signed book as part of the day on Bullo, but instead I had signed name labels that could be put in books later, down south. So it had started and it had started on Bullo; Charlie would have liked that.

It was a long day, especially for Marlee. And by the time the plane took off late in the afternoon, we were weary. But it was worth every minute of the hard work just to see Marlee laughing and smiling—the first time since the operation. She was back in the world of the living.

We were into the next muster when 'D' day arrived, or I should say 'L' day, Launch Day, the 13th May. Charlie's lucky number.

The launch started with an article in the *Good Weekend* colour magazine. This was followed by '60 Minutes' the next day and then the book was finally in the shops.

It was a funny day. I kept saying to myself, 'Well, it's out there now. You'll soon know.' But you don't. Maybe the publishers get the feedback straight away, but the author has to sit and agonise and wait. Unless you called the publishers on the hour every hour you had no choice but to wait for weeks for results. Sometimes it was months before a book started to sell. Sometimes it never happened! Of course, if Marlee had had her way she would have had an open line twenty-four hours a day, which would have given minute by minute updates of all sales all over the country. I wouldn't have minded that myself, but I would never have asked for it, and I had to stop Marlee from doing just that. To her this was the only book in existence.

So although this was a significant day in my life, after saying 'Whoopie!' to myself a few times it was business as usual. No, I can't say I really was as matter of fact as all that—I would every now and then let out a 'Yahoo! It's launched!' and give the book a quick flick-through, still finding it hard to believe I had actually written it. But my mind housed a mixture of emotions. I knew that wonderful things were expected of it, yet was terrified it wouldn't meet those expectations. Marlee wanted to celebrate with champagne but I wouldn't let her. I thought it might jinx it.

For days I would find myself sitting staring at my face on the cover of the book, wondering, 'What happens now?' I was quite hopeless work-wise, had to force myself to get anything done. I wandered around the house telling myself how I should have changed this part, how I left this out, why didn't I add this? Marlee finally told me to go to Darwin to have a few quiet days to collect myself before the tour. Sound advice. I was showing very definite signs of stress. Instead of being excited about the greatest event in my life, I was dreading it. I was so tired and worried and just plain down, that I lacked the confidence to carry it off. I had always wondered why people wanted to be hermits, it seemed so strange to me. But the week before I was due to leave on my tour I had a strong desire to go and bury my head in the sand and forget everything.

I busied myself with packing. I had to pack for every climate—from the tropics of Cairns to the cold of Hobart. I tried desperately to get everything into one suitcase, and failed miserably.

I had to arrange the 31st May payment before I left. It was due to fall in the middle of the tour, and with the schedule I had I would have no time for anything outside of the book. Money was now coming in from cattle, so it wasn't as desperate as the other months had been. But still, doing this again so soon after the last payment had my stress level to breaking point. The stress was caused by the anger surges and by worry. I was worried about Marlee doing too much too soon, I was worried about the tour; I was worried, period! I had fifteen days of speeches, television appearances, newspaper interviews, book signings, literary luncheons, literary dinners and non-stop travel. I was still writing speeches, sorting out the most comfortable clothes, there was no room for 'hard to wear' or impractical dresses. I was edgy. And I wasn't totally sure I could last the fifteen long days of touring.

We had another muster on the 15th and Marlee was busy handling, branding and drafting cattle. But she managed to stop for long enough to tell me once more to go!

'Mummy,' she almost begged, '*please* go to Darwin. Get a massage and stare at the hotel walls for a few days, till you feel human again.'

I said it wouldn't help, but she insisted and just packed me onto the small plane and kissed and hugged me goodbye and said to me, as she always seemed to be saying, 'Go on, Mum. You can do it! Go wow them. I know you can!'

I arrived in Darwin late Tuesday afternoon. The tour started on the Friday. Somehow I had to get this wreck of a body and mind into working order. I was still worrying about leaving Marlee with all the responsibility, but she assured me that with Franz she would be just fine. They were deliriously happy—they had each other, so they could be strong together. I was the problem at the moment and I had to do something about it immediately or I wouldn't get through the weeks ahead.

I checked into the hotel and called the beautician I go to whenever I'm in Darwin. I asked if she could give me a massage straight away. She agreed, and I was there within minutes. I told her I felt like death on legs; she didn't comment, because that was obviously how I looked. She just asked me to get up on the massage table. I told her I had to survive fifteen days of intensive touring and asked her to do her utmost to get me into shape.

I closed my eyes and tried to relax and she went to work.

That afternoon, Zelda worked on me for hours before she could make any impression on my muscles. She said my neck and shoulder muscles were like steel bands. She massaged and applied hot towels and repeated the process over and over before she could feel any signs of me relaxing. Eventually my neck muscles became too sore to touch, so she rubbed in a soothing lotion and left them for the next day. She worked on the rest of the knotted muscles in my back and all over me. When she had finished, neither of us was sure if I would make it to the hotel on my own, my legs were so wobbly. I crawled into a hot bath, but was too weak and exhausted to get out and kept falling asleep. Every part of my body was relaxing with a vengeance. I remember pulling out the bathplug because I thought if I fell asleep in the bath I would drown. I woke up the next morning in bed, with no recollection of having got there. It took me some time to get out of bed and coordinate my legs. I couldn't believe stress could get you in such a state, but I was walking proof ... well, just walking, proof. My next massage was at 8 a.m. Again, Zelda worked until she could see improvement. I was back again at twelve noon. She finally broke through the stress barrier on the 5 p.m. massage. My neck muscles now felt other than steel cords and were starting to become pliable.

Marlee called me Wednesday night, just after I'd managed to crawl out of the bath and make it to bed without falling asleep on the way, but I could hardly articulate. Marlee was alarmed. I assured her it was because I was relaxed. She replied that she had never heard a relaxed person who sounded like me. I told her I was getting better, even though

I really didn't feel that way. I only had one and a half days to go before the tour, and I must admit I wasn't all that confident. But so many people were relying on me, I had to give it my all. So I banished all other thoughts from my mind and tried to focus on what I had to do. Oh, I still worried day and night, but I kept that in the background.

Thursday, 'D' day minus one. I arrived at the salon early and had the works: facial, massage, leg wax, massage, fingers and toenails painted, eyelash tint, massage. It was the first time in my life I'd spent the entire day in a beauty salon.

I woke Friday morning feeling reasonably human. After a third night of twelve hours' relaxing sleep I was feeling that maybe I could survive. I certainly wasn't jumping out of my skin, but the important thing was I felt I was together. I had Zelda to thank for that.

Friday, 22nd May. This was it! I had two interviews and a literary luncheon—Darwin's first literary luncheon. As I looked out at the sea of faces I saw many old friends looking back at me. It was a good thing I decided not to have notes because I had to stand up at the table and hold a microphone and talk. You can hide a lot behind a lectern, even a small one. Notes and tissues for sweating hands, etc. But there is nowhere to hide a thing just standing at a luncheon table.

The nerves were there in full force so I couldn't eat, hungry as I was. I felt if I put any food into that turmoil in my stomach it would just throw it straight back where it came from. I passed the time pushing the food around my plate, thinking this would be a great way to diet. If I had thirty speeches, one each day for thirty days, I'd be slim. Probably dead, but slim.

After the speech I did a television interview and signed books. It finished about three, and for Darwin's first literary lunch I thought it was a successful affair. More than 120 people had booked and more seemed to have turned up on the day. I knew there were a lot of things I could do along the way to improve my speech and so I concentrated on those changes as I soaked in a long, hot bath back at the hotel.

The next day saw another first—my very first book signing session. People came in a steady stream, and a few times the line banked up. But it would be classed as a quiet morning, and gave no inkling of what lay ahead in the eastern states.

I had coffee with Ruth, the owner of Bookworld and Tony, state manager for Pan, and about three o'clock went back to the hotel. Tony wanted to know if he could arrange dinner, but I told him I was in training: no drinking, no late nights; it had to be early to bed and plenty of sleep. I'm sure he went away thinking I was an eccentric nut, but I knew this was the only way. If I started going to dinner and having late nights and glasses of wine here and there, it would be the end of me.

I spent the rest of the afternoon putting my clothes in order and packing my suitcase. After finishing the packing I kept a hair appointment I had previously arranged for a cut and dye and I was now completely overhauled from top to toe! I had an early dinner, watched the news on television, put in a wake-up call for 4.30 a.m. My flight to Cairns was six o'clock.

As it turned out, I didn't need the wake-up call. My nerves did it for me. I was wide awake at 4 a.m. I left the hotel in time to have coffee in the departure lounge at Darwin airport. I was greeted and congratulated by all the staff and after a quick coffee and a chat I was off again.

My publicist, Jeannine, met me at Cairns airport and it was straight into the first interview. I posed on a bridge over a swimming pool, peeped out from behind a tree and a few other places, and all the while I couldn't help but think 'why am I doing this?' However, as I was soon to find out, there was a lot more to writing a book than just the pile of papers that make up the manuscript.

It was another newspaper interview an hour or so later

and then a television station, a late lunch, and a short break before a cocktail party to meet the reps. This was then followed by a literary dinner. I didn't need to go to the gym for a workout—we were staying at one of those tropical resorts that covers acres and acres, and being a good ten-minute jog to the reception from my room, after four appointments and getting lost a few times I had clocked up a fair few miles by cocktail hour.

The dinner speech seemed to go well. Jeannine was pleased and she had attended quite a few of these affairs so I considered her an expert. The guests certainly said they enjoyed it.

Next stop was Brisbane. We got into the airport at 10 a.m. and were straight into the radio and television interviews. This continued for most of the day and the next morning was more of the same. At midday we left for Toowoomba for a book signing. That finished at 5 p.m. and it was on to a dinner.

My mouth fell open when we arrived at the restaurant. It was packed and they were turning a lot of people away. I could hardly get through the obstacle course to the microphone and had to step over all the wires from the power-points. The MC was holding my hand, helping me up to the lectern, when my heel caught in my hem. I was hopping on one leg, with the man holding my hand and everyone clapping, waiting for me to step up to begin my speech. I was saying, 'Let go of my hand'—I needed it to free my heel—but he couldn't hear me, and thinking I was suffering last-minute stagefright was gripping me even tighter and encouraging me to come forward! I was wobbling and pulling back and he was smiling and pulling forward. I could see myself falling on the wires and the whole apparatus coming down on me in a heap. Luckily a nice man at a table right behind me saw my dilemma and quickly unhooked me. I cleared the wire, thanked him, and stepped up to the microphone.

It was a great night. There were many photographs taken

and many, many books signed. I was relaxing more and the speech was coming easier, and I thoroughly enjoyed talking to all the people. At conferences, a lot of people are reluctant to approach you. One man once came up to me at a conference and said, 'I know you don't have time to talk to me, but ...' And I said, 'Yes, I do.' And he said, 'Pardon?' And I said, 'Yes. I do have time to talk to you.' To which he was very surprised and said most speakers just leave straight after the speech and the audience never has a chance to speak to them personally. When I told him I wasn't your regular run-of-the-mill speaker 'so speak on', he did. The people at the literary dinners, however, weren't like this at all. They were very friendly from the word go and were all around me, asking questions about the book, the station, the way I wrote the book, how was Marlee, had she met any other nice man ... endless questions.

At last it was time to leave. We drove back to Brisbane, arrived around midnight and went straight to bed.

The slow pace of Darwin had now well and truly disappeared, and I could feel the pressure slowly building up. Jeannine was rushing in all directions; how she coordinated the whole tour and kept it running smoothly and on time I'll never know. I, on the other hand, spent most of my time walking around in an organised daze. I had no idea of where I was going, most of the time didn't even know what city I was in. Jeannine would have to whisper in my ear where we were, who my next interviewer was, or what radio station we were talking to. I would repeat the name over and over and then someone would shake my hand and start saying how much they enjoyed my book and I would forget everything I'd just been told. At one stage of the tour I was asked, 'And what do you think of our great city?', and if you'd offered me a hundred million dollars to answer that question in ten seconds, I would've lost! Maybe in five minutes I could've worked it out. But a snap answer? Forget it. However, I was learning on the run, and quickly replied, 'This is, without a doubt, a great city.'

The next day was more television, shows taped in the hotel for programs later in the week, radio stations; and finally a rush back to the hotel for a literary lunch.

The luncheon was in the Hilton Ballroom. Six hundred and fifty guests! A record. Up till now the record was a Sidney Sheldon luncheon of 630. Our lunch was booked to capacity and people were being turned away.

And what a wonderful event it was. You could see the work, thought and attention that had gone into it. There were tablemats with a caricature of me leaning on a post and rail fence; and as I walked up to the stage a band played 'Some Enchanted Evening', which of course I'd mentioned in the book was 'our song'. Charlie's and mine.

By now I was trying to vary my speeches. I felt if I repeated the same words over and over they were sure to sound sing-song. So I kept to a basic outline and filled in the stories I thought each city or town would appreciate.

After the lunch there was just over an hour to sign books and talk to hundreds of people—we had to leave for the airport at two-thirty. The signing line was amazing and very well organised. It was 'assembly-line' style. Jeannine had people moving down the line explaining I had a plane to catch and that if they wanted other than my signature they should write the message on a slip of paper they'd been given and put the paper in the book. They were also asked to keep the chatting to a minimum so I could sign everyone's copy.

I sat at a table with Jeannine on one side directing proceedings. She would put the book under my pen and if no slip of paper was in evidence I would sign and the book would then be whisked out from under the pen from the other side. After that I would look up, smile at the person in front of me, thank them for buying the book and say I hoped they enjoyed it. They each had a thoughtful, quick remark and would slip away and another person and book would appear. I could have stayed all day and chatted, everyone was so friendly, but the time was limited. Even after an hour I couldn't see the end of the queue. Fortunately people were very thoughtful of those behind them, and of me and the pressure they could see I was working under. I remember signing frantically, while hearing someone say, 'I used to know her when she was normal.' Whoever it was never made themselves known to me. But I loved the remark!

After a hundred or so signatures my hand developed a mind of its own and went merrily along signing as I talked. I don't know how but I signed every book right down to the last person in line. Two hundred and thirty books all up. Another record! At one stage I was signing, thanking people, and being interviewed by newspaper reporters, all at the same time. I ended up thanking the reporters and answering the book owner.

Incredibly, we just made it to the plane. I was still signing books while getting in the car to the airport. The adrenalin from an event like that doesn't wind down for many hours. Maybe I was new at the game, but I was racing at 2000 rpm when we hit Sydney. There was a cocktail party arranged for 6 p.m., which left me fifteen minutes to dress after I arrived at the hotel—if of course everything went according to schedule!

Marlee and Danielle came to Sydney for the party, as did my sister Susan and her husband Ralph and my brother Tod and his wife Frances and many more friends. I met more journalists, more people from the publishers, people from Qantas and the *Bulletin*, more booksellers, and Andrew Olle. It was Andrew's interview that started me on this long and amazing path. He was interviewing me on ABC Radio, the day after the Business Woman of the Year Awards, and my publisher, James, was listening in on his car radio. He immediately made an appointment to talk to me.

That appointment changed my life forever, and was doing more so as each new day unfolded on this incredible tour. What a difference a day makes!

There were a few more interviews with newspapers and photographs and I could at last talk to friends and family. I thought this would be 'Time Out', but no. There were more books to sign. I had left my glasses in my hotel room in the rush to get to the party in time and was now signing books without them. The signatures were done by feel.

By this time I was having difficulty even thinking. Earlier in the day, when signing books in Brisbane, I was being told a lady's life story at the same time as signing her book, and her favourite adjective was 'wonderful'! I was concentrating on the message she had asked me to write, but her voice kept repeating 'wonderful' this and 'wonderful' that and I ended up writing 'to wonderful'! I apologised profusely. 'Oh no, that's just wonderful!' the woman said, and picked up the book and wandered away with a satisfied smile on her face. I was showing signs of pressure then!

But now, at eight o'clock, my mind was a hopeless jumble, and I was past thinking clearly. I was only just capable of smiling. And that is what I was doing, when Ross Gibb, the managing director of Pan Macmillan, asked me if I would autograph a book for him. I had a complete memory blank and could not remember his name! I couldn't say, 'Oh, by the way, I've forgotten your name.' What did come into my mind was the silly joke about the chap who couldn't remember someone's name and tried to get around it by saying, 'And *how* do you spell your name again?' To which the man replied, 'S-m-i-t-h.'

I decided to sign my name first, I was at least sure of that. Then I worked up the page, writing a message. But the brain was only transmitting 'smile'. I told it to *think*! *Think*! I was ending the message with 'thanks for everything', while screaming at my brain to think, think, and promptly wrote, 'thinks for everythink'! I couldn't see clearly without my glasses, so not sure if I was on target or not, I did my best to put an 'a' and 'g' in the right places, and apologised for the mess. It now looked like two cats had had a fight on the page!

'I am sorry, but I'm only capable of smiling at this stage of the proceedings,' I mumbled, embarrassed now.

Ross had apparently seen other first-time authors in this state, because he tactfully said, 'Put "To Ross" in there.'

The next day was panic stations. All day was radio interviews, newspapers, then 'Midday with Ray Martin', and I was running on adrenalin and nerves! When we arrived at the television studio I was so nervous my teeth were chattering. We were taken to make-up and a bright brown face was painted over my face. The next stop was the hairdresser. Then we were taken to a waiting lounge where the producer ran through what would happen out there before the cameras, finishing with, '... and at the end of the segment Ray will ask you to read the last paragraph from the book, about Charlie.'

Read on television? Visions of my first school play flashed before my eyes, my mouth opening and closing like a fish, but no words coming out! *Read on television!* I was sure I would fluff this. But it had been arranged, so that was that. I had done plenty of TV interviews, but not before an audience. I suppose it is the same, but nerves throw events all out of proportion and I had quite a few nerves in action at this point. I like the taped interviews. If you did the wrong thing, it was, 'No, next time I want you to do ... Okay, let's try that again.' This time it was a different story. If I fluffed it, I fluffed it nationwide!

It was time. We were led out before the cameras during a commercial break, were sat down and wired up. Ray Martin was very nice and ran through a few things, asking questions of his own and then there was a countdown and it was 'showtime'.

Ray Martin is an excellent interviewer; he makes the time very enjoyable. We were on air for more than ten minutes and it seemed like a few seconds. Suddenly he was handing me my book and asking me to read the closing paragraph. I made it through without getting tongue-tied, but I was gripping the book so tightly there was a perspiration-soaked thumbprint on the page, which penetrated a few more pages.

I wanted to stay for the rest of the show and see how it was all done behind the cameras, but it was on to the next appointment.

A lot of the letters I've since received remark that my reading on the Midday show reminded them of *Gone with the Wind* it was so moving. A lot of people watch Ray Martin, and the next day the publishers received the biggest number of orders from bookstores they had ever recorded in one day.

The rest of the afternoon passed with more interviews. We had time for a quick snack—my diet was coming along nicely—then it was on to 'The World Tonight' with Clive Robertson. This was taped around seven-thirty so I didn't have to sit around until the eleven o'clock show. I could go back to the hotel to watch myself on television. That was strange. Up to this point of the tour I hadn't seen myself on TV or heard myself on the radio. I had resisted the temptation to look at myself on the monitor on the Ray Martin show in case I made a face or became mesmerised.

Friday morning Marlee flew back to the station. Danielle had left for Queensland on a Thursday flight, and Jeannine and I went to Canberra, where I was speaking at the Canberra Press Club. We checked into the hotel and I sat in a hot bath to get the circulation moving again in my feet. It was decidedly chilly in Canberra—everyone there thought it was a lovely day but I knew it was freezing!

The Canberra Press Club is very, very formal. We had to line up and be introduced to the Board, and were asked to partake of a sherry before lunch. I declined, saying I was speaking. No one smiled. We all filed out of the boardroom, very ceremoniously, and went to lunch. The pace of the tour and my constant nerves were working wonders on my weight, but I knew I had to eat a reasonable meal fairly soon before I ran out of steam. I managed to get some of the food into my stomach, and could have eaten more, but the idea of these luncheons is that someone talks while everyone else eats. You have to leave your meal and go up on stage to do your bit, and by the time you get back to your table everyone has finished and is up to coffee and chocolate. I think that's how I accidentally stumbled upon the coffee and chocolate diet.

Yet again, the audience was very friendly and seemed to enjoy the day. There were a lot of good questions and the book signing took hours. I didn't have to rush to catch a plane and didn't have another interview for a while so I could chat with each person in a relaxed manner.

There was one more radio interview and that signalled the end of the day. We were finished at 4 p.m., and had the whole night free! The shock was too much. But I knew I was still very tired, even though I was feeling well, and that I had to be careful not to overdo things. So with that in mind it was dinner in bed and an early night.

The next morning saw more book signing at a big shopping centre in Canberra, then it was back to the hotel to pack and off to Melbourne.

The following day—Sunday—was free! A whole day to do nothing but savour my most exciting news: the book had hit number one on the bestseller list in the Sydney *Daily Telegraph*! It had actually gone straight to number five the day after it was launched, but now, one week later, it was at the top! I was over the moon. The sun was shining and I felt good inside. I was still a bit dazed though. Still coming to terms with the realisation that I had written a book, was touring Australia to promote it, and now it was number one. Yes, I was definitely in a daze.

Jeannine and I went for a walk to celebrate. We walked and talked for so long we ended up lost, somewhere in Melbourne but no idea where. We caught a taxi back to the hotel. After lunch, the first quiet, relaxed meal for the whole tour, Jeannine told me of another surprise: she had arranged a massage for me.

May 1992

What a day! What bliss! Top of the bestsellers, a walk in the sunshine, good food, the best company ... it could have only been topped if I'd had a nice man in my life ... then a massage, and the rest of the afternoon with nothing to do but get nervous about the following day! Oh joy! Even the fact that it was the 31st of the month and the third handover of $50,000 was about to happen in Darwin on the Monday morning couldn't dampen my spirits.

The next day in Melbourne was a lu-lu. Our first interview was 7.30 a.m. on radio, with Richard Stubbs. No one should be that cheery at seven-thirty in the morning! He is very natural but very go-go, and he really enjoys what he is doing and puts you at ease in the first few seconds. It was a good interview.

It was then over to Channel 9, for 'In Melbourne Today' with Denise Drysdale and Ernie Sigley. What a pair of characters! Again, they relax you so much you forget you're on camera, and are lost in chatting and laughing. Then you get up and walk away still wired for sound, which of course I did.

We then raced back to our hotel, I had a thirty-minute break for essentials—like the toilet and a quick shower and change—and it was downstairs to the Dymocks literary lunch in the ballroom. I was relaxed with the speech by this point and was starting to enjoy myself. Every audience had been wonderful in their response and applause, and their interest was shown in the many questions asked. This audience was no exception. I was still signing books and answering questions when time ran out and I then had to concentrate on just signing so I could get through all the books before I left for the next radio interview.

We arrived back at the hotel, exhausted. It had been a long day, up at 6 a.m., back finally with my shoes off at nine-thirty. I was now living proof that there was a lot more to writing a book than your thoughts and pen and paper!

The next day was only a shortie—eight hours—and we

ended up in Hobart for dinner. I loved Hobart, I felt the land welcomed me. It is difficult to describe: the land just greets you, makes you feel you are coming home, as if you belong. The only other place I get this strange sensation is Bullo, but that's only in recent years. Bullo terrified me in the beginning. In retrospect, however, I think that was me. The land has always been the same, I'm the one that has changed.

I loved everything *about* Hobart—the buildings, the people, the countryside; even the weather was perfect, sunny but brisk. The day was more of the same: radio interviews, book signings in stores, then a literary lunch at the Wrest Point Casino convention centre, a book signing after the lunch and off to the airport to fly to Adelaide.

Although it is great to be the centre of attraction day after day, it does eventually take its toll. Jeannine was suffering badly from a terrible flu and I was still in my dazed state, doing what I was told, smiling at anyone and everyone—one man in the hotel elevator thought I was trying to pick him up! I would sign the nearest thing if someone put a pen in my hand and would start talking if a microphone appeared. I'd probably cracked up days before, although I'm sure I was getting worse by the day.

We arrived at the airport, checked in and went to have a cup of tea, although I think a whisky might have been more beneficial for Jeannine and her flu. And then it was off to Adelaide, via Melbourne. We arrived in Adelaide at 7.30 p.m. It would have been nice to go out on the town and have some fun—I had been in all the capitals in Australia and had not gone to one restaurant—but by the end of each day all I wanted to do was put my head on a pillow and sleep. I think it would take a six-month, fulltime, training program to get me to the stage where I could do what I was doing each day and still have the energy to stay out late at night. You needed to be young and fit and I was neither. One look at the next day's schedule was enough for me, and so it was a hot bath and off to bed.

The next day saw a 5.30 a.m. start and another early morning radio session. The same routine followed, only this time with a little twist—I was speaking at a girls' school. This news did put me off the track slightly—children are a much harder audience to please. I knew this instinctively, being the mother of three girls. I had never given a speech before a young audience and this change in the routine right at the end of the tour was the last thing I needed. The base speech I was using and adapting would not be suitable, but I didn't have the time or energy to think of anything different.

We were led into the library, and there they all sat, waiting! No microphone, no lectern, all my little security blankets gone!

I thought quickly and decided to tell them all about the children and their life and experiences and schooling during the time they grew up on Bullo, and the mischief they got up to when I sent them away to boarding school in Adelaide. It went over very well and there were a lot of questions about the Bullo River School, mostly if it was still in operation!

We just made it to the airport at the end of the day and were thrilled to be upgraded to first-class. We really were exhausted and to be waited on hand and foot in first-class style was very soothing.

The last day was another 'up with the birds', or long before the birds, I should say. We arrived at the first radio station so early that the doors were locked and we couldn't get in and had to telephone them to say we were downstairs waiting.

From there to Channel 7; then a radio interview while still at the television studio, as time was running out; a bit of food on the run; and off to Channel 9. Then it was on to ABC Television, and back to the hotel for a literary dinner! The diet was progressing fabulously. And at this stage of the proceedings I was a strong contender for an endurance race for the Olympics. Fortunately I had a two-hour break before dinner, so I could recoup some energy.

I was comfortable now with the speeches, but was to be surprised yet again. Little did I know that arrangements had been made for a live hook-up with the 'Tonight Live' show in Melbourne. Again, this was a first for me, and I didn't want to fluff it on the last night, or on national television. Yet again, my nerves were now back in force.

However, it turned out to be a great last night, with a very happy audience, and there was lots of laughter and questions—like, 'If another woman decided to tackle what you have, what would be the most significant advice you could give her?'

My reply to that was simple. 'Don't.'

Another question: 'Do you think men are scared of you?' This one surprised me a little. It was something I'd never thought about. I knew I'd been so busy, and it was true I had no private social life, but I'd assumed men didn't ask me for dinner and the like because I was never in one place long enough. Except of course Bullo, and that is a hell of a long way to drive to pick up a date for dinner. But *scared* of me? Why should I frighten men?

My answer: 'I hope they're not afraid of me, but I suppose you'd have to ask a man.'

After a while I had to stop question time and go up to the suite for the cross to Melbourne. The dinner guests carried on with dinner, so now I was missing dinner as well as lunch!

The room was full of lights, technicians, equipment, cameras and more people, all of which were trained on one chair—and it wasn't hard to guess whose chair it was.

I have watched many live hook-ups on television, with two people talking to each other in different places. The interviewer looks at the other person on a screen and directs questions to them. But the poor person being interviewed doesn't have it that easy. You have a funny little plastic plug in your ear, which talks to you, not always clearly I might add, and you have to hold your conversation with a camera lens. Now, if you don't think you would feel a right gig sitting in a roomful of people, all staring at you, while you chat away to a camera lens, then you are very wrong. The technicians waved instructions at me all the time, but told me not to look at them! How you follow instructions and don't look at the person dishing them out, I don't know. I was told just to keep talking to the camera. So I did. All the time thinking what an idiot I must look. It is obviously something you get used to, because a lot of people do it very well. But the first time around it is very disconcerting. Months later I saw the tape of this interview and was pleasantly surprised. The ear plug was not working very well and I had visions of myself on the television with this pained expression of concentration on my face as I struggled to understand the question then a look of relief when I did. But luckily it didn't show up like this at all and the interview was acceptable.

That one last hurdle cleared, I went back downstairs. Apart from a few more hours of questions and books to sign, we had finished the tour. We had made it. I could sleep in the next day and relax. We didn't finish until late; Jeannine finally had to drag me away with the excuse I had a late interview. She could see how tired I was and knew the only way I would get away was if she took me away.

It was a wonderful crowd for our last night. One of the kitchen staff said he heard so much laughter coming from the dining room that he came and listened to my speech to see why everyone was laughing. He said he bought my book because if it was as good as the speech then it would be good reading. That pleased me no end.

The tour was considered a success. The book was still on the top of the bestseller list and orders were coming in thick and fast from all over the country. The publishers were looking at a second print already.

I am a great believer in the saying, 'You don't really know something unless you experience it yourself.' Well, I certainly experienced this wonderful tour, but I cannot find words to describe my feelings adequately. It was an amazing two weeks of my life and a time I'll never forget. Something I wish everyone could experience. To have people accept you totally does wonderful things to your overall being. And to receive only constant praise warms your soul. My year up to this point had been a neverending black nightmare, except for a few brief shafts of light, so to have this completely successful tour, with daily reports of huge book sales, healed my battered body and heart.

I know there are many, many, many people involved in making my first book and tour such a success, some of them I don't even know. I met so many people, they are all mixed up in my brain. Faces, names, places; all jumbled up and out of context. But nevertheless committed to my memory bank forever.

CHAPTER 7

June 1992–
July 1992

It was June. It should have been 'tour recovery time' but no such luck. It was the middle of the mustering season. We had full staff, some of whom I hadn't even met, running around, bringing messages from Marlee or Franz asking me to order parts for some piece of machinery that had broken down thirty miles away.

When I arrived back on the Sunday, Marlee had cooked a lovely dinner and we had a bottle of champagne to celebrate the successful tour and the book hitting the number one position. She'd been calling regularly so I was fairly up to date on everything that had been going on. Now it was just nice to sit and rest and talk.

But I wasn't over my jet lag by a long way.

Monday morning I bolted out of bed at 5 a.m., thinking I was late for the first radio interview. My Rottweiler, Jedda, snapped awake, hair bristling, growling and ready to defend me. I wandered into the office around 6 a.m. to be greeted by the mail piled up against the wall. There was another smaller pile of faxes and phone messages next to it.

'Welcome home, Sara,' I said quietly to myself.

Marlee breezed into the room, told me how great it was

to have me home and gave me a long list of the spare parts needed and the food we were out of.

'Gee, I'm certainly glad you do all that and not me!' she said as she disappeared.

I attacked one of the piles. The phone interrupted me around 9 a.m. It was my sister ringing to tell me my book was number one on the bestseller list in Queensland. I didn't tell her it had been there for a while. Still, it was exciting news and improved my mood. But it also made me want to celebrate, kick up my heels, let go, instead of tackle all the work on the desk, and the lists of things to be ordered. Later, I told myself. Now I was starting to sound like Charlie. I'd been hearing that promise for thirty years, ever since I married him. He conned me the first twenty-six years, now I was conning myself. So as much as I would've liked to have spent the time daydreaming and generally doing nothing for a while, it was down to hard work. We were mustering at the end of the week, there were several business people calling by, and in ten days I had a speaking engagement at a luncheon at the Regent in Sydney.

For the next week I caught up on the backlog staring at me from two desks, bruised my ear making the necessary hundreds of phonecalls and organised the household, ready for our next batch of tourists in a couple of days.

Soon it was time to leave for Sydney again. The ten days had just vanished into thin air. I was up at 5 a.m. and it was straight through from the station to Kununurra airport on a small four-seater plane. I was so tired I even fell asleep in it, which is near impossible because there's no place to rest your head. I boarded the jet to Darwin with only a few minutes to spare, had an hour's wait in Darwin and then caught another bigger jet to Sydney, via Adelaide and Melbourne. And I was told the flight was direct! I asked what time we landed in Hobart and the air hostess gave me a strange look.

I finally arrived in Sydney in the middle of the night and continued to sleep through what was left of the night in a bed. Sleep was something I couldn't get enough of lately.

Perhaps my body was trying to tell me something. I spoke at the luncheon on the Saturday, had dinner with friends I hadn't seen for a while, got back to the hotel at a reasonable time and put in a wake-up call for 5 a.m. My flight home left Sydney at 6 a.m.

I got home at 7 p.m., thirteen hours' travelling. And that was after another so-called 'direct flight'.

I sat down in the living room, too tired to move. The cook bombarded me with complaints about all the special food that hadn't turned up on the order. I was very close to saying it didn't make any difference because he'd have ruined it anyway, but held my tongue. Some day I will find a good cook. Uncle Dick was doing last-minute repairs to the guests' room and the house girl was following him with a vacuum cleaner, cleaning up after him. She didn't know it, but by the look on Uncle Dick's face she was dangerously close to having a vacuum hose tied in a bow around her neck! Marlee and Franz were thirty miles out of our road helping a cattle truck that was stuck on one of our jump-ups.

I went to my bedroom, took a hot shower, locked the door with Jedda inside, so every time someone knocked she attacked it, and drifted off to sleep to the sounds of growling and snarling at the door. However, the locked door didn't stop Marlee—she came around to the window and just stepped inside. It was around midnight. The cattle trucks were waiting at the yards ready for loading. She would start before first light so the driver could be over our dirt road and onto the sealed highway in the cool hours of the morning. This was better for the cattle. So she'd be gone at 4 a.m. and I wouldn't see her. We had to talk now.

We sat out under the stars, ate sandwiches and drank cold beer. Franz was in the shower getting the dust and grime off.

Ours were the usual problems—too much to do and not enough people to do it. The running of the house, entertaining the tourists for the next three days, and the general office work were my responsibilities. The cattle were Marlee's. Marlee said that after they had loaded, drafted and branded they would come back to help me.

She left at 4 a.m. and I was up at five to get some office work done before I started on the staff. There was a note on the desk, from Marlee: 'Have left Franz in bed. He has a high fever and does not feel well at all. Please look after him till I return. Love, M.' I just knew it was going to be one of those days!

The tourists arrived at eleven o'clock and I walked out to greet them. All the people we've had over the three years have, without exception, been delightful—we still get Christmas cards and letters from many—so I suppose Murphy's Law dictates we had to strike-out some time. And strike-out we did, in a big way.

There was no pleasing this particular visitor. He complained about absolutely everything. After a few days he announced that he and his entourage were leaving early. I quickly handed him the phone so he could book the plane, and had to tell the staff not to cheer until the plane took off, just in case he heard. He reminded me of 'Gloom and Doom' out of *Dick Tracy*, only Gloom and Doom had more appeal than our guest.

All week we had trouble with cattle trucks breaking down or getting stuck on the road somewhere. It took longer than usual to move the cattle out of the yards, so it was only a few days before the next lot of tourists. We were dreading them, after that last miserable man. But these people were lovely, and enjoyed everything they did. On the last day they asked me to sign a copy of my book which they'd brought to the station with them.

We had a few quiet days before the end of June and another celebration, in a peculiar sort of a way. On 30th June I made the last payment to Trippe. Nothing to celebrate of course, paying out money, but not to have to find that same amount of money again in thirty days took a tremendous load off my sagging shoulders. I could now push

(Photo: David Hancock/Skyscans)

Me in the cattle yards.

Bullo River Gorge.

(Photo: David Hancock/Skyscans)

ABOVE: The homestead, 1970.
BELOW: The homestead now, 1993.

(Photo: David Hancock/Skyscans)

ABOVE: The homestead.
BELOW: When the roof blew off.

The girls when young.
ABOVE: Marlee. BELOW RIGHT: Bonnie. BELOW LEFT: Danielle.

(Photo: David Hancock/Skyscans)

ABOVE: Murray Lee, me and Danielle.
BELOW: Charlie's angels.

ABOVE: Bertha damaged. On the Bullo airstrip having her tail repaired in the 70s.
CENTRE: Bertha the seaplane, Oshkosh, 1991.
BELOW: Woo.

ABOVE: Danielle with Honky-Tonk.
BELOW: Early dawn. If you look closely, you can see Bleep standing by Woo. This was when she was just learning to fly and fell in love with Woo. She stayed with the plane whenever it was on the ground.

ABOVE LEFT: *Bleep walking with one of the dogs.*
ABOVE RIGHT: *Bleep deciding if she could get on the tractor with me.*
BELOW: *Bleep dancing with me.*

ABOVE LEFT: *Danielle and Bleep.*
ABOVE RIGHT: *Danielle trying to help Bleep to fly.*
BELOW: *Bleep coming in for one of her disorganised landings.*

ABOVE: Troubles waiting for her morning grooming.
BELOW: Troubles in the 'golden Rolls' waiting to go shopping. She went from the pound to riding in a Rolls, and she seems very pleased with herself.

ABOVE: This is a wild turkey (bustard) who crash-landed on the roof and hurt his leg. Marlee took care of him until the leg was better and he flew away.
BELOW: True love in the Bullo River piggery, 1975.

ABOVE: Charles with his crewmen aboard USS Enterprise *in 1944.*
BELOW: The 'Big E' homeward bound. USS Enterprise *steams towards the Panama Canal and New York to be part of Navy Day ceremonies, 27th October 1945.*

Charlie's last sail.

ABOVE: *One of the many army exercises on Bullo.*
BELOW: *The Hercules on a take-off.*

that aside until the following year, when I would have to start the battle over the court costs, and would again have to find extra money. But that was a whole year away!

By July I was very close to a nervous breakdown. Instead of losing weight when I worry I eat so much I put it on. I weighed more than I had ever weighed in my life, I wasn't exercising and I worried day and night.

The crops had failed, months and months of backbreaking work had dried out and crumbled before our eyes. You could not believe that green fields as far as the eye could see could just turn into dust. In only a few months there was nothing but bare dirt. Only the ridges of the ploughed ground lay as evidence of all that work. What was left of the sorghum, after lack of rain had dried it out and the grasshoppers had had a feast, we baled. We knew we would need every morsel of feed we could get together for the animals. This was not going to be a good year; any amount of hay would help at the end, especially if the rains were late. Our cavalcade crop had just crumbled and blown away in the wind, in those fields we only had bare ground.

However, the seeds were still there and we were assured that they would regenerate with the next rains. We only had to wait. Still, it does something to you to watch your crops die! The past months of worry, finding and paying the money in an unjust court judgement was still very much affecting me. The pressure of the book tour and the worry that I had to succeed were also taking their toll. And the running of the station for a season was always such a challenge that I needed a rest just from that at the end of each year. For six years there had been no rest at any time. We had been working seven days a week without a break. I was starting to show signs of cracking. The throat infection that started in February at the IBM conference would not go away. And to add to it my ears were now affected. The only time they felt normal was at 30,000 feet, up in a plane. The doctor told me it should be the other way around, and I said I was well aware of that but my ears seemed to think differently.

I walked around in a daze; I hardly smiled. I suppose it's called 'withdrawal'. I found I avoided people, dreaded meeting anyone, wasn't interested in the next day. Everything seemed to be piling in on me; the world seemed to be going too fast and I wanted to get off. The doctor suggested anti-depressants. I said no.

I was still working from daylight to dark, every day—as were Marlee and Franz. Marlee was faring much better than me, but I could see that if we both didn't have a break soon, we would be in serious trouble.

I was now like a robot. I went through the day's work with one thing in my mind—to get to the end of the day and into bed. Bed became my only sanctuary. Yet I knew everything I had done that year had had to be done to enable us to survive. But to survive I was tearing myself apart. I would crawl into bed at night wondering how we could do all the work required to get to the end of the year. Having paid out all that money I now had to find enough in the next few months for us to get through to the beginning of the next season in April. The income from the next few months of cattle had to last us through the six months' rainy season. The droughts in Queensland and New South Wales had brought down the price of cattle by fifteen per cent, so on top of losing all that money our income for the season was also down before we even started.

I suppose it's therefore not hard to understand why I withdrew. But the rest of the year was waiting and my head-in-the-sand approach just didn't work. I had to get on with living. People wouldn't stop knocking on my door, and I had to answer.

Whenever my life gets to these darkest moments and my general feeling is, 'Stuff it! It's just too hard,' fate or God offers a hand and pulls me out of the black hole. Little shafts of light flicker through, and before you know it you are back in there fighting. And in the latest shaft of light we saw our next tourist: five-foot, one-inch Katie Barkell from Sydney.

When the travel agent booked Katie in the beginning of the year, he said she was seventy-eight years old. I told him this was very rough country, and that I wasn't sure a person of that age would enjoy it. He assured me she was very healthy and very determined to come to Bullo. So Katie arrived on a plane with a load of horse feed, beer and food supplies. She walked into the house and I knew it would be A-okay. Katie was just so full of life, eager to find out what the next minute would bring. I'm sure she was very much like Marlee when she was her age; well, she still *was*, at seventy-eight!

She wanted to experience everything that was going. She even went bullcatching with Marlee and had her photo taken sitting on the trussed up wild bull. And loved every minute of it. She had probably been just as spunky in her younger days. These days she is expending her energy exploring the world. She read about Bullo in a magazine and decided it was one place she wanted to go. The travel agent realised she could not be put off with a trip to sand and palm trees, so she arrived at Bullo.

Katie was a good tonic for everyone, a breath of fresh air. We all loved her and she boosted my spirits considerably. Made me realise that problems were just problems and they would pass, but what I had—my home and family—were there forever. I felt I really had no right to feel sorry for myself. I was healthy, I had people that love me, friends, a home, options in my life, freedom to choose. I had the lot! Self-pity only delays progress. Other friends dropped by for a few days and being surrounded by those who are close to you was good for the soul.

We had three days before the next nine tourists arrived, so there was no rest. This group was made up of two families, five children in all. And we were lucky again. They were delightful people and they lived not far from Katie in

Sydney. The children had a great time and that is, I think, the measure of a good family holiday: if the children are happy, the parents relax. It was our first batch of young children so it was a challenge for us. But the station so completely captivates youngsters that we really don't have to do much, just sit back and let Bullo weave its magic. Which it did.

Soon afterwards I had a speech in Coolum at the Hyatt and so I tried the 'cure' again. Two days in Darwin, on the magic massage table, under the expert hands of Zelda. I added to this cure by going to stay with Susan and Ralph for a few days' rest before the conference. I was looking forward to three blissful days staring at the waters of their quiet creek and out to sea, surrounded by bushland. A noiseless retreat from the 'life out of control' style of living I was caught up in at the moment ...

And that was when I was first introduced to 'Troubles'.

Susan had not been well for a long period of time over the past year or so. Nothing serious, just different complaints, one after another. Marlee and I had decided she had been too long without a dog. She had always had dogs in the past, and taking care of them occupied a great deal of her time. We felt she now had too much time on her hands and that a new dog would cure this and most of the complaints. That was our opinion, anyway.

We offered her a puppy by Hunter, or a puppy from the same kennels, but she refused, saying she was too old to train a puppy. We offered to train the puppy to the 'well-trained' stage and then hand it over, but she felt that this breed of dog, although gorgeous, was just too much for her to handle. I could understand this—there are certain dogs for certain people. Susan was simply not a Rottweiler person. But Marlee couldn't understand how anyone could not love a Hunter, and was sure that when we gave Aunty Sue a Hunter puppy she would fall madly in love with it. With that, she went ahead and ordered a Rottweiler puppy from the same kennels as Hunter and Jedda had come from.

She arrived a few months later and we called her Emi. Jedda and Emi were like sisters and had a wonderful time growing up together. Of course everyone fell madly in love with Emi, including me, and I could see the writing on the wall—we wouldn't want to send her away when the time came. But we followed the plan and sent photos of Emi playing, Emi sleeping, Emi eating, etc, etc. As Emi grew in size and into our hearts there was less and less talk about 'when she goes to Queensland'. Marlee would say, 'when she is bigger', but I knew I couldn't part with Emi. She was part of our life now. So the departure time was always put back a bit. But fate had decreed Emi was not to belong to anyone.

She was only eleven months old when she disappeared. She and Jedda would race and play for hours in the early morning, before the heat of the day. Then one morning only Jedda came home. She was very upset and shaking and would stand and stare out across the paddock towards the river.

We went looking for Emi after a little while but there was no sign of her. We never found a trace. One of the stockmen who had been repairing fences along the river said he had seen Jedda and Emi playing along the river edge each morning during their playtime. We don't know for sure but it looks as though Emi was taken by a crocodile. This seems the only explanation for her disappearance—if she'd been bitten by a snake she would have made it home before the poison took effect, or we would have found her during our search. Also, to support the crocodile theory, Jedda got very nervous the next time we took her fishing down by the river, and no amount of coaxing would get her out of the back of the Toyota.

We decided not to tell Susan, because I knew she would immediately blame herself for Emi's death. She would reason that if she had taken her the dog wouldn't have died. So we continued to talk about Emi as if she was still with us. And had been following this line of action since the end of the year.

When I called Sue and said I was speaking in Coolum and could I stay with them for a few days, I noticed she was not her usual happy self. I asked if everything was all right and was it convenient for me to visit at that time?

'Oh yes,' she said. 'It has nothing to do with you. I'll tell you when you arrive.'

When they met me at the airport, there sat 'Troubles' in the back seat of the Rolls. This was why Susan had been acting strangely about my visit. They had a new dog, a Great Dane. Susan had been worrying for months about how to tell me and I had been worried how to tell her about losing Emi.

You could see that Troubles had captured Susan's heart. She was a gentle giant, with big soulful eyes that would melt your heart. I did not mention Emi.

I confused Troubles. I sounded like Susan and acted like her and Troubles would rush up to me and stop and sniff and a puzzled expression would come over her face and you could almost see her thinking, 'You act like her, you sound like her,' sniff, sniff, 'but you are not her.' And she would rush away to find Susan. But that night, when we sat down in front of the fire, she finally realised there were two of us. She sat for hours staring first at Susan, then at me, and having now solved this dilemma, she went to sleep in front of the fire, happy. If you asked any member of our family or any close friend what they would like to come back to life as, without hesitation their answer would be, 'Aunty Sue's dog.'

From an early age Sue and I wanted to spend our lives driving around picking up lost, sick or abandoned animals, nurse them back to health and find new homes for them. Well, it didn't work out exactly as we planned, the RSPCA took over that dream, but we do our bit for any animal we find. Susan and Ralph have never bought a dog or cat. Lost or abandoned or starving cats and dogs seem to find their way to their door. And they take dogs from the pound. There is one newspaper that prints a photo of the 'dog of the week' at the pound. Ralph can't buy that paper because if Susan saw the picture she'd have to give the dog a home.

They always end up with the large dogs, because they are the hardest to find homes for. But they are always 'gentle giant' types rather than strong and muscular. So it has always been Great Danes, German shepherds and Afghans. Status dogs, which people buy as cute puppies and watch in horror as they grow into half a horse or grow a massive coat of hair that requires hours of maintenance per day to keep it in reasonable condition. Or the dog grows to twice the size of the garden, or eats more than the whole family combined. Because of one or all of these reasons the big dogs end up in the pound or out wandering the streets.

Susan and Ralph have been taking these dogs into their home for thirty-plus years. There are endless wonderful stories about the long line of animals that have passed into their loving care over these years, but the most recent lucky dog that has had the good fortune to become the 'Pet of the Potts' is Troubles.

Troubles was around twenty months old when she was found wandering the streets of Marsden, a suburb of Brisbane, and was picked up by the pound. The Great Dane Society has an arrangement with the pound that whenever a Great Dane is brought in the Society is to be notified and they take it upon themselves to find the owner or a new home for the dog. When Troubles' week was up and no owner had been found, one of the people from the Society took Troubles out of the pound and agreed to look after her until a home was found. The Potts were listed as previous owners of homeless Great Danes and so Sue and Ralph were called. Ralph spoke to the man about Troubles and said to just bring her to the house and he was sure Susan would change her mind about not wanting any more dogs. When the dog arrived Ralph told Sue that if the dog could not be placed in a home, she would have to be put down, and Troubles just stood there with doe-like eyes, shivering with fear and generally looking miserable; and Susan was hooked.

As the name implies, it was not an easy transition, even

though the dog appeared to have had good training. Susan said the man who was taking care of Troubles while a home was being found must have been very kind, because for days after he delivered her to the house Troubles would go and stand and stare at the spot where the car had been parked. But she soon realised that she had struck it lucky a second time and as she learned to love and trust her new owners she blossomed into her real self.

One of her first hurdles was 'Ginger Boy', the resident cat in heaven. Ginger Boy is a very, very big ginger marmalade cat who wandered into Potts paradise about eight years earlier. Susan and Ralph were living in Bargara at the time and already had two cats and two big dogs. Poor old Ginger was only a kitten born to a stray cat in the sand dunes and was wandering along the beach looking for a home. Every time he came into the garden the two resident cats, Tabbather and Gemma, would bash him up and send him on his way. But he wouldn't give up and kept coming back. He would hunch over, close his eyes and take the beating, without fighting back. Susan and Ralph tried to discourage him and would spray him with the hose, but when he took that punishment also, they decided to let him stay, telling the other cats to leave him alone.

He had never seen a square meal in his short life, and when Sue started to feed him he quickly realised how lucky he was. He went from being so starved he could hardly walk, to being so stuffed with food he could still hardly walk. That was all of eight years ago and now Ginger Boy has Aunty Sue perfectly trained. He has three meals a day, has definite likes and dislikes, and now when Sue goes shopping she has to go to more than three supermarkets before she has Ginger's weekly requirements. He is combed and brushed and checked for fleas, twice a day—Sue will not put a flea collar on him because she doesn't think they're good for the animal. So every morning Ginger sits on a stool in the sun for his first groom of the day. He then retires to a comfortable sleeping spot and waits for morning tea. The vet once told my sister if she didn't put Ginger on a diet he would die of a heart attack. He was so fat he couldn't reach over his stomach to clean himself. The diet was a very traumatic time; no one believed Sue would survive the wailing that Ginger would come out with when he wanted more food. But she was strong, for him, and he slimmed down to a nice, reasonably overweight cat, who can clean his back legs and tail and does not have the threat of a heart attack hanging over him.

Ginger Boy was a problem for Troubles, not the other way around. Ginger had shared paradise with many a big dog during his reign and was not the least daunted by a three-foot-high, 130-pound giant towering over him. He just stiffened his tail, in a controlled quiver, and walked calmly under the Great Dane's nose. Troubles sat back on her haunches and stared at this curious creature. She showed no aversion to cats and they soon settled into a harmonious relationship, which has never changed—although every now and then when Troubles' tail connects with Ginger's face the cat will turn and give the offending tail a whack.

Troubles' psychological problem was, now that she had found paradise she lived in fear of losing it. The thought of going without her three meals a day, lined trampolines for sleeping, rides to the shopping centre in a Rolls-Royce, daily brushings in the sun and all the other perks she had discovered, made her a little edgy. This manifested itself in her behaviour. She wasn't going to let these two wonderful human beings out of her sight.

If both Susan and Ralph left the house, the neighbours informed them Troubles started up a terrible mournful howling that only stopped when the car turned into the garage. So they started to take her on some of the short trips in the car and she slowly came to realise that when they did leave they would return. It took some time, but she is now less frantic when they leave together and although she doesn't like being left behind, when she is told to stay she obeys.

When she does go shopping it causes quite a stir at the local supermarket because she sits regally in the back of the Rolls.

Susan was walking back to the car one day when a very down-to-earth couple walked past. The wife looked in and saw Troubles reclining on the back seat and said to her husband in very 'Dad and Dave' tones, 'Ere, if you had a Rolls-Royce, would you let a dog in it?' The husband replied, 'If I owned a bloody Rolls-Royce I don't think I'd let you in it!' Then the wife pointed to the window of the car and he looked in and saw the Great Dane sleeping peacefully. 'Now I've bloody well seen everything,' he said, as his voice faded down the street. 'Only a bloody idiot would ...'

When she is left at home, all shoes have to be safely locked away because when she's alone she consoles herself by taking only one shoe of any pair and burying it in some part of the garden. Ralph has found a few, but it was a while, and quite a few single shoes missing, before they realised what was going on. This problem has not been solved to this day, so shoes are either on your feet or safely locked in a cupboard.

Troubles is slowly putting on weight and her coat is starting to shine, due to all of the care and attention she has received. And as long as Susan doesn't feed her on the same scale she did Ginger, Troubles will become a picture of perfection.

Every morning she walks with Ralph down to the corner shop to pick up the bread, and on the way home she collects the newspaper from the lawn and brings it up to the breakfast table. She struts around the breakfast room, throwing her head around and prancing, with the paper still in her mouth, and only when she's told how clever she is will Ralph be given the paper.

She is terrified of the swimming pool and as yet no one has been successful in coaxing her into the water. This could have something to do with her first day there, when she tried to walk on the plastic cover of the pool. As a result

Troubles slowly sank into the water, with the cover engulfing her. I suppose it is easy to understand why she still gives the pool a wide berth.

When she arrived it was mid winter, and being very thin she felt the cold badly and would sit near the fire and shiver. Sue decided she needed a coat. It was night and the only woollen material Sue had in the house was some very fine wool kept aside for a good winter skirt. No prizes for guessing what happened to the thirty-five dollar a metre fine wool material—Sue was still sewing way after midnight. And Troubles had her first winter coat.

Troubles still has her hang-ups and is still doing strange things. Not long ago, when Sue and Ralph returned home from shopping, they found that Troubles had rearranged the living room for them. She had taken cushions from the breakfast room chairs and put them in the living room, and cushions from the living room were found in other rooms. A few of the mohair blankets Sue uses for lap rugs on cold nights when watching television were taken out of the sewing room and were on the chairs in front of the TV. She had also been snooping around the guest room, had found my sneakers, and had one between her paws and was resting her head on it when they came home and found her. Nothing had been damaged or chewed, just rearranged to pass the time of day until they returned.

Susan named her well, but along with being a trouble she has been a complete joy for them. She really is a unique dog.

Soon it was time to go to the Hyatt in Coolum. Susan and Ralph drove me, as I was speaking at a conference dinner that night. I waved goodbye and as the golden Rolls drove away saw Troubles' head resting on the ledge at the back window and those wonderful eyes looking at me until the car drove out of sight.

It was back to a hotel room again, waiting until it was time for my speech. I had been invited to cocktails before dinner and had met a lot of the people. Nerves kept food-intake to a minimum, but this time it was fortunate because three days with Susan had put on a few pounds. She feeds people on the same scale she feeds her pets. Copiously.

You would think by this stage in my speaking career I would be over the nerves, but I'm not. I get very nervous before the speech and this continues for a few minutes after I start but then I relax a bit and I seem to be okay thereafter. I don't know why I get like this, because without exception every audience I have spoken to has been truly a pleasure to be with, so I've had no bad experiences that would cause this reaction.

Anyway, the speech went well and afterwards quite a few people came to the table to ask me to sign my book. By the time I did this and danced a few times it was midnight. I had a 5 a.m. wake-up call booked, my flight left at 8 a.m. and I had nearly a two-hour drive to Brisbane. So it was off to bed.

I would have loved to have gone back to Caloundra to spend another few weeks with Sue, but July was just too busy on the station and it took all our time—mine and Marlee's—merely to get through each day. Apart from the cattle to be handled we had more tourists arriving. I had to get home.

One of the biggest pleasures of my year would have to have been reading the letters I received from those who read my book. Each week the mail plane brought piles of these incredible letters. I also received faxes and phonecalls. They always cheered us when we were going through a particularly rough time or when we were down. I often found Marlee reading the letters to cheer herself up. Letters started to arrive while I was still on tour and Marlee would read some of them out over the phone. By the end of June they numbered in the hundreds. The phone did not stop ringing for months. These wonderful letters and phonecalls gave us the strength to keep going.

When my book first came out, some people were labelling it a 'woman's book'. Men were standing back. They might have thought it was another book tearing them apart. When I wrote it, that thought never crossed my mind—I didn't write for any particular sex or type of reader. I just told the story I had to tell.

Although it did appear that at the beginning my audience was mostly women, by the end of the tour in Perth there was a good percentage of men coming to listen. The word had spread that I was only criticising one man, poor old Charlie. As I said, I just told a story, and the fact that the leading man just happened to be a cad and a bounder doesn't mean all men are such. I obviously picked the best in the 'cad and bounder' field.

At one luncheon a lone man stood impatiently in a long line of women, waiting to get a book signed. I saw him each time I looked up. As he got closer his discomfort increased. Finally he was standing in front of me. I asked would he just like a signature or his name also.

'It's not for me! he shouted. He then went on to say that his wife had told him to buy it. She couldn't come to the luncheon so he had been sent to buy the book. He was very annoyed he had to do this. I signed the book and said I hoped his wife would enjoy it and that maybe he might find it interesting.

'I'm not going to read a woman's book!' he snarled as he stomped off.

I was a bit taken aback by his aggressiveness, but fortunately that was the only negative response I had from anyone.

My favourite 'male' story, however, and the one that has to take the prize, was a phonecall. On this particular day I answered the phone to this very down-to-earth, fair dinkum Aussie voice.

'Gidday,' he said. 'I'm calling you 'bout your book.'

Uh-oh, I thought. 'Oh yes?'

'Yer. I'm just callin' to say thank you.'

'Oh really?' I said, mystified.

'Yer. I didn't read it, of course.'

Now I was completely confused, but thought silence was the best policy. So I reduced my reply to, 'Oh?'

'Naar. Don't read much. But I'm thankin' you for not makin' your book any longer, see.'

I stuck to the script. 'Oh?'

'Yer. Because if it'd been any longer I would've bloody well starved to death! My wife didn't take her bloody head out o' your book till she finished it. I've been livin' on beer and chips for three bloody days! So you see that's why I'm callin'. T' say thanks ... So thanks.' And he hung up.

I sat holding the phone for ages afterwards, too amazed to laugh. But it has given me many a good laugh since.

The letters came mostly from people I didn't know who had read my book. Now and then there were letters from friends, people I had met over the years and people who had visited Bullo.

Some letters instantly brought back memories. One such letter was from a man who came to the north as a land valuer back in the early sixties. His letter ignited a spark way back in the recesses of my mind.

The year was 1965 and Hooker Pastoral had been our neighbours since the early sixties. Bullo at the time was one million acres and one third of that was over a mountain range from the main valley, with the mountain plateau almost impossible to cross.

The only way to get to the other side of the property was to drive out our road, 48 miles, along the Victoria Highway to Western Australia, 80 miles, then out along the Legune road to head about 60 miles in the direction of Bullo. It was almost a complete circle. To say that that part of the property was not easily accessible to us would be an understatement. There were very good pockets of feed and rockpools of water right along the range on that side of the mountain, as there were on the valley side. In those days, with all the herds still very wild and with most owners just starting the big job of cleaning up the land and bringing the herds under control, there were large numbers of cattle to be had. They were just standing around under trees, munching on grass, without a care in the world, all wild and clean-skinned (not branded). There were hardly any fences, and the whole set-up was a rustler's dream!

At the beginning of the season our manager mentioned to Charlie that we had quite a few cattle on the other side of the mountain. He had seen them when he went into that part of the property the previous year, and he thought we should either bring them back to the main valley or, if leaving them there, brand them and put up a boundary fence between Bullo and Legune. He explained our boundary went within twenty miles of the Legune homestead, which made our cattle very close to that property and a long way from us ... When Charles realised our cattle were so close to the neighbour's yards he arranged for the stockcamp's immediate departure. They had to cross rough, rocky mountains and gorges to get there, so there was quite a lot of preparation. The only way to cross was on horseback; no vehicles could get through. They had to take a big mob of spare horses in case of injury, because most of the three-week journey would be over rough rock and all of the horses had to be shod, otherwise they would get stone bruises. All their supplies were packed on mules.

It took many weeks of preparation but they were finally ready for departure. Once again the children and I were left in the care of the Aboriginal women, and all the men rode off into the wild blue yonder, seeking adventure. When I later heard of the adventure, I realised for once I had the better deal. For once Charlie suffered without me!

They made it to the other side and into the lovely valleys of Bullo on the West Australian side of the property, still in the Northern Territory, but only just. Charles was pleased to see that a boundary fence had been erected which doubled as a fence for one of the neighbour's paddocks. But after a few days' ride up the valley, Charles saw a lot that didn't please him. The boundary–paddock fence was miles into our property with spear gates at regular intervals along the fence and it conveniently enclosed all the watering holes on their side. Our cattle had to walk through the spear gates in order to get to the water, but they couldn't walk back to Bullo country because the spear gates only work one way. After riding over most of the area it was evident where all the cattle were: on the other side of the fence, which in places was as much as ten miles into Bullo country.

Charles was furious, and after doing a few sums of the cattle lost in the last five years he said to our manager, 'Okay let's go get them.' The manager said he couldn't do that, and that maybe he should talk to the neighbour. But Charles believed that would be a waste of time and that it was time for action! So Charles with the stockcamp went to get his cattle back, not in broad daylight of course. They waited for night and for the next few days by moonlight and dawn they mustered the paddocks along the boundary fence.

They mustered all the cattle they could find, and the calculated figure of stolen cattle went right out of Charlie's mind. It was open season on anything with four legs that mooed! They then assembled them on the Bullo side of the fence, turned their heads in the direction of home, and it was 'Bullo Ho!'

Charlie said the return trip was a nightmare! It was very difficult for both animals and men. The horses were foot-sore, the cattle were foot-sore, and the men were sore a little further up! They had to rest the cattle many times when they reached flat ground and water because of the slow periods over rocks with no feed, no water and too much heat. In fact they were so long getting home that they ran out of food and had to camp at a watering hole while they killed a steer for meat.

This stop saved Charlie's skin. Back at the boundary, the heavy tracks of cattle clearly going through a fence that was still intact had been found by a fencer. (Charlie had opened the fence to muster the cattle out of the paddock and then the wires were strained up again.) The fencer mentioned this to his boss who went and looked at the tracks, checked the paddocks, found the cattle missing and then called his boss down south. The managing director, carried away with his new cattle empire up north, then rushed straight to the scene.

The managing director started looking for the culprits in the company plane. When Charles heard the plane, he was resting the cattle and men in the canyon on Bullo, about three days from home. He realised they were onto him and that they could very likely have the police waiting at the Bullo homestead on his return. I knew nothing of this however, as Charles and I had not been in communication since he left. The plane then flew low over Bullo homestead, not long after missing Charlie hiding in the canyon. It swooped low over the yards, saw they were empty and then flew away.

The next day the same drama was played out again. Charlie was now travelling at night and hiding during the day. He was days overdue and I was worried sick. He said he could be up to ten days late and not to worry before then. But I did, and by the tenth day I was in a state, wondering what I should do. Charlie knew this would be the case, so he had sent a rider on ahead with a note telling me that he was three days' away, that they were all right, and that he would see me soon.

The same plane flew over every day until Charlie arrived home early in the morning, quietly pushing the cattle down the airstrip past the house. After the cattle were yarded Charlie and the men ate non-stop for a good part of the morning and then spent the rest of the day washing in the creek. Sleeping was also high on the agenda.

I was surprised at the small herd of cattle they had returned with. There were so many men, they had been away such a long period of time, and returned with such a poor result. It turned out that most of the herd had stampeded the night before, and the men and horses were just too tired to round them up. But it wasn't all bad because the cattle were inside the paddocks and could be mustered easily the next season.

We were soon interrupted by the sound of a plane circling the homestead and the manager disappeared out the door saying he was going to check fences. Charles told me to stay put as he went quickly to the caravan. The plane with Hooker Pastoral painted on the side then taxied to a halt. Charles then emerged from the caravan with his gun holster on! I screeched 'Charles, what are you doing? What's happening?' And finished on high 'C' with, 'What are you going to do with that gun?'

He told me to put the children in the caravan, and then I went out into the garden to stand and watch. Watch what, I had no idea, but knowing Charlie, it definitely would not be dull! Charlie walked out to meet the plane with the pistol hanging on his hip, just like a scene out of *High Noon*. A man stepped down from the plane and I noticed Charlie did not shake hands. By his dress I guessed he was the manager from next door. There was a lot of arm waving and pointing in the direction of the cattle yards and finally more men got out of the plane and then they all marched towards the cattle yards.

They then walked back up the flats, with arms still waving and with quite a bit of shouting by all, except Charlie. So I knew whatever the situation, Charlie was in charge for the moment. They eventually reboarded the plane and departed. It was not a social visit by any means, no morning tea and they didn't even come to the shed to say hello!

Charles walked in with a smug expression on his face and I demanded to know what had happened. Charles said he would tell me in the next few days, after it was all over, so I wouldn't be implicated! Then I really started to worry. I had visions of Charlie in gaol and me out there in that terrible wilderness alone brought tears to my eyes. But Charlie said not to worry, that he had just helped justice along and the whole thing would be over in a few days.

The next day the plane was back, this time with the big boss from down south. The props of the twin engine clunked to a stop, the dust spiralled and finally settled, coating the entire plane, and only then did the plane door open. When the steps were in place, out he stepped. He was close to retirement age, fairly tall, with a portly figure giving evidence to a life of good food. He wore fancy tooled American cowboy boots that no Australian ringer would be caught dead in, moleskin trousers, a matching shirt with dark fringing across the yoke, a hat with a fancy dark leather band which matched the leather belt around his large stomach. What a sight he was out there in the Outback. He should have been on the stage.

The moment Charles saw this apparition he knew he had the upper hand and he played it to the hilt. They walked towards each other, this man had also seen *High Noon*, overdone the clothes but had the walk down pat, and Charlie who was perfectly cast, both in his walk and clothes. They stopped each side of the gate and sized each other up. He was a shade taller than Charlie, but no match. Charlie was perfection, standing there in his scruffy clothes, dusty hat old enough to be the genuine 'Outback' thing, on his head at just the right angle, gun hanging low, the leather ties loosely secured around his thigh, shirt sleeves rolled up to show strong sunburnt arms, white teeth beaming in a large smile out of a sunburnt face, a cigar clamped firmly in the corner of his mouth. They began to verbally spar and as the conversation continued the other man's complexion became redder and redder. He finally stormed off, leaving Charlie standing at the gate. When he reached the top step of the plane he turned and shook his fist at Charlie and Charlie returned the gesture by taking off his hat in a sweeping gesture. The door was slammed and the plane disappeared in a cloud of dust.

There were a few repeat performances, so at least the man was getting fair wear out of his new outfit! Each time the plane landed, Charlie would strap on the gun and walk out to the gate and wait. When the plane didn't return I was finally told the whole story.

Charlie had brought back the cattle he considered his. He told me of the fence miles inside our land, the spear gates, and the fencing of all our watering holes in their paddocks. When the plane flew over the canyon Charlie knew they had discovered the cattle missing and wanted to take aerial photos for evidence. It had taken days longer than expected to get the cattle through the rough mountains. Otherwise he would have been home days before they had found the cattle missing. So Charlie, who always loved an impossible challenge, started the game of outfoxing the other side. He moved the cattle at night when he could not be spotted from the air, as in those days planes could not fly after sunset, and during the day he would split the herd into smaller groups and graze them under thick tree cover. The plane flew over many times, but never even came close to spotting them. Charles walked the cattle through the mountains and into the upper Bullo valley and when they were behind our block fence at the end of the valley and inside one of the large outer paddocks he let them go. The next two days he mustered our branded cattle and put them in the yard. He was very pleased with the whole operation. They had taken his cattle over the last five years and now he had returned the favour. 'If I had gone to court,' Charlie said, 'it would have taken years, and a lot of money. I would have been up against a big company with money, influence, power, connections … Why, even if I had all the evidence in the world, I wouldn't have stood a chance! No, I just helped justice along a little bit. Got it all over in a few days without a lot of fuss.'

Our neighbours did not go to the police as they had threatened to do. It would be a bit hard to explain the spear fence miles into Bullo land. They also couldn't prove Charles and the stockmen had been on their land, because no-one saw them coming or going. And they had to have proof of Charles and the cattle, proof of the cattle on Bullo, and there were no cattle to be found.

During one of the many discussions at the gate Charles was told the boss would get a court order to muster all of Bullo to find his cattle. Charles was delighted and told him to go ahead. Of course when his manager explained what this entailed in time and money, that rash statement fell by the wayside. It would have cost many times the value of the cattle in question and still wouldn't have been concrete evidence. Charles could say he had no idea the cattle were there, and that they must have just wandered onto Bullo and then hand them back, as a good neighbour should.

The big company soon realised the little man had won. The only way they could have caught Charlie was red-handed, hence the plane flying all over Bullo for days. As they didn't catch him in the act the only thing to do was to forget the whole thing and go away.

Charles's estimate of cattle lost over the five years was around nine hundred and fifty. But by the smile on his face as he finished the story, I think he might have evened the score … and more!

When we visited Charlie's mother in America the next year we were told a story about Mrs Henderson at a church function. The Bishop had asked her how Charlie was.

'Oh he's out in the wilds of Australia somewhere, rustling cattle.' 'No Margaret,' the Bishop replied, 'I do believe the correct term is mustering, not rustling which would be illegal.'

'Of course,' she said, 'how silly of me to get that wrong, yes, he is MUSTERING cattle.'

Another letter I received told me what a lucky woman I was to have had the powerful, intelligent and dynamic Charlie as a husband. Well … best leave that statement unchallenged! But the letter did remind me of Charlie's second Hollywood gun scene. Charles always demanded my full attention whenever he decided to grace us with his presence.

One particular day was very hectic. Nothing was going

right and I was racing from the kitchen to the office, to the school room and back again.

Charles complained to me regularly as I delivered beer and cheese and crackers and larger snacks to him half-hourly. He wanted me to sit with him so he could tell me of a new infallible scheme that could make us a fortune and solve our money problems. I told him I did not have the time to sit around all day and do nothing as he did. His mood changed abruptly and he replied very bluntly that it was my job to do all the things I had been doing, and so I shouldn't be complaining.

Well a few thousand words passed my lips over that chauvinistic remark. But the bottom line was, I thought he had fallen down miserably on his job. We were close to financial ruin and he was just sitting stuffing his face, and reading pirate books, and I ended by saying I would be very happy to be free of him and the endless duties that went with him.

Our conversations often ended in this bitter way, and his recent romps around the house after some of the female staff had ceased our communications altogether. He knew he was in hot water and was even answering the phone instead of screaming out to me to do it. I was very weary and just ignored his actions. His reasons for chasing females were not of interest to me, nor were his latest plans to make millions. I had to simply handle one day at a time, and try to get through the work.

I marched out of the room and he said in a sulky voice, that I would have a hard time surviving without him. I shouted back, 'Ha, try me!' He did!

I went back to the kitchen to find black smoke billowing from a frying pan of charred onions. I was swearing and cursing under my breath when a hysterical governess collapsed at my feet, clawing my apron. She was sobbing and blurted out something no-one could understand.

I told her I couldn't understand a word she had said and told her to speak slowly.

'Mr Henderson!' She blurted again and went through the motions of holding a finger to her head, indicating a gun.

'Good heavens!'

I rushed to the office. The door was closed and with my heart pounding I tried the handle; it was locked.

'Charles!' I called and waited ... Nothing.

By now the governess had told the children in the classroom that their father had shot himself! I had to calm them down, and assure them that nothing of the sort had happened, while glaring at the blubbering governess over their heads. I wasn't very calm myself, but I knew if I joined the bawling brigade, the children would really be upset. I just kept clinging to the fact that Charles was too arrogant and self-centred to kill himself.

I pounded on the door, with my back to the children; tears were streaming down my face. I looked along the wall to where it joined the flyscreen across the front of the living room. There was a gap between one of the large tree trunks that hold up the roof and the straight timbers of the flyscreen and I managed to squeeze through. Of course the logical thing would have been to walk out the front door, around to the front of the office and peer in. But panic put this logical solution out of my mind! The noises coming from the other side of the door were unbelievable so my squeezing through the gap was unheard by Charlie. He was sitting in an armchair with his back to me. He had not shot himself, as he had announced as his intention to the governess. When he had fired a shot, she had thought he had carried out his threat and came screaming to me in the kitchen. He was sitting calmly, listening to the hysterical ravings from the other side of the door. My panic immediately disappeared and anger took its place. He had nothing to do but play stupid games! How dare he! I voiced my thoughts with all the emotions that had built up.

'How dare you, you god-damned S.O.B.!' I screeched loudly, scaring the living daylights out of Charles who was dramatically positioned for an audience he hoped would ultimately force the door open. He hadn't planned on a rear attack.

He launched out of the chair with such fright that the gun went off again! The wailing on the other side of the door started up again, now screaming my name, thinking I had suffered the same fate. I shouted to them I was okay, and so was daddy, so far! This brought the hysteria back to a soft blubbering. I looked at Charles in complete disgust and was about to launch into endless abuse, then thought what's the use, and walked towards the locked door.

Charlie, still recovering, said, 'God damn it, Sara, you gave me such a fright, I nearly shot my foot!' I told him I was glad.

I asked him to put the gun away, because when I opened the door his daughters would rush in and I didn't think he would like them seeing him as a quitter! I opened the door and the children crowded around him asking questions. I could see his expression of bemusement. So except for me frightening him out of his skin, his little performance had gone exactly as planned, and except where I was concerned he was again the centre of attention. As I walked away I heard him telling the children it was all a silly mistake, that he had been cleaning his gun and it had gone off accidentally.

That governess, like many others, wasn't with us for long. She wasn't an Outback type nor a very good teacher, but she did try to help whenever she could. Well ... if one could call it help ... One particular day, as pandemonium and panic prevailed, we had twelve guests for lunch. I told Charles I could either type the urgent letter he needed to go out on the plane or I could cook lunch for them, but I couldn't do both at the same time. In his usual manner he told me to type the letter and he told the governess to stop teaching and go and cook lunch. After she had asked me three-hundred questions about the meal, Charles ordered her out of the office, told her not to disturb me again, and to make all the decisions on her own. I had to keep typing through lunch to finish the letter.

The governess had been preparing lunch all morning with

the children helping. The girls would regularly appear at my side, I would ask how it was going in the kitchen, and they would just roll their eyes and walk away. I kept on typing.

All the guests were men and they had all been to Bullo many times. They always looked forward to a hearty meal of a pound of steak with onions, chips and vegetables, followed by chocolate or banana cake or usually both, all washed down by cold beer. Most of them cooked for themselves or were on the road so much they really enjoyed a good wholesome meal.

Blue, our stock inspector, entered the office and said to me in an amazed voice, 'She forgot to cook my hamburger!' and poked the plate under my nose.

After spending all morning in the kitchen, all that was on the plate was a little pile of chopped raw meat and a green salad! Charles was hot on Blue's heels and said he thought I should go and do something about some lunch, everyone was waiting.

I couldn't believe the scene that greeted me in the kitchen. Such devastation for a green salad and raw meat! She was now working on a dessert, with some unbelievable French name, which was made from egg whites. The egg whites were supposed to have some exotic cream sauce over them, but she hadn't checked if we had all the ingredients. We didn't. She discovered this after she had all these balls of egg white floating around in saucepans of boiling water. When I asked her why she had not cooked the hamburgers and that the men would eat ten times what she had on their plates, she burst into tears and ran from the kitchen, crying she could not cook for barbarians!

With the children's help I quickly cooked steak, chips and onions. The children fished the balls of egg white out of the boiling water and put them on a plate on the table, but there were no takers. The guests settled for coffee and biscuits.

When they were leaving one asked as he stopped to thank my for the lunch, 'Cook staying long?'

'Not if I have my way!' was my reply, and he nodded in

a satisfied manner, knowing I would have my way, and knowing he could look forward to a good outback meal on his next visit.

I was told later, when she finished crying, she had served Steak Tartare, not raw hamburgers and I informed her, that if the only ingredient of Steak Tartare you had was meat, then you did indeed only have raw hamburger!

As for the dessert, even with a special sauce, it was not the working man's idea of a good meal. She then rushed off to her room again in tears.

Nearly every letter I have received starts with 'I have never done this before, but I feel I must write and tell you how much I enjoyed your book.' So after reading hundreds of letters from such sincere and caring people, I knew I couldn't walk away from my latest problems. It was just not possible to quit and let all of those wonderful people down.

So stubbornly I worked on, and as the end of July approached, I realised the constant flow of kind words and concern was healing my battered soul and giving me the strength to go on.

CHAPTER 8

August
1992

On the 2nd August the ABC 'Holiday' crew arrived by road. They drove up from Alice Springs and were coming to Bullo to film a segment for the show. Sarah Henderson of the ABC soon found out she was in Sara, without the 'h', country. They were another great crew—Sarah laughingly told us the reaction when she'd gone into one store to pick up some prearranged goods.

'Hello,' she opened with. 'I'm Sarah Henderson ...'

'No you're not.'

'Yes I am!' she insisted.

But she was told in no uncertain terms that Sara Henderson lived closeby and that she was definitely not her. And to clinch the argument the man smugly said, 'And I know her.'

So while Sarah was in 'Sara' territory she had to change her introduction to, 'Hello, I am the *other* Sarah Henderson from down south.' This was accepted, and everyone patiently waited for her to state her requirements.

By the time they'd arrived in our road most of the day was gone. They were on a tight schedule so it was a quick snack and straight into action.

Marlee started with bullcatching, or I should say a tame version of bullcatching. To catch the really wild scrubbers further away from the homestead would take a fair bit of driving, so Marlee took them into a nearby paddock and picked out the meanest, semi-wild bulls. The sound and camera men soon discovered the bulls were wild enough, however, when they found themselves doing a few fast laps around the truck and bullcatcher, with the bull on the wrong side of the camera. Being enthusiastic, they got carried away with the action and closed up to film the bull's reaction to being chased. They found out, very graphically, how he felt.

The next morning saw a long drive down to the Victoria River looking for crocodiles and fishing for barramundi, but both were very elusive. Franz had caught a large barra the day before so Marlee cooked the fish whole on the barbecue for dinner and the film crew met all the Bullo crew. We were in the middle of a muster out at 22-Mile camp (called this because it is twenty-two miles from the homestead), and Sarah and the cameraman went up in the choppers to film the cattle coming into the yards. Then, to complete the sequence for the day, they took shots of the cattle being drafted and branded.

The next stop was Leslie Lake, a very beautiful expanse of water at the foot of the mountain ranges on the north-western part of the property. Sunset on the lake with all the wild birds feeding, the mountain as backdrop, the setting sun casting shadows across the water is a very beautiful picture. The camera captured it to perfection.

Too soon, the time was up, and bags were packed. The crew had covered quite a lot of territory in just a few days and were very pleased with the scenes they had captured on film. Sarah was sure it would be a good segment on the show, due to air some time in November.

The dust settled, the departing vehicle disappeared down the road, there was no more 'Camera rolling ... Action!' drifting around on the morning air, so it was back to work.

We still had cattle in the yard that had to be dealt with.

The drafting finished, only the sale cattle were left in the yards to be trucked. The new calves had been branded and were let out into the waiting arms of their mums. They all ambled back into the bush, until the next year. Now all we had to do was wait for the road-trains to arrive to take the steers to a grazing property near Darwin, where they would wait until they were shipped to the Far East.

We had been lucky this season, we had had good 'off the road' experienced drivers. In other words, they drive on station roads, not just on highways. We had gone the whole season without one truck being stuck on the road. This time was no exception—the big rigs rolled up to the yards, ready to load their cargo. The stockmen opened the gates and started moving the cattle up the race and onto the double-decker truck. The driver was on the lower deck moving the cattle up the ramp to load the top deck first. When it was comfortably filled he winched the ramp into position, leaving the lower deck clear to start loading.

The stockmen slowly moved the cattle onto the truck in a steady stream, keeping the smaller round yard full. The gates at intervals along the race discouraged the cattle from turning around to go back. It is only wide enough for them to go in one direction, but many a time I've seen an animal twist itself round and get jammed so tightly that a panel of the race has to be removed to release it. This loading had its fair share of stubborn ones, but on the whole the cattle loaded reasonably well. The first truck, both trailers loaded, pulled slowly away from the loading ramp. The noise of the powerful engine as the driver shifted gears echoed through the surrounding mountains as the rig gradually started on the long journey to Darwin.

The second truck then moved into position and lined up the loading door of the truck with the edge of the loading ramp. The cattle stepped off the loading ramp onto the truck. The first trailer was loaded and the driver moved the second trailer into position, the cattle rocking the rig and mooing, shuffling and butting as they got comfortable. The loading was repeated, and the rig was ready to follow the other truck out the road. I listened as the sound of the second engine faded up the valley, the sounds reverberating back to the yards. You could clearly hear the drivers changing gears, calling for more power as they climbed higher into the mountain range, heading for the pass that would let them out of the valley and into the world on the other side of the mountains. I listened until the power finally faded and only a hum could be heard, if you were listening carefully.

The yards were empty.

The sun was slipping behind the sandstone mountains, sending shafts of light through the trees and into the yards. The dust was still filtering down to earth, having billowed high into the air from the churning wheels of the road-trains. A smaller cloud of dust created by the station vehicles leaving for the homestead mingled with the cloud of dust caused by the slow-moving herd of cattle. It would take the next hour or so with the cool change in the air at sunset for this vast area of floating dust to settle.

For some reason I love a just-emptied yard at sunset. I can still hear the cattle mooing, the clang of the steel gates, smell the cattle in the dusty air. The shout of 'Look out behind you!' is still so alive, you keep turning in response to the imagined call. I can sit for hours by an empty cattle yard while memories go flooding by. In 1992 the thought is clearly how things have progressed and changed.

The yard at Bubble Springs, or 22-mile, was the second camp stop on the long walk out of our road in the old days. In those days the road was so horrendous that cattle trucks could not get into the property, so to get our cattle to market we walked them fifty miles to the front gate to load them onto trucks at the highway. They were the days of pack mules—used to carry all our requirements; and horse-tailers—men who take care of the herd of forty or so horses needed to keep mounts up to the stockmen while they're chasing the wild cattle. One man would use three or four horses a day, so he'd need to change horses regularly every three hours or so. They were also the days of dried vegies and salt dried beef, strong black tea and dry damper, day after day on the trail. Then a special, very special, dessert on Saturday night: bread dough, fried in extremely hot beef fat until golden brown and fluffy, then flipped into another saucepan holding bubbling hot plum jam, rolled around a few times, then dumped in a sea of hot custard. Sounds amazing, doesn't it? But after a week of dried vegies and beef it tasted like nectar of the gods. On Saturday night, after being in the saddle from before first light till long after sunset, to finish your meal with the special Saturday night treat, have a couple of swigs of OP rum, roll out your swag under the stars, beside the flickering of the camp fire, the smell of the billy boiling and the lowing of the cattle as they settle down for the night, is something any old timer will tell you he wouldn't swap for the world. No matter how hard I try I cannot remember the name of this Saturday night Outback delight; however, if I close my eyes sitting on the stockyard rail I can conjure up the taste, even after all these years.

Those were also the days of bathing in the river after sunset, freezing cold in June and July, then collapsing for a few hours' sleep before taking your turn to ride watch on the herd. You're woken by a hand shaking your shoulder, no noise for fear of spooking the cattle; you give a nod to signal you're awake and then crawl out of a warm swag, fully clothed. Quietly shaking then slipping on your boots, along with a heavy coat and hat, even at night in case you're still out there somewhere chasing cattle at sunrise, you walk the horse slowly and quietly to your position to take over from the stockman finishing his watch. And all the time the cattle quietly graze to the night-sounds of feet swishing through grass.

Hand movements indicate that you've arrived and the stockman slowly moves off towards the camp, fully aware that any sudden noise or movement could catapult the night into a thundering mass of confusion and dust.

By the early morning watch, just before dawn, the cattle are settled. You are alone with your thoughts and the sounds of the night.

That old camp had been further down the road from the present yard site, on a part of the river where a little waterfall formed a large pool and a perfect swimming hole. The grassy area around the river was good for grazing and was a natural holding position.

Now, twenty years later, things have changed considerably. Musters that took weeks, sometimes months, to complete, now, with helicopters, take days! The cattle are brought in from a range of about ten miles in a complete 360-degree turn around the yards. They are then drafted, branded, the sale cattle loaded, the road-trains depart and it is all done in three days.

I was still contemplating these changes when Marlee brought me back to the present.

'Good muster,' she said as I opened the door to the Toyota and climbed in.

'Yes,' I replied, still reminiscing. We now had half an hour's drive back to the house, but twenty years ago it would have been a four hour ride on a horse ...

I snapped out of it and listened as Marlee outlined the changes we are always planning, changes which we seem to discuss when driving. I watched her profile as she elaborated on the endless exciting ideas she had for improvement. Dreams and ideas, mind you, which would cost millions. But which were slowly, slowly becoming reality.

I couldn't help but wonder how different her life would have been if her father hadn't made the decision to leave America to come to Bullo. I needed the slow horse ride of four hours to ponder that one. But despite the fact I only had half an hour I found myself slipping back to my memories of the children's life on Bullo.

When I analyse their lives in the Outback, I can only come up with 'non-stop adventure' as a description. It was constantly full of new challenges, daily; full of wonderful animals; with lots of hard work thrown in—a little too much—when their father could find them to issue more orders, that is. Charlie seemed to have the notion that if he kept the children, and me, for that matter, working all the time, this would keep us out of trouble. But keeping out of Father's way was a fun game in itself …

The children would be in the kitchen, telling me of some adventure they had just had and begging to have a few more, just a few more minutes of play before school, when they would hear their father approaching. Charlie had the habit of clearing his throat whenever he was about to say something important. Well, Charlie thought everything he said was important, so he was perpetually clearing his throat. This could distinctly be heard as he approached the kitchen, and was the signal for evacuation. One minute I would be in the midst of chatting children and playful animals and the next minute I'd be alone. The dogs were always the first to be alerted to the impending disaster approaching. They would sit bolt upright with ears pricked, waiting; then, when the familiar throat-clearing was heard the ears would droop and the dogs would scatter in all directions, followed closely by the girls, eyes searching for a place to hide, an escape route. Children would disappear into the storeroom, under the kitchen bench, out the door. The dogs would head for the nearest door—Charlie didn't like them in the house and they knew it. It was his rule, and only he enforced it.

The day was spent with the dogs one step ahead of Charlie as he moved around the house looking for someone to issue orders to. The children were right behind the animals—not because they weren't allowed in the house, but because they'd get issued with orders about more work. They considered the dogs had a better deal, they were only told to get out.

I must admit there were a few occasions I downed tools and disappeared with the mob, just to avoid the deluge of instructions I would get because he couldn't find the girls.

So, by the time Charles arrived in the kitchen, a full seventy feet from the bedroom, there would only be me standing there with a vague expression on my face. He would demand to know where the children were and I would mumble something along the lines of having seen them not long ago, and they were probably out in the garden, etc. He would walk outside and bellow their names, to no avail. Then he'd return to the kitchen and tell me to have them report to him immediately when they showed up. After stocking up on cheese, crackers and beer he would retire to his bed and book at the other end of the house.

And only when the coast was clear, would the children and dogs slowly emerge from their various hiding places and things would return to normal.

'Avoiding Father' would've had to have been one of their favourite games. I assisted them in playing it, as I did feel he was far too strict. Even on Sunday, when the staff were allowed a day of rest, Charlie expected the children to work all day in helping with the various activities—such as arranging for horses to be saddled and ready for anyone who wanted to ride. Because most of the staff couldn't ride anyway, the girls then had to go along to take care of them.

So again I would help them get out of these jobs. If the children wanted to go on picnics by themselves to one of their secret places they would pack the picnic goodies the night before and then hide the lot away in the bottom of the fridge ready for an early take-off on Sunday morning. They would saddle the horses and quietly ride away.

It was a very covert operation, and very exciting—except for me. I would have to stay and face the music, although one could hardly call Charlie 'music'. He would go to their rooms around 7 a.m. to hand out the orders for their day's work and for the outings he had promised the staff. He expected the girls to do everything while he, as usual, would sit with his beer, cheese and crackers and read all day. When he didn't find them he would rush back to me demanding to know where they'd gone.

'I'm really not sure,' I'd usually reply. I did know, of course, but if I told him he would send someone to bring them back.

He would then proceed to tell me what punishment they could expect for not staying home and doing their job. This in turn would prompt a good, heated argument about how he expected too much, and what about *their* day off? He would relent then, and actually try to con me to either go and do the work or tell the staff the events were off. I would flatly refuse to get out of bed and, having had a snack with the children at 5 a.m., I knew I could outlast him, food-wise, for at least three hours. Finally he would go and tell the waiting staff that the planned Sunday excursions were cancelled.

Even though Charlie was impossible to live with, most of the time, by working together the children and I could make life bearable. As little girls they really did love and adore their dad. As they grew older they realised he was less than perfect in many ways, but they still thought he was a wonderful and very brave man. And they were always, well, maybe almost always, proud to be his daughters as I am sure they still are today. He inspired them to always reach for the stars, and through life as they achieve each separate goal, I am sure they pause and think of him.

I know Marlee wants to make Bullo the place of his dreams. Danielle is determined to succeed in Martin's and her dream to be on the land and they plan to get married on 12th September next year, her father's birthday. Bonnie hasn't told me, but I think she wants to be the best in the world at aerobatics.

So yes, I think it would be safe to say that all the girls still think the world of their father ... with some reservations ... and still wish for his approval.

When they were younger this constant desire for his approval meant they often tried to achieve the impossible, and would regularly find themselves in dangerous situations. Challenges came along at a rapid pace, and life was a non-stop adventure. These adventures were so numerous I don't know where to start. One of the first that comes to mind was a fishing expedition to the end of the airstrip with Honky-Tonk, Danielle's pet donkey.

Marlee and Bonnie with Danielle tagging along, always seemed to be harnessing some animal for some task. If it wasn't poor Honky-Tonk, it was Herbert, their favourite horse, a truly patient creature.

This day, however, I found them busily trying to strap a mule pack to Honky-Tonk's back. Try as they might, it just kept slipping round; they couldn't pull the girth strap tight enough.

They finally accepted defeat and decided to design their own carry bag, donkey-style. With rope and hessian bags, they made a fair replica of the original. All this hard work was in preparation for the enormous haul of fish they were expecting to catch and which the donkey would be carrying back.

They started out after lunch, in time for the turn of the tide. I told them to be back before sunset. I kept a watch-out down the strip, waiting for them to come up over the edge of the river bank. Right on time three small figures appeared, towards home. It didn't take long to realise the donkey was not with them, and I could see, even at that distance, there was something wrong. I was out the gate and running down the strip at a flat sprint. Halfway there Honky-Tonk came screaming out of the trees in front of me, squealing and snorting and bucking, then he disappeared into the trees again, ignoring my calls. I kept running towards the girls.

I stopped in my tracks and looked in horror at Marlee's face. She was covered in blood. It was dripping down the front of her clothes and was splashed all over her arms. Bonnie had blood through her hair and all over her face and arms. I couldn't tell who was hurt the most or indeed if they both were hurt. Bonnie was crying the loudest, but on closer scrutiny I could see Marlee was the injured child.

The story came out in torrents of words and tears, there, in the middle of the airstrip. They had caught four beautiful big barramundi and the whole operation was going along as planned, until they loaded the fish into the carry bags. Marlee packed all the fish and was about to turn Honky-Tonk around to lead him home when one of the spikes on the fish stuck into his side. He went crazy trying to dislodge the spike and in the process swung around and let fly with a kick that caught Marlee full in the face. The hoof hit her cheek with such force it cut a line just under the top teeth—in places the teeth had come right through the cheek. Already half of her face was badly swollen. I had no idea, but feared her jaw was broken.

We walked the rest of the way back to the tin shed, all three of us crying. Honky-Tonk still kept charging back and forth across the airstrip, wanting to stop to be with us, but not knowing what was hurting him and preventing him from standing still. I told the girls he would have to wait till the men got back from the yards. It would take quite a few strong men to slow him down long enough to get the fish out of the carry bags, something I would not attempt.

I took Marlee straight into the radio room to call the doctor, only to realise it was after five-thirty. We had no medical help until seven o'clock the next morning. I was now sure Marlee's jaw was broken, the swelling had increased even in the short time it had taken to walk home. The first thing to do was to get the wound clean. Bonnie and Danielle were my little assistants, and helped me make Marlee as comfortable as possible. I bathed the wound in warm salt water, but most of the damage was on the inside of the mouth so I made Marlee gargle salt water for hours. I gave her medicine for pain, but she still had a very restless night with very little sleep. As she drifted in and out of sleep she'd mumble, 'Honky-Tonk has my fish,' and then the pain of moving her jaw would wake her and I would have to assure her that the fish were safe before she'd doze off again.

Honky-Tonk was eventually caught and relieved of the

spike sticking in his side, and he immediately became the calm, quiet pet we all knew. The fish were cleaned and put in the fridge.

By morning Marlee's face was so swollen she couldn't see out of one eye and the other eye was almost closed. I was now absolutely convinced her jaw was broken. The flying doctor arrived and agreed that it did look serious. Wyndham Hospital did not have the facilities to handle this so we had to fly her to Darwin. By the time we reached Darwin it was midday and very hot. Marlee was miserable, both eyes were closed and I had to lead her. She couldn't now breathe through her nose because of the swelling, and when she did try to take a breath there was a gurgling, rasping sound. The nurses took one look at her and quickly went to work.

After a lovely bath, X-rays and an injection for pain, she was resting in bed. She could not move her face, let alone smile, but what I could see of her eyes through the swelling said it all.

Thankfully the X-rays showed no breaks in the jaw, so it was now just a matter of waiting for the inside of the mouth to heal and the swelling to go down. Some of the wounds were deep and came right through the cheek. I told Marlee that, as bad as it was, it had to be better than a broken jaw. The expression in her eyes indicated she didn't believe this statement.

Her face did eventually return to normal, the salt water bathing had worked its magic and she had no visible scars. There was just the tiniest mark where the large back molar went right through the cheek.

The girls realised at an early age that we were always short of money. This was not a difficult conclusion for them to reach—they heard endless arguments about money, and money affected their lives at every turn. They had to ride bareback because there weren't enough saddles to go around. Their father said it was to teach them to be better riders. The stockmen got the saddles and the children went without. We didn't even have a truck that could make it to the local gymkhana without breaking down. Even if we did find a truck to take their horses, they were told we couldn't afford the time or the money. Which was in fact true.

They decided at an early age that if they wanted their own saddle and belongings they would have to earn the money themselves. There were many long and serious discussions on this subject among the girls and me. They mainly wanted my assurance that if they did manage to earn their own money Daddy wouldn't take it. I told them he wouldn't. Pleased with this guarantee, they set out to find ways and means of making money.

There were many, many schemes over the years, but my favourite has to be the ferry ride from the house to the abattoir. We hadn't yet built the staff quarters in the early 1970s so all the staff lived in the tin shed with us. It was the only building on the station, except for the abattoir.

The abbatoir operated twelve months of the year, so there were problems with flooding during the Wet Season. Homestead Creek ran along the back of the tin shed, or 'homestead', as it was charitably called. When the creek came up overnight the staff would be greeted the next morning with water from the garden gate to the abattoir door. The abattoir was air-conditioned, so they didn't relish the idea of working in wet clothes and subsequently freezing.

It was during this time the children came up with their first money-making scheme. They harnessed Herbert the Horse to the boat and started the Bullo River Ferry Service. A painted sign was placed at the back gate, stating how much per ride. The staff were very good humoured and would line up. Bonnie rode Herbert and guided him, she was still too small to swim in the strong current. Marlee walked behind the boat to hold it straight and stop it swinging off course, while shouting orders to Bon about which way to go. Two of the staff helped by rowing. In the deep and fast-flowing part of the creek Marlee could only hold onto the back of the boat—it was too deep for her to touch bottom. At this stage of the journey she did a lot of shouting because most of the staff were hopeless rowers and Herbert would have to pull the full weight. It was then that the trouble would start. He would bolt and gallop off in the wrong direction, and the boat would run aground on one of the many high points of land and someone would then have to help Marlee push the boat back into the water. Or if he didn't run it aground Herbert would just gallop off and the boat would be rocking madly until Bonnie could stop him. Many times the boat would come close to turning over in mid-stream.

The girls also planned to serve Vegemite sandwiches for morning tea during the crossing, but the operation never seemed to get out of panic stations long enough to eat a sandwich.

After delivering the passengers on the other side of the creek in a reasonably dry condition—at least, not soaking wet—they asked for the fares, and were told to 'charge it' to their wages. The girls tallied their takings and rushed back to me to ask for the money. They were bitterly disappointed when I told them I couldn't take it out of wages. If anyone had to pay to get the people across the creek to work it would have to be Daddy. The girls knew they had no chance of getting anything out of their father, so they quietly unharnessed Herbert and left the boat tied, ready for the people to row themselves across the creek.

They had worked so hard at their little business I couldn't bear to see their disappointment, and I promptly gave them each some money to start their saving fund.

They tried other money-making schemes and worked hard on each new idea, but, like their mum, found that they worked long and hard with no cash up-front, or back, or anywhere, just the satisfaction of helping to keep the station going and their home together. It was very hard for the children to understand that this was their only reward for endless hard work. But accept it, they did.

Their next adventure, which entailed a lot of hard work and no money, was the piggery. The abattoir was expanding and Charles decided that a piggery was to be added. There were many reasons for this decision—the pigs could eat the offal from the abattoir and then be sold. We were supplying meat to most of the Aboriginal missions around Bullo, and as the missions grew and more white staff were employed, requests for meat other than beef started to come in. So we branched out into pork, fish and eggs, and even started a smallgoods section. At one stage Charles asked me how I felt about making fresh bread, a few hundred loaves a day. I'm sure you can imagine what I told him.

The fish, Charles had some of the older stockmen catching; the eggs, we already had a large chicken run, so we just added to it; and the pork, well that was why the piggery was started. Years later it became quite big, up to 400 pigs, but in the early days there were only about thirty. Charles put the children in charge of it. I didn't necessarily agree with this for many reasons, not the least being the state and smell of their clothes. Even after a hot bath I still couldn't bear the smell of them and had to hold my breath when I hugged them. But Father said we couldn't afford to hire someone just to look after a few pigs, so with older step-brother David they became piggery supervisors, after school.

Being typical children, they had fun every possible moment. There were beauty contests, where they would crown 'Miss Pig of the Month'. Every afternoon after school they would disappear down the flat to the pigpen with their stockwhips in hand to train the pigs to perform like circus lions. They did teach the pigs to be very well behaved and mannered—the pigs would line up and wait for their dinner to be put in the troughs and if any pig stepped out of line before they were given the order the crack of the whip had it scurrying back in line in a flash. The girls even made the pigs eat politely—if one of them put its feet in the trough the whip would be flicked on its rump and the pig would jump in the air, squealing in protest, but would go back to the trough and be careful not to put a foot in the food. If the pig was really bad mannered it would have to sit and wait until all the others finished, then eat alone. I could see all this from the kitchen, and as far as I was concerned that was as close as I wanted to get.

But there were times when I was asked to come and judge the beauty contests or to watch a rodeo, and on these occasions I would drown a few dozen tissues with eau de cologne, stand as far away as possible without seeming difficult and watch the events they had so patiently prepared for my enjoyment!

They did have fun with their piggery, in spite of their mother.

Another of their responsibilities was the chicken run. This they did not like at all. There was a mean rooster who bailed Bonnie and Danielle up in the laying coop. Marlee would regularly have to go to their rescue with a big stick to fight him off. I had to constantly remind them that the eggs needed to be collected, or the water changed.

Added to this, every day before school they mustered the steers into the yards for the day's kill in the abattoir. So at the ages of fourteen, twelve and seven they had very full days. If the cattle were low in numbers in the close paddocks, they mustered further out to bring in more cattle. This was only during the wet when the stockcamp had gone to town.

Consequently, during the mustering months of April to November, it was very difficult to get any school work done. They were always rushing out of school, saying that Daddy told them to do something. Charles and I would argue regularly because some of the jobs he gave these little girls not only kept them out of school but quite often endangered their lives. He would argue that he was making them tough and resourceful. Of course if the job was just a little beyond them and something did go wrong there was a pact not to tell Mummy, otherwise, their father would point out, Mummy would not let them go out with him on the musters. This was a fate worse than death in their young eyes, so Charlie would regularly put their lives in danger and I never heard a thing about it till years later.

The children, again in their quest for their father's approval and the praise of a 'job well done', would also not tell him of their near-death experiences—if they happened to be out of sight and could cover their tracks effectively. On one such occasion, when Marlee and Bon were only thirteen and eleven respectively, they were out with their father in the stockcamp, mustering at Number Two Bore camp site. This camp site is opposite the homestead, but over the other side of the Bullo River, only about one and a half miles as the crow flies. However by road you have to drive or ride six miles along the road to the hard river crossing, cross the river and then ride another six miles to get back to the camp site. At low tide the horses and cattle can cross at a very muddy crossing opposite the house.

Charles told the girls to come back to the homestead to pick up more hessian, which was needed for the wings leading into the yards. (The wings are two fences built out from the main gate of the cattle yards, which form a funnel for the choppers to push the cattle into the yards.) Hanging hessian on the barbed-wire fence makes it look solid to the cattle and they are less likely to try to knock it down. They see the open gate, and the theory is they will head for the open space. Because of where this yard was situated, the two wings had to be fairly long to get around some heavy scrub, and they ran out of hessian. Charles had instructed the girls to cross the river, come back to the homestead, catch one of the mules in the home paddock and load him with a few more rolls of hessian. He took them down to the river and watched them ride their horses into it, the deepest part coming just up to their stirrup irons. Charles then returned to the camp, assured that the task was easy.

The girls caught Snowy the mule and loaded him to capacity with rolls of hessian. They tied him and the horses to the back gate and exploded into the kitchen, eating everything in sight and talking nineteen to the dozen about all the exciting things they had been doing, until it was time for them to leave. They took a little bag of cake to munch on the way. Danielle and I waved goodbye, Danielle remaining outside to watch them cross the paddock, calling back to me in the kitchen with a running commentary of their progress until they were out of sight. Then she came quietly into the kitchen and started to tell me what she would do when she was old enough to go on a camp muster.

The girls arrived at the river and led Snowy into the water and started to wade across. During the time they'd spent catching Snowy and eating, the tide had changed. They knew they would have to swim the horses and Snowy across, but what they didn't account for was the weight of the hessian when it was wet.

They took a few steps into the river and started to swim the horses with the mule in between them. By the time they reached the middle they knew they were in trouble. The wet hessian was now so heavy that Snowy was losing the battle to stay afloat. No matter how fast he paddled he was sinking. The girls couldn't release the harness—Snowy's legs were working like pistons and that made it impossible to get anywhere near the girth without being kicked to death. And if they let go of the harness he would sink anyway! Besides, if they lost the hessian what would they tell their father? Their only option was to save the donkey *and* the hessian. They got a strong and secure grip on each side of the halter and started towing Snowy to the far shore. But he kept sinking as the hessian became heavier. The girls' arms were aching by now as they took more and more of the load. Most of the hessian was underwater, as was most of Snowy, with only his head and neck above, in between the two horses. He knew he was in trouble—his big eyes would look from one girl to the other, at the shore ahead, then he would let out a squeal. By this stage he had stopped swimming and was a dead weight just hanging on the harness and the girls' arms.

The girls huffed and struggled as they physically pulled

Snowy and his load through the water. If they tired and relaxed their grip more of Snowy disappeared under the brown water. His neck was now completely under and the water line was covering his ears. As more of him slipped below the water Snowy squealed in alarm and the girls would try to lift him higher, but their arms were just failing them.

By the time they were almost across the river only Snowy's nostrils showed, breathing furiously. The girls were battling and their breathing was coming as fast as the mule's. The few times when they relaxed their arms he disappeared completely. At these times he would lurch out of the water, snorting and squealing, only to sink back again, to let the girls take the load.

At last his back feet touched the soft mud of the riverbank, and he started walking on his hind legs. The release of weight on aching muscles was wonderful—and not a moment too soon as the girls were really struggling. Then the mule started lunging forward and pulling the girls with him. All he could see was the dry riverbank ahead and when his front feet touched the mud his speed increased. However, it was only a fleeting relief because when the water was no longer bearing the weight of the hessian and the full weight was once again on Snowy's back he collapsed and for the second time went under. The girls were gasping for breath themselves, but had to go to Snowy's rescue. He had now stopped kicking—exhaustion had set in, and the load was so heavy it was burying him. The girls reached down once more and dragged him to the surface. When he stopped coughing and wheezing and snorting the three very shaky survivors slowly waded out of the clinging mud and dropped on the edge of the riverbank, still in the water, but with their faces resting on the solid mud.

It took a good fifteen minutes for them to feel like moving. Snowy was first, he got to his feet and staggered a few extra yards, but the soft mud was tough going and he collapsed spread-eagled in the mud again, looking like a cartoon character.

But they couldn't rest long. There was still work to do. They took rolls of wet hessian from the load, until Snowy could stand, and headed for the camp. It took three trips before they delivered the whole lot. They quickly unrolled it and hung it on the wings before their father arrived at the yards. And he never found out about Snowy's near demise.

Marlee told me of this near-disastrous adventure many, many years later, and about Snowy's sudden aversion to water. Apparently, when the stockcamp started to cross the river at low tide, returning home, Snowy took one look at the water and took off into the bush with his heavy load swaying madly. The stockmen caught him but there was no way they could get him into the water, finally someone had to take him all the way up to the six-mile crossing, where he walked quietly across the dry, built-up road. That night, during the discussion at the homestead about Snowy's peculiar behaviour, the girls just sat like little angels, looking at the ceiling.

As for Snowy, for the rest of his life he flatly refused to go anywhere near water. Not a hoof could he be persuaded to put in anything that slightly *resembled* water. And who could blame him?

Our lives continued at this speedy pace with unusual, but normal for the Outback, events happening daily. Then, every now and again, an extraordinary interlude would occur to make us realise just what a unique experience life truly is. Such an interlude was approaching in our lives ...

It was about ten o'clock in the morning, the heat of the day was just making its presence felt. I was walking in from the garden, and looking out across the paddocks I saw a large column of dust forming where our road bends into view. It was blurred through the dancing heatwaves, but the dust-cloud soon rose clear of the heat distortion and climbed high into the sky. I then saw a vehicle.

As the vehicle continued along the last two-mile stretch and the dust increased, I thought to myself, 'There's only one driver who churns up that much dust.' I was right. Bluey Lewis, our stock inspector, screeched to a halt at the back gate. I walked slowly out to greet him, giving the dust time to settle.

He jumped out of the Toyota, walked to the back and dropped the tray.

'Got something for you,' he said as a bundle of something rolled into the bulldust.

Bluey carefully picked it up, gave it a bit of a gentle dusting and two scrawny legs unfolded, the long feet clawing at the air for something solid. Standing the feet firmly on the ground Bluey coaxed a head and a long neck out from under a large wing. Two big eyes blinked at me with a dazed expression, asking the obvious question, 'Is it over?' The obvious question of any living thing that had just completed a journey with Blue.

'Oh, Blue, it's a baby brolga.'

'Yair. What did you think it was?' he said, as if it were an everyday event to unload a baby brolga from the back of your Toyota.

'Well, after rolling around in the back of your truck it really doesn't look like anything— except maybe a feather duster gone wrong.' The bird couldn't coordinate its legs and was staggering everywhere.

'It's all yours,' said Blue, heading for the driver's door.

'Wait a minute! What do you mean, "all mine"? I don't know anything about brolgas. I've only ever watched them dancing off in the distance or flying overhead. What on earth would I do with a baby?'

'Oh there's nothing to it. Just give it food and water a few times a day.'

'How did you end up with a brolga anyway?'

That's when he told me that Judy and Mike Walsh at the BP store in Timber Creek had been raising it. Some Aborigines had found it as a newborn and given it to them. 'Must be a few months old by now,' he said. 'Very friendly, and loves people. Well, that's all the bird sees—people. Has no idea it's a bird yet. Anyway, they can't keep it at the store any more because it's becoming a bit of a problem. Greets all the customers when they pull up for petrol and scares some of them half to death. But the main problems are it pecks at its own image in the side mirrors on the cars and pecks the insects out of the radiator grilles. Gets the insects all right, but punches holes in the radiators. Doesn't make the customers too happy and is becoming an expensive pet. Mike's a bit worried what the bird might do when it grows bigger. So I told them this would be a great place for the bird to grow up.'

'What is its name?'

'Don't think it has one. You'll have to decide that.'

With that, he started the engine, gave me a wave and took off at the super-sonic speed of MAC-I. Dust showered all over us. I gave a few coughs and the bird sneezed repeatedly.

'Well, what am I going to do with you?' I asked the brolga as we stood there eyeing each other. It had been shaking its feathers over and over again in the last few minutes and was finally getting them under control. It now looked like what it was. So much so that when the children rode up on their horses the first thing they said was, 'Where did you get the baby brolga?'

'Bluey just brought it in.'

'Oh boy! Is it ours?'

'Seems so.'

At the sight of the horses, the brolga backpedalled in alarm, but when the girls dismounted and kneeled down to talk, it immediately stepped forward again. It wasn't long before they were all around the bird, talking and stroking. It was definitely used to children, but I still warned the girls to be careful, it could peck at their eyes. However, it seemed it was love at first sight. The bird followed the girls for the rest of the day. When they went riding it waited patiently at the garden gate until they returned. When dinner was ready it took its position at the kitchen door. We sat down to the meal and in the background I could hear a strange continuous sound.

'What's that strange sound? I've been hearing it for hours.'

'That's Bleep!' said Danielle enthusiastically.

'Bleep?'

'That's what we've called the brolga. Bleep the Brolga!' said Marlee. The name described the noise perfectly: a constant bleep bleep.

'If that's all it does all day, then it's well named,' said their father. 'But there's no way I'll put up with that racket all night, so you'd better find some way to silence it.'

'She's lonely. Can she come in, pleeeease ...?' this plea from the three girls in unison. All eyes on their father.

'Ask your mother,' he quickly retaliated. All eyes then swung to me.

'No. Sorry. You can't bring a bird like that into the house. It belongs outside.'

Nevertheless, within a few days Bleep had managed to wheedle her way inside. The children would dash through the kitchen, rushing in or out of the house on some adventure, and there she'd be—right in the middle of the bunch.

It was decided Bleep was a female; never actually announced or stated as fact, just assumed.

She was toilet-trained within a few weeks. This wasn't because she was clever but because the children were regularly taking her into the garden. But I would say it was more thanks to me swinging a broom at her every time she even looked like disgracing herself. On the occasions she did have an accident, she found herself on the end of a broom, flying out the door, without the aid of wings.

She was a delightful bird, however, and very soon was firmly entrenched as one of the family. Whenever the children planned anything, there was Bleep right in the middle of all the action. Every night she settled down outside the children's rooms. The walls were only flyscreen so she could see them and was content with that. When the lights went out she positioned herself comfortably on one leg, the other leg disappearing into her feathers. Her head and long neck would curl gracefully under one of her large wings and after a few rufflings of feathers to get everything sorted out, she would be snug for the night.

But the moment one of the girls put a foot out of bed, in the morning, Bleep would unwind, stretch her neck, lower the folded leg, flap her wings, give a few shakes of her feathers and be ready for whatever the day would bring. She would then dash into the kitchen to join in the morning activities. At breakfast she was very messy trying to spear her Rice Bubbles. I would put a plate for her on the sink with a handful of cereal and she would amuse herself, patiently trying to spear each little piece while keeping one eye on the children. She knew the routine well and waited for the mass exodus she knew would come as soon as the girls were given permission to be excused. At that moment they all exploded out the door for a few minutes' play before school.

Bleep had to be locked outside the house during school, as she was too much of a distraction during lessons, and of course the girls would use any excuse to interrupt school lessons. She would stand at the nearest flyscreen to the schoolroom and peer in. She knew the time of morning tea and lunch breaks—you didn't need to look at the clock. As the time drew closer, Bleep's pacing became more and more frantic, her neck weaving back and forth, so excited she could hardly contain herself. When the children raced out the door she would jump in the air and trumpet loudly. Some days Bleep would be so impatient to play and cause so much commotion that I had to lock her in the storeroom to get any school work done. Somehow she would still manage to create enough disturbance to disrupt everything and get the children out of the school room early.

A few months after Bleep had been with us I realised we hardly knew anything about this beautiful creature that was growing in our midst. I decided to do some research, and got out our many animal and bird books.

In Aboriginal legend it is said the brolga was a famous

dancer named Buralgo, who rejected the advances of an evil magician who in turn changed her into a graceful crane. I had no idea there were magicians in Aboriginal folklore, but there you are. The book was right about the graceful dancing. Watching brolgas dancing in a swamp at sunset is one of the most beautiful things I've ever seen. Many's the time I've sat mesmerised by the elegant movements of mauve and grey fluttering wings and feathers. Their red heads darting in and out of the water and throwing it high in the air, the rays of the setting sun turning the water into cascading diamonds, perfect dancing partners.

I have yet to see any scene as breathtaking as that.

The book went on to say that brolgas live into their thirties; stand about one and a half metres tall when fully grown; are easy flyers, slow but powerful. Pilots have spotted them cruising at 3500 feet. They are one of Australia's largest birds, and they mate for life. They eat a variety of insects, frogs, roots and their favourite habitat is a swamp. There was more information, but I closed the book thinking, 'Well, we certainly do have an interesting bird among us.' Bleep definitely loved insects, but also Rice Bubbles—and hamburgers, which she stole from the frying pan, before they were cooked. But the swamp as favourite habitat was not in evidence yet—Bleep seemed to prefer being high and dry in the homestead. Although she did give the shower recess a curious glance every now and then.

There were no guidelines that I was aware of for raising such a bird in captivity; not that Bleep was locked in a cage. Most of my day I spent locking her out of the house, while most of her day was spent waiting for an opportunity to slip inside.

She grew rapidly and it wasn't long before we were eyeball to eyeball. When I told her she was naughty for something she had done, she would stretch herself to her full height and tower over me, staring down her long beak with those strange eyes. I would take hold of the end of her beak and give it a good shake, then she would sidle up to me and put her head under my arm and hide her eyes. This was to say she was sorry. Her beak was a menacing length and quite a dangerous weapon, if she ever chose to use it thus.

She never did show any tendencies towards viciousness, and was always the most amicable of creatures. Until, that is, we employed a manager with two little boys. Bleep adored the girls, so it was a surprise when she displayed an instant dislike for the boys. We found out later she had good reason: their favourite pastime was throwing stones at her. Bleep had very expressive eyes, when you looked into them you knew immediately if she was happy, curious, frightened, excited, or anything else. When the boys came into the kitchen her eyes would turn to a cold, steely glare. It was very frightening. The boys would do a 180-degree turn and run. She had them terrified, but it didn't stop them from throwing stones at her from a safe place.

One day she came limping into the kitchen, one knee so swollen she couldn't bend her leg. There was a terrible gash right across the joint. Whatever had caused it had been quite a blow because the joint was swelling as I watched it. The next morning the joint was the size of an orange and Bleep couldn't walk.

The vet told me to mash penicillin tablets into her food to prevent infection, and to keep her quiet and continue the medication until the swelling went down. I bathed the wound in salt water and kept it covered with a bandage and healing ointment. All the time I bathed the leg she would watch closely and with her beak gently nibble all around my fingers and hands as I worked. If I spoke to her she would look closely into my eyes, she was fascinated with everything I did. After her leg was wrapped she would go through the same nibbling action all over the bandage.

We took turns carrying her around or sitting down to give her good leg a rest. She could not bend the bad leg so could not squat, or fold it up. With a lot of manoeuvring she could sit on my lap, but this meant bending her good leg into a squat position and hanging the sore leg straight down, resting on the floor. I had to sit on a high breakfast stool for her sore leg to be comfortable.

I fed her as she couldn't chase insects. During her illness she lived on cereal and mince meat and the children would catch her favourite bugs. This very close relationship with me for all that time formed a lasting bond. After she could walk again she would sometimes be off with the girls on their adventures, but for the most part she tended to stay around the house with me.

The naughty boys continued to throw stones, unbeknown to anyone except Bleep. The day came when she had had enough and she attacked. I heard terrible bloodcurdling screams and rushed outside to see Bleep in hot pursuit of one of the boys; even at a distance his fear was evident. I think Bleep was teaching him a lesson, because she was quite capable of catching him but chose to stay a foot or two behind, breathing down his neck. It was having the desired effect—he was red in the face from screaming and every inch of his face was etched in fear. I couldn't take the risk that she was playing—if I were wrong, and she did attack, it could be fatal. I reached the boy in record time; he was very close to collapsing and was hysterical. I stood in front of him and scolded Bleep, but she would not back down. She was defiant. The expression in her eyes was, 'Let me at him.' I asked him if he had done anything to her and he shook his head and said she was just mean. I knew this wasn't true, told him I could not protect him every time and that eventually Bleep would get him, so he had better tell me what he'd done. I saw him move his arm behind his back. I reached for his hand, opened the closed fist and out dropped a stone. Bleep had terrified him so much he was still clutching it in fear.

'You've been throwing stones at her, haven't you?' I said, furious.

His mum appeared on the scene at this moment, and when she discovered what he'd been doing he was quickly hauled off to receive a good spanking. As the howls of indignation floated from the manager's caravan the expression on Bleep's face changed to one of satisfaction. The manager left not long after, so the problem of the little boys throwing stones at Bleep stopped. And I didn't have to spend my time sprinting around the garden saving them from having their eyes pecked out when she deliberately ambushed them.

After the boys left, Bleep never showed any aggressive tendencies towards anyone, ever again. Life once more returned to the three musketeers and Bleep. Indeed, the girls could do anything with her; and when I was out of sight, they did. I came into the kitchen one day and there was Bonnie instructing Danielle to feed Bleep lumps of bread while she had her fingers around Bleep's neck to stop the bread from going down. There were several lumps down Bleep's neck up to Bonnie's finger, and a very strange look on Bleep's face! The expression on Danielle's face was warning enough to Bon that someone was approaching, she quickly let go and all the lumps continued their journey. Bleep made several elaborate stretching movements of her neck, ruffled her feathers and was ready for the next adventure.

The girls and Bleep were with me in the kitchen one day, hindering my attempts to prepare lunch, when Marlee asked, 'Mummy, why doesn't Bleep fly?'

I really hadn't thought about it, but it was true—she walked, or trotted everywhere. Flapped her wings a lot, made a lot of fuss, but I'd never seen her attempt to fly.

'Has she tried to fly when she's been with you?' I asked.

'No,' came the chorus.

'Well, I suppose the parent bird teaches the baby bird to fly. And Bleep, being an orphan, I suppose we'll have to teach her.'

'Oh boy!' they exclaimed. At the sound of the girls' excitement, Bleep bounded up and down and flapped her wings furiously, knocking most things off the kitchen bench. The girls raced out the door yelling, 'Come on, Bleep, we're going to fly!' and she was out the door in a flash.

And so started the saga of 'teaching Bleep to fly'. Every spare moment found the girls running up and down the lawn, flapping their arms and shouting, 'Fly, Bleep. Look, like this,' and they would flap their arms vigorously. Bleep would dash back and forth with them, trying to figure out what this new game was and what part she was expected to play. The only result was lots of dashing to and fro and furious flapping. So to make their arms look more like wings the girls tied towels to their wrists. Then, to really get serious, they moved out onto the airstrip. I was asked to join them during these sessions, to contribute any further suggestions. Things were not progressing fast enough for the girls, although Bleep was having such a great time, being the centre of so much attention, she didn't mind if it went on forever.

The children were running up and down the airstrip, pleading with Bleep to do something, other than just run, when they heard their father approaching in the Super Cub. The girls picked Bleep up and carted her off the strip and stood on the side while the plane whooshed by. The Super Cub is a two-seater, high wing, fabric aircraft. Ours was painted a bright yellow and was called 'WOO' because its call sign was VH-WOO, or Victor-Hotel-Whiskey-Oscar-Oscar. When WOO flew past Bleep a strange expression came into Bleep's eyes. And as if a switch had suddenly been flicked she let out a tremendous trumpet and went running after the plane.

It was love at first sight. Bleep thought the plane was a bird … well, we assumed this. But whatever she thought, she bedded down under the wing of WOO that night and there was the devil to pay the next morning when Charles wanted to take-off. Bleep wouldn't let him anywhere near the plane. She would flap her wings and arch her neck and run at him in a very menacing way. The girls and I had to take her away and hold her while Charles took-off. When we did let her go she raced down the strip after the plane and stood at the end and watched wistfully as the little yellow plane disappeared into the distance. This performance continued whenever WOO took-off or landed—someone would rush to hold Bleep, for fear of her being chopped up in the propeller. It was almost as if she knew she should be doing what the plane was doing, but she had no idea how. She didn't relate running up and down the airstrip with the girls as anything to do with flying.

While the love affair with the plane continued at night, during the day while the plane was away Bleep returned to normal and the girls continued with the flying lessons.

I knew it would just be a matter of time before she would fly naturally ... One afternoon Danielle came rushing into the kitchen, breathless.

'Quickly Mummy! We think Bleep is going to fly!' she panted.

I ran out onto the airstrip with Danielle and there was Bleep, flapping her wings furiously and leaping into the air.

'Okay!' shouted the girls and off down the strip they ran, waving their arms and towels as fast as they possibly could. Bleep usually did the running, but this time she was also flapping as she loped along beside the girls, and in a short space of time she was airborne.

The girls collapsed on the ground, shouting and cheering with what little breath they had left. Bleep kept flying, encouraged by the girls shouting, 'Flap, Bleep! Flap!' She kept on flapping, then looked around for the girls. When she saw them still on the ground, she stopped flapping in midair and fell like a stone to hit the ground with a thud. We all rushed to her side. She was dazed, but luckily there were no bones broken. We stood her up gently and talked to her to settle her down and reassure her. But the eyes kept asking, 'What happened?'

They tried again. This time, when Bleep was airborne, the girls kept running, flapping and shouting all the while. It wasn't long before Bleep got the hang of flying and the thrill of it all. She finally accepted that for some reason the girls could not join her in the air so she had to fly alone.

The problem we now had to solve was her watching the girls all the time instead of concentrating. Because the moment they stopped flapping she also stopped and fell out of the sky. She was still flying very low, almost alongside the girls, and we were worried that when she discovered she could go high, if she stopped flying then she would really hurt herself.

The lessons continued. The girls were becoming long-distance runners, while Bleep's flying skills improved daily. But her landings left a lot to be desired.

'Mummy, Mummy! Come quickly!'

I dropped what I was doing and rushed out with Danielle. She pointed high up in the sky and there was Bleep. She had certainly found her wings and was flying around the house and airstrip, having a wonderful time.

'Goodness! I thought something was wrong.'

'There is. She doesn't know how to land!'

'Well she's soon going to find out,' I said.

Having seen me, Bleep now came in for landing. It was fair to say she didn't know how to land. She was coming in like a Kamikaze! Dive bombing at a dangerous pace.

'Quickly, start flapping!' I yelled, and we all started flapping and calling to Bleep to get her attention. We managed somehow and she started flapping again, which slowed her speed considerably and stopped the death dive. But she still hit the ground with a terrible whack. It was a perfect crash-landing, beak first. She tumbled over and over, all legs and wings and feathers. We ran to her side as she lay in the dust. She managed to stand and after a while shook all the bulldust out of her feathers and walked back to the house with us, not too sure what it was all about.

The next step was to teach her to back-flap with her wings and put her feet out first, like landing gear, when she came into land. I told the girls to take Bleep to watch the other big birds down at the billabong. We all went down for a lesson, with Bleep in tow, hid in the bushes and watched the birds as they approached landing. The watching was easy, but we wondered how on earth we could teach this to Bleep. I think these daily visual lessons did the trick. She wasn't too sure what these strange creatures were, but she saw they could fly and was very interested in the way they landed and didn't crash-land as she did. So each day she watched their technique, fascinated.

We were all desperately hoping Bleep would learn from these other birds, because at the rate she was going she would be a write-off before she soloed.

The children persevered and for the next week went through the back-flapping techniques, with Bleep copying the big birds' actions when they landed. It was then time for Bleep to solo. We all watched as she flew around the house and finally the girls called her down. She started her shaky gliding descent towards her little group of anxious family on the ground, an intent look on her face as she approached touchdown. We all held our breath. She went into her back-flapping action about eight feet above the ground and awkwardly thrust her long legs out in front of her just before contact. Her claws stretched, waiting for contact with the ground. And somehow she managed to remain upright. It was far from a professional landing—most birds would have totally disowned her—but her human family was thrilled, and so was Bleep, just quietly. We jumped around, clapping and squealing, and Bleep soon joined us after recovering from the shock of still being in the upright position and in one piece. Jumping high in the air, she trumpeted continuously and strutted around, as if to say, 'Who's a clever bird then?' After tiring of this celebration, she promptly took off again, circled the airstrip and came in for another famous landing. This went on until sunset. There were a few outright failures, but she definitely had the hang of it by the next day.

There was great festivity. Bleep could finally fly—the girls had officially given her her wings—but what was most important, she could finally land.

Flying, and landing, changed her life overnight. But she

still stayed close to home, even though she now had the sky at her disposal. She was puzzled as to why we didn't join her and I think because of this she stayed close by. If she lost sight of the children or the homestead she turned around and came home. We were still the centre of her life and she didn't feel comfortable when she couldn't see us.

Since she was born, people had been her whole life. She trusted humans implicitly, and this trust was clearly demonstrated when we had an old friend visiting for the weekend. He got into a heavy drinking session with Charles and when it came time for him to go home he wanted to take Bleep with him. I patiently explained that this was not possible, but he was beyond the reasoning stage. He kept picking Bleep up and tucking her under his arm. He was very drunk and fell over a few times, still holding on to her. I was worried that she would get hurt, but more worried that if she tired of this game and this person who would not leave her alone she might peck him.

But she didn't show any signs of hostility, even when he fell into the half-dug swimming pool. I watched in horror as he stepped out in midair and disappeared over the edge with Bleep securely tucked under his arm. I rushed out to the pool, thinking they would both be injured, but found them sprawled out on the bottom in the dirt, he softly stroking Bleep, telling her it was all right and she patiently listening to everything he had to say. It was an amazing reaction. Whenever he grabbed her she would go limp and just hang there like a rag doll, letting him carry her around the house. I finally got the chance to rescue her while he was visiting the bathroom before his long trip home. I quickly hid her in one of the bedrooms and told her to stay there until he was gone. She seemed to accept this and waited until we let her out when the coast was clear.

When he came out of the bathroom and started to look for her I told him she had gone off flying. He staggered out to his truck and drove off with a clashing of gears. Charles said he would sober up by the time he reached the highway.

This wasn't the case, as his wife later told me. When he did reach the front gate he took the wrong turning and ended up hundreds of miles away in another town and didn't get home till the following night.

Bleep had still not had any close contact with birds. The closest she'd got was watching them at the landing lessons down at the billabong. If any bird came near while she was flying she would promptly land and walk with the children until it was out of sight; if the bird remained curious and hung around she stayed with the children, the look on her face clearly indicating that she did not know what this weird creature was and moreover had no interest in associating with it.

After she could fly, she went everywhere with the girls and me. One afternoon we had to move cattle into a new paddock, so she came on her first muster. It was quite a menagerie. The dogs always followed me everywhere I went, also Honky-Tonk was very fond of mustering. As I was only a reasonable horsewoman, I rode in the lead, followed by the various dogs and donkey. The cattle were fascinated by this strange collection, and would follow closely, trying to sniff all the animals. This made my job as lead easier. Even with the new addition, Bleep, tagging along, the cattle were not in the least disturbed. She walked quietly on the edge of the herd, eyeing them all and keeping quite close. Every now and then, when she got bored, she would take to the skies, circling the herd. Sometimes she would fly away and disappear for a few minutes, but she'd soon swoop back, land and start walking again.

She loved flying next to me at about shoulder height. Trotting was just the right speed for her, but most of the time when we were moving the cattle it would be at a walk. So she had to do a fair amount of circling to slow down enough to stay with us. When the cattle were safely in their paddock she would wait until we were trotting back to the house and then she would fly wing in the middle of all of us. This was her favourite part of the day. Sometimes if the horses weren't too tired the girls would gallop back to the house and Bleep would be in her element, flying wing at shoulder height. She would then watch the girls wash down the horses, supervise the storing of the saddles and join us on the front porch at the end of the day for the sunset, very much a member of the family gathering.

She was a great assistant hunter. When their father sent the girls down to the billabong to hunt for ducks Bleep would always go. Of course she didn't know she was being a Judas, helping hunt her own kind. She just wanted to be a part of everything the girls did. And that included a duck shoot. It was a strange sight watching two little girls with guns over their shoulders walking through the paddocks with a brolga. The girls would push Bleep ahead of them in the billabong and she would walk casually into the water while the girls crawled along behind her in the long grass. The other birds feeding in the billabong would look up and only see the brolga. Thinking it was very heavy-footed and made a lot of noise, but was no danger, they would go back to eating. Bleep, egged on by the girls, would wander closer and closer to the feeding birds. She was a perfect cover; the girls could get almost alongside the ducks before the ducks realised that even a big bird couldn't possibly make all that noise. But by the time they had worked this out it was too late for them, and the girls would have an easy shot as the ducks took off.

With Bleep as their cover the girls were very successful hunters. There were times when Bleep would have nothing to do with the hunt and wouldn't follow orders, just wandered off in the opposite direction, away from the ducks. No matter what the girls did they could not convince her to cooperate. On those days the catch would be very small. Bleep was always interested in the ducks the girls had shot; on the way home she would poke and peck at the strange, lifeless creatures. She still showed no interest in any live bird, however.

On one hunting trip with Bleep as decoy Marlee shot a

duck and laid it next to her gear on the edge of the water. She was wading back to her hiding place to wait for more ducks to land when she heard a terrified squawk from Bleep. Quickly swinging around, she was just in time to see Bleep reeling back in horror as the duck charged with its wings spread and neck stretched in the attack position. Marlee's immediate thought was that she hadn't killed the duck and it was now racing around the billabong wounded. She was off after it in a flash. By now Bleep had regained her composure after being scared out of her senses, and joined Marlee in the chase.

Marlee, aided by Bleep, chased the duck up the billabong and down the billabong and across the billabong. Marlee thought it had to be badly wounded because it couldn't fly, but was darting around the billabong at breakneck speed. Trained never to leave a wounded bird, Marlee had a rest and resumed chasing the duck. During her rest, it would sit at a distance and just watch her. Marlee and Bleep continued to give chase, all around the place, but never even got close to catching it. Marlee decided she would just have to shoot it again and headed back for her gun. As an afterthought she walked over to her gear to get a few more bullets, just in case this duck was as hard to shoot as it was to catch, and there, lying next to her gear, right where she had left it, was the duck she had shot! She had chased a perfectly healthy duck for miles. It had been hiding in the grass right near her gear and had jumped up when Bleep wandered over to look at the dead duck. Bleep had scared the live duck out of its hiding place. It was a young duck, not yet old enough to fly, except for skimming across the water at high speed.

Marlee picked up her duck and headed for home, completely exhausted and in no mood to have any more to do with ducks for the day.

Bleep grew into a very big bird, but in all the time she had been with us we had never seen her with another bird. She just didn't appear interested. However, she was now flying further afield than before and would go out of sight and stay away for well over an hour; but she'd always come home at sunset to spend the night sleeping outside the girls' bedroom.

We talked many times about when Bleep would probably leave us and go into the wild. I certainly didn't want to lose her and I know the children felt the same but we had to face the fact that this was inevitable. I worried about her own kind accepting her: she was a very peculiar brolga and had developed some unusual habits living with humans. I told the girls we could only wait and hope, but in the meantime we should all just enjoy this rare creature because we had to accept we wouldn't have her for long. Changes were taking place ...

I was cooking dinner one evening when Bleep came into the kitchen carrying something in her beak. She was making the soft krrrr, krrrr sound she made when she wanted to be intimate; the loud trumpeting was usually reserved for wide open spaces. She had used it a couple of times in the house but after a few scoldings learned to keep it for outside.

'What do you have there?' I asked her, whereupon she dropped a stick into the frying pan, in the middle of the onions I was cooking.

'Bleep!' I scolded her and picked the stick out of the onions and put it on the kitchen bench. She promptly picked it up and threw it into the onions again. This time I threw the stick out the door. It was not long before she was back in the kitchen with another stick, heading straight for the onions.

'No!' I said very sternly, but it was to no avail. In went the stick. I held it up and, shaking it, told her 'no' many times. She suddenly spread her enormous wings and started bounding up and down. This was pretty disastrous in the kitchen—she merely succeeded in sweeping most of dinner off the bench. But she was bounding so high I could see the fan lopping off her head if I didn't get her out of the kitchen quickly. So I picked up the stick and ran out of the house and she bounded after me. Once I had her outside I locked the door and raced around to the other doors and did the same. While I finished cooking dinner, the flyscreen on the kitchen windows received a severe pounding as she pecked repeatedly at it to show her displeasure. After I threw many jugs of water over her, she went off sulking, but kept returning to the screen, throwing sticks at me.

This change in her behaviour, we were soon to find out, was here to stay. It became a nightly event. One way or another she would get into the house and head straight for the kitchen with stick in beak, ready to dump it in whatever I was cooking. It soon became habit that I would take her outside the minute she started this strange behaviour, and so began the dancing session each evening at sunset. She would throw sticks high into the air and dance around me; if I tried to go inside before she was finished she would block my way. It was soon conveyed to me that I was expected to dance with her. I would throw sticks and twirl around and flap my arms and generally look ridiculous. But work through the routine I had to. There was a certain amount of trumpeting by both of us, and dipping of the head and closing of the wings across the chest. It was straight out of *Swan Lake*. I couldn't cut it short; some evenings I would be running late with dinner and after rushing through most of the routine would declare, 'Enough,' and head for the kitchen. But she would block my way, stand close and fold her wings around me, flutter them against my arms, and nestle her head down onto my shoulder. Then she would spring back, leap into the air and majestically float back down to earth, and the dancing would start all over again. The message was, we haven't finished yet.

For some reason I was the favourite dancing partner. Well, she was smart enough not to try Charlie, and the girls were always, or most of the time, away from the house working. I suppose I was the only one she could rely on to be at the homestead each night at sunset, so I got the job.

We thought this change in her habits might indicate that

she was ready to mate. But on reading more about the brolga, it was stated that even though dancing was part of the mating process, brolgas just loved to dance and it didn't necessarily indicate that she was ready to take this great step.

The next year, however, the dancing did become a very serious part of her life. Sometimes when she was out mustering with us she would see brolgas off in the distance feeding or dancing in the billabong, and she would go closer and land to watch them. She started watching them more and more, sometimes for long periods of time. There were times when she stayed out in the paddock and didn't come home to join us for a sunset drink. She would fly away after she had brought us safely to the gate. Gradually she was staying away overnight and sometimes it stretched into days.

By the end of the year we had to accept that Bleep was moving towards living in the wild. After weeks of absence I would think she had finally gone, but then she'd walk into the kitchen and act as if she'd never left. We would make a fuss over her for the next few days and she would be part of our day again; then suddenly, without warning, she would be gone.

I knew she was trying to hold onto two worlds—having a foot in both camps, so to speak. She was having great trouble trying to accomplish this because, as much as she loved us, the call of her own was very strong and was winning. I would turn to see her looking at me with the strangest expression of love, confusion, wonderment and sadness. And the next day she would be gone, and we'd have to adjust our lives to another long period without her.

'Mummy, Mummy! Come quickly!' Danielle dragged me out the door and pointed excitedly to the airstrip. There was Bleep, with another brolga.

'She's brought her boyfriend home!' the girls said laughingly. However, she wasn't having much luck convincing him that we were family. You could follow what was happening: Bleep was trying to get him into the garden, but he wasn't having a bar of it. She would walk a few steps towards us then turn and beckon him to follow. He would stand his ground and just ignore her. She finally came into the house alone, keeping one eye on him and one on us. There was quite a lot of calling back and forth, and you could imagine him telling her to hurry as he wasn't going to wait too long. She would then go to the door and tell him to be patient! But he obviously laid down the law because she raced out the door in a fluster as he started to take off without her. She made a hasty depature, flapping across the lawn, taking off on a path crossing his and joining him in midair. We waved to her from the ground and she broke away from him and circled the house a few times, trumpeted loudly, then flapped away at double speed to catch him up, disappearing into the sunset.

The visits became less frequent. Mostly she'd trumpet loudly as she circled the house, until we came out and waved; then she would fly away, with her boyfriend close by. While we were happy a wild brolga had accepted our crazy, mixed-up Bleep, we were sad in our hearts that we had lost this wonderfully unique bird. But love was in the air, there was no doubt about it, and he had won her over to his world. A few times when visiting she broke away and glided down to land, but he called her back each time. So it was a surprise when the girls came rushing in one afternoon, screaming with excitement!

'Oh quickly, Mummy! Quickly!' they shouted as they dragged me out the door.

There on the airstrip stood Bleep and her mate, in the throes of a serious conversation. But the reason for the girls' excitement was the two baby brolgas standing patiently by as their parents had a heated discussion. Bleep finally won and she marched triumphantly towards us with her babies following tentatively behind her.

What a proud mother she was. The babies watched their mother's every move. They watched how we patted and hugged Bleep, while all the time she 'krrred' to them quietly. It wasn't long before they let us near them.

Father bird performed as he always had in the past. He stomped up and down the airstrip and let out a continuous stream of complaints—obviously his opinion of Bleep's outrageous actions. She would go to the door and give him a piece of her mind on a regular basis; but most of the time she would ignore him.

She stayed as long as was possible. He was so anxious about the babies that she would take them to the door to show him they were safe. We knew as darkness approached that she would have to leave.

We all gave her a gentle hug and lighly patted the babies, and with a heavy heart watched them slowly walk towards the airstrip. Bleep paused a few times and looked back. Then she left the babies and returned to us. We all stood there for a while, in silence—there was nothing to say. We knew this was the last time we'd see her. She was in a turmoil—not wanting to leave her human family, yet knowing it had to be. She looked at us with sad eyes, and turned and walked back to her waiting babies.

She never came home again. Over the years, when a brolga trumpets as it passes the house, I like to think it's Bleep saying hello from afar.

But over the years even these contacts have gone, and she is now very much a part of the wild. We will never forget her—she was a wonderful part of our life for a long period of time. She was such an important part of the development of the children's love and understanding of all creatures.

One other longtime resident is Honky-Tonk. Apart from his disastrous fishing expedition, his life so far has been spent growing up peacefully with the girls. He has taken his part in a series of fun adventures ... well, almost all fun adventures, starting with his arrival at Bullo as a very small donkey.

His arrival was definitely out of the ordinary, even for a donkey. Honky-Tonk was swapped for a pig. Bradshaw Station wanted a boar to start a small piggery. We were up to our forty-plus piggery, so Charlie made this great deal—to swap a pig for a donkey for Danielle's birthday. The manager of Bradshaw said he would 'drop' the donkey by, and that's exactly what happened. Honky-Tonk arrived by plane. Dick Gill, another character of the time, and like Charlie a brilliant pilot, arrived on the big day with the donkey sitting in the co-pilot's seat strapped in with seatbelt and safety harness. Honky-Tonk was about the size of a large dog.

The children were waiting for the plane and when the propeller stopped they rushed over to the door and there was this small donkey sitting in the seat just like a person. It had thick bushy hair sticking out around large eyes—which were a little larger than normal at that moment. Marlee and Bonnie lifted the dazed animal out of the seat and carefully stood him on his feet. He stood swaying for a while, but it wasn't long before the girls had him trotting after them for his first adventure in his life on Bullo.

Dick was on his way to town so he couldn't take the pig with him, but said the mustering helicopter would pick it up on the way to Bradshaw later in the day. So the pig in his crate was put in the shade with some water to await his transport. The helicopter pilot was not too pleased with his cargo. He was on his way to muster cattle and didn't take too kindly to carting pigs around, even cute ones. But it was only a ten-minute flight to Bradshaw, so he grudgingly agreed. We assured him the pig was squeaky clean and had been shampooed that day, which it had—the girls used all my hair shampoo! This didn't impress the pilot at all and as the squealing pig and the crate were placed on the seat next to him, he had a very pained expression on his face. He started the engine and we moved back as the rotorblade started to whirl. The helicopter lifted off, but the pig didn't want to have anything to do with the unfolding events—we could see the crate rocking against the safety belt as the pig thrashed around. After one almighty thrash he came hurtling out of the side of the crate and straight out of the chopper, momentarily airborne, as the chopper was almost eight feet off the ground at the time. The pig only had time for a few frantic running movements before he went *splat* on the ground at our feet. The pilot shrugged his shoulders and quickly made his escape.

Our eyes went to the poor pig, spread-eagled in the dust. There hadn't been so much as a twitch since he hit the ground. Thoughts of 'poor little dead pig' were going through my mind ... when he jumped up and ran off squealing, disappearing into the trees on the other side of the airstrip.

A sturdier crate was built and another pig was finally picked up by plane, and made it to Bradshaw Station.

I don't think the swapped pig lived as long as Honky-Tonk, or had the same exciting life. Honky-Tonk went everywhere with the children and turned into a very patient animal, as did every animal that shared their lives. But he seemed genuinely interested in whatever they were doing and tried to do what they expected of him. He was hitched and harnessed to an endless array of wagons and carts. He was dressed appropriately at Christmas and became part of countless nativity plays. They dressed him in clothes and wheeled him around in the wheelbarrow, and they couldn't wait for him to be big enough to wear a saddle.

It was a daily question: 'Can we put a saddle on him now? Is he big enough?'

To keep them busy as they waited for this day they started horsebreaking Honky-Tonk. They went right through the book, a page at a time, and subjected the donkey to every step of the technique the book recommended. As I said, Honky-Tonk was a very patient animal, and always so sweet—you could see the interest in his eyes as the girls put some harness or rope on him. He would look at it and sniff all over it, the children telling him it was all right, it wouldn't hurt him. And he would listen and believe.

As he grew older we were told that he should be 'cut', otherwise he could turn nasty and kick. But if we had him castrated, we were told, he would stay quiet and be safe around the children. Because he and the children were inseparable Charles said we couldn't risk him kicking, so we took the 'expert's' advice.

The stock inspector who was on the station inspecting the cattle killed in the abattoir offered to do the job, and he botched it. Honky-Tonk became just what we were trying to avoid—our dear, sweet, gentle pet grew unpredictable and nasty and started kicking. He became very hard to handle and there was nothing we could do but banish him to the outer paddocks, where he was no danger to the children or indeed anyone else. A few stockmen, however, did come very close to losing their manhood and Honky-Tonk came close to losing his life. Men were not his favourite species, after his encounter with the knife.

Honky-Tonk would spend his days trying to get back into the home paddock. When he did manage to make it back home he would amuse himself hiding behind trees and jumping out and chasing people. His favourite victim always seemed to be the staff cook. He would wait for her return to the staff kitchen with her supplies, such as sugar. When she was halfway down the flat he would trot out from behind trees and fall in behind her. She would start running and screaming, with him following her closely, breathing heavily down her neck. He would keep this up until she dropped the sugar and ran off screaming into the safety of the garden. He would then leisurely lick up a kilo of spilt sugar.

Of course, as soon as he knew he could scare a person he played it to the hilt. Most of the men had his measure—if he couldn't bluff or intimidate them he would leave them alone and concentrate on the scared types, who mostly seemed to be the female cooks.

We lost a lot of cooks because of Honky-Tonk. But I found that the cooks who were chased regularly and therefore left were, without exception, very bad cooks. Good cooks didn't seem to get chased by Honky-Tonk. So I think it would be safe to say that some of the staff might have had a hand in helping Honky-Tonk into the home paddock so he could do the deed.

Chasing cooks was not the only reason he was sent to the outer regions—he would also sneak into the kitchen and steal the bread by the loaf. He could flip up the lid on the bread tin and lift a full loaf of bread out and be through the door in about twelve seconds. But this time the same stockmen who would laugh when they saw the cook running screaming down the paddock with the donkey breathing down her neck did not laugh so heartily when there was no bread for breakfast.

After being banished to the outer paddocks we only saw him yearly, when he came into the yards with the cattle from that area. Occasionally when a gate is opened to move cattle he will slip through and work his way back home.

I see him from time to time when I'm out in the paddocks. I can call his name and his head will come up from feeding and his ears will prick as they hear the familiar voice. Every now and then he must remember the early days, because he will suddenly appear at the back gate of the homestead and stand there, wistfully staring into the garden. His playful days are over—he doesn't chase the cook any more—but if anyone annoys or teases him he can still give a good, swift kick, so it isn't long before he is sent back to the outer paddocks.

He is twenty-one this year, is fit and healthy, and still loves the girls. If he sees Marlee he will walk up to her and put his head on her shoulder for a pat.

I suppose it was only to be expected, with a river running down the middle of the property and cattle paddocks on both sides, that crocodiles would play a major part in the girls' lives.

Marlee's most unforgettable brush with a croc happened when she was around sixteen. She was swimming across the river with her horse, heading for Number Two Bore camp site. It was the choice of riding twelve miles, out the road to the six-mile crossing and then six miles back to the camp, or swimming straight across the river, a journey of one mile and a bit. She decided on straight across. The river was up so she had to swim next to the horse, holding the saddle and the reins. They were in the middle of the river when Marlee spotted the croc. He was drifting down with the tide, immobile, looking just like a log being carried along. There was nothing Marlee could do, except stay on course for the shore and make certain she didn't collide with the creature. She slowed the horse, took a tighter hold on the reins and waited.

He drifted closer and closer—as long as he stayed on the surface Marlee felt she had some chance; if he submerged, she was in trouble. If he started to move or manoeuvre she was in big trouble.

She slowly edged the horse around, treading water, and monitored the croc's movements by peering under the horse's neck. All the time hoping the horse presented too big a prey.

They drifted closer, they were almost level, the distance about thirty feet and closing. Marlee stayed as motionless as possible, but under the thick, muddy water her legs were going at double time keeping on course and avoiding a collision; the horse was working overtime just keeping them afloat. Above the water only their eyes and Marlee's mouth showed any signs of activity as she whispered in the horse's ear to steady him. She had no idea if the croc would continue on his way and ignore her or float up to her and lash out at the last minute and attack.

He glided by, a yard or so away; the horse and Marlee remained still and silent, even their feet had slowed down just to treading water. The croc remained lifeless, letting the tide carry him. For a brief second Marlee looked into those terrible eyes. They stared at her, cold and expressionless, like chiselled stone. They didn't dart about, surveying the scene, but stayed immobile, as did his whole body. Marlee had never seen eyes so completely devoid of life or emotion; dark holes of nothingness.

Then the tide swept them away and she and the horse

were thrashing for the bank. Eyes returning every stroke to the evil shape drifting aimlessly down the river.

The next time her father wanted her to ride to the Number Two Bore she went via the six-mile crossing.

Marlee met her next crocodile at her favourite fishing spot. She was fishing near six-mile crossing when a small salty decided she was encroaching on his territory. Every time she threw the cast net to catch some live bait he would try to steal the catch, net and all. Marlee threw rocks at him and hit him with a few lumps of wood and he barked at her and rushed her, in an effort to scare her off. But he was only around four feet in length and Marlee did not scare easily.

He retreated down the riverbank and watched and waited. Each time she pulled in a fish he would rush up the bank barking and generally trying to look ferocious. After several heavy lumps of wood landed on his head he got the message and retired further down the river to do his own fishing. A few times during the afternoon, however, he slowly edged his way back to eye her pile of fish on the bank, but as soon as Marlee brandished a large piece of wood over her head he scurried away.

At sunset when Marlee picked up her fish and climbed the bank she saw him scuttle back and take over her position once more, which was his spot in the first place, according to him.

The last eight-mile yarding of cattle saw an encounter of the dangerous kind, involving a very big croc. Marlee sent one of the stockmen out to give water to the cattle in the yards. The water was pumped from the river up to a holding tank and into the troughs and the pump was down the bank on the water's edge. The stockman climbed down the riverbank to see an enormous crocodile curled around the pump. Marlee went back with the shotgun. It took quite a few shots to convince the monster to move—when a croc gets over twelve feet there isn't much that scares it. But finally some well-placed buckshot convinced it that it would be more comfortable somewhere else.

The shotgun then became standard equipment when starting the pump at six-mile and only stockmen with gun experience were allowed to do the job.

The latest croc Marlee has crossed paths with was only a few months ago. She was driving back to the homestead, late, when the headlights picked up the yellow glow of eyes in the night. She slowed the Toyota. Thinking it might be an injured animal, Marlee approached slowly. When the eyes were in full light of the direct beam, Marlee saw it was a very large croc, sitting in the middle of the road. He was of the size that you didn't throw stones at, or hit with lumps of wood, and Marlee was very glad she was sitting in a vehicle and not walking. He took his time and ambled slowly across the road and down to the bank towards the river. The road runs between the river and a large, freshwater billabong. He might have been on his way back from a freshwater bath, or a dinner of a few wild birds. As Marlee drove past his tail, heading home, he swung around and gave an annoyed bark and a few snaps of his jaw, to show his irritation at being disturbed. It was not a pretty sight and one Marlee definitely would not like to meet floating down the river.

It wasn't only crocodiles that were life-threatening, however. The seven-ton, red Toyota truck was slowly crawling, clawing its way up the side of the steep mountain, to the top of the Bullo River jump-up. A slow painful journey, bumping from rock to rock. Like any vehicle, Charlie had the truck loaded to its limit, and then some. Marlee and Danielle had been to Katherine on a twelve-hour round trip and had made it back to within thirty miles of the front gate when a wheel bearing seized. Marlee contacted us through the two-way radio and Uncle Dick and Charlie drove out to repair the wheel. They were in a Toyota utility, behind the truck, waiting for it to get over the last hump coming up the first jump-up to the pass into Bullo. The last section of the climb was particularly steep and the old truck was taking its time, Marlee coaxing every ounce of performance out of the straining engine. She was only twenty feet from the crest when the engine finally gave up the ghost. She stamped on the brakes as she felt the truck rolling backwards, but her foot hit the floor with a jolt as the brake cable snapped. Adrenalin surged as her foot pumped the lifeless brake pedal. When she turned to look back she saw her father and Dick in the utility, the truck bearing down on them at an alarming speed. There was nowhere to go; the road was only wide enough for one vehicle—on one side was the cliff face, on the other side a sheer drop. And behind was the ute, about to be crushed.

Marlee swung the back of the truck into the cliff face. The back of the tray hit the cliff with a crack, and checked the runaway truck's speed. But one set of wheels ran up on a pile of rubble and the truck tilted and rolled over, across the road. When the dust cleared, the tray and load were on the road and the cabin was hanging over the cliff. The heavy load of fuel drums was anchoring the vehicle.

Charles jumped out of the Toyota and sprinted up the road, his heart in his mouth. He had watched helplessly as the truck careered down the jump-up. But was relieved when he saw Marlee turn in towards the cliff face, and thought the drama was over. However, the next turn of events had taken him by surprise. He watched in horror as the truck rolled and skidded towards the cliff edge. Now he could see nothing as the dust billowed everywhere and clouded his view. He ran into the cloud and straight into the truck, which was luckily still on the road and not over the side as he had feared.

He found Marlee and Danielle standing on the road, a little dazed and still coming to terms with the last few seconds. Marlee's upside down window had ended up close to the edge of the road; Danielle's window was hanging out in midair.

Marlee had carefully crawled out and stretched to the edge of the road as the truck creaked and groaned. She told Danielle to follow her. But Danielle was stuck! Marlee knew the truck could go over the side any second and with a full load of fuel on the back no one in the cabin would have had a chance. She reached in the window and grabbed both of Danielle's arms and heaved with all her might. Danielle ended up on the road beside her. The truck, held down by the heavy load, stayed put.

So now they had a big job ahead of them. The girls got into the back of the Toyota, their father asking regularly if they were feeling okay, while all the time telling Marlee he would never let her drive again. Marlee knew this was because he was going over in his mind how he would have faced me if he had had to go home without my daughters. Having been saved from this fate, he kept repeating, 'That's it! You will never drive again!'

The girls collapsed in the back of the Toyota on two foam mattresses rescued from the truck and Uncle Dick drove carefully to Timber Creek, 60 miles down the highway. Maxie Duncan, the owner of the Timber Creek pub, had his own truck and he offered to come back to the crash site with them and offload the cargo onto his truck and take it into the station. The Department of Works grader was at a camp site very near the turn-off into our road, only 11 miles, so they were contacted by radio and it was arranged they would meet them on our jump-up, at the truck.

They drove back the 60 miles to the truck and the grader driver managed very skilfully to put the truck the right side up. It came down on all four tyres with a mighty crunch, after being perilously close to going over the side of the cliff a few times. The engine was very sick and refused to obey any of Dick's requests. The brakes were just as bad. The grader held the truck in position while rocks were packed behind each wheel; the load was then transferred to Maxie's truck and the 48-mile journey to the homestead began.

Charles called me from Timber Creek to tell me what had happened. Even though he told me they didn't have a scratch on them, he knew I would go over them with a fine tooth comb, so he was being extra careful, making sure he delivered them in mint condition. As the Toyota climbed the jump-up he looked back at the truck and a cold shiver went through him, despite the fact that he was hot and sweaty from loading Maxie's truck. It was the realisation that he could have been leaving much more than a forlorn old truck on the side of the mountain—a few more feet and the truck would've tipped over the side ... He stopped thinking as he couldn't bear the next thought.

As the Toyota laboured over the crest of the mountain the truck disappeared from sight. Charles turned around and faced the road ahead.

He was right. I did check every inch of the girls when I had them safely home. Charles looked on, a guilty expression on his face. He knew it was his fault they had been so close to death. Because of the continual shortage of money he was always making Dick cut corners, only allowing him to order the most desperately needed parts, so Dick had repaired the brake cylinder with wire. This had snapped at that vital moment Marlee needed the brakes. Dick told Charles this sobering fact after he had checked the truck.

This was certainly in the forefront of Charles's mind for many weeks. For the want of saving on spare parts he had almost lost two of his children. Dick got the new parts the next week. When Dick finished working on the truck there were lots of bright red patches of new paint where he had hit the dents out of the body. The truck still looked a sore and sorry sight, but at least the brakes were in top condition!

I don't suppose the girls could count the times they have had close brushes with death. Maybe it's part and parcel of growing up in the Outback, or just being Charlie Henderson's daughters, but close shaves seemed a normal part of life for them. So much so that most of the time their only remark, after being one inch from a horn, or hanging over a cliff in an upturned truck, or gliding into land in an aeroplane with a failed engine, tended to be: 'Gee, that was close,' or, 'Wow, that was lucky.'

I was a nervous wreck all through their childhood and teens, always wondering if I would ever see them again as they departed each day with a cheery, 'See ya, Mum!'

But they have grown up into very unusual women, so maybe there is something in Charlie's 'walk the edge' type of training. The girls will tackle any situation and like their dad are very brave; but thankfully they also inherited a bit of my practical sense. As a result, Marlee and Danielle do not run headlong into danger, but approach a situation with fearlessness and logic, giving them capabilities to handle unusual situations.

In December 1988, Marlee and Danielle had to walk a herd of cows the 48 miles from the Victoria Highway when we had the chance to buy a second lot of drought cattle from Queensland.

The rainy season had well and truly arrived and I could see only wall-to-wall problems trying to get a truck in our road. But Marlee was sure she could handle any problem. Besides, the cattle would not be available after the rainy season.

The trucks from Queensland arrived at our turn-off from the highway just one day too late. It had rained non-stop all night and as a result, the first 11 miles of our road were under water and very boggy.

The truck could not get in the road and could not wait around, so I arranged with the manager of our neighbouring Newry Station to hold them in their yards, which were close to the highway.

The plan was for the cattle to wait there until our road dried out enough for the trucks to drive them in. But by the look of the sky I could see the cattle spending the season in Newry's yards.

Finally there was a break in the weather and the road seemed dry, so we booked the trucks again. It started raining while the cattle were being loaded, and by the time the trucks reached our turn-off the driver wouldn't risk driving in. Luckily Marlee had planned for this turn of events and during the days of waiting for our road to dry she had left Danielle in charge of the cattle and had come back to Bullo to organise everything required to walk the cattle in the road from the highway if necessary.

She packed food, camp gear and saddles into the utility, loaded horses into the old red truck and with Rex, one of our Aboriginal stockmen for that season and Stumpy, the stock camp cook, the convoy started for the front gate. Marlee had arranged with Danielle when they would meet at our turn-off.

The red truck lived up to its reputation and the engine stopped again—no, not on the jump-up, but in the middle of the river crossing. It could not be persuaded to start. The Bullo River crossing now looked like a used car yard: the red truck was in the middle of the river, the Toyota utility was on the homestead side, completely blocked and unable to cross the river, and the international two-ton jeep was on the highway side. Marlee had parked it there when the river had come up suddenly a few weeks before and she could not get the jeep home.

Stumpy carted all the gear in the utility, across the river, and loaded it into the jeep. Marlee jumped the horses off the red truck, then towed it out of the river with the jeep and parked it on high ground. Rex saddled one of the horses and herded the others the rest of the way to the front gate. Because of the delay at the river crossing they had to go at double time to meet the road trains with the cattle at the arranged time. But when they arrived at the turn-off they had to sit for half a day because the trucks were late. The cattle were unloaded, the road trains departed, and the girls and Rex turned the cattle and horses towards the distant cliffs and headed across the Auvergne flat ... to the Bullo pass ... and home. With Stumpy following in the Jeep.

The first stop was Turtle Creek yard, a small wire yard twenty miles in the road. Because half a day had been lost, Marlee now had to push the cattle to get there before dark. Along with the usual problems of keeping the herd together, she had to contend with the worry of a stampede in the rough, mountainous country. Another problem they soon discovered, and had not anticipated, was that these cattle were young breeders born in the drought years in Queensland, and had therefore never seen rain, either falling from the heavens or water running in rivers. Marlee had endless problems every time they came to a running creek as the cattle would just stand and stare in amazement at the water. After long sniffing sessions they would jump across, 'pogo stick' style, to reach dry ground on the other side. There were lots of creeks to cross so there were constant delays. But when they saw the expanse of the Bullo River they just dug in their heels and refused to budge, the leaders sniffing and snorting at the fast running water. It took a while to convince the cows it was safe to cross. Even with no rain for a few days the Bullo River had dropped enough for the Jeep to get through without the engine going under. Marlee had all the calves that had been born in the last few weeks in the back of the Jeep, they were too small to walk the distances required each day.

Stumpy now carefully carried the precious cargo into the river with the lead cows, who just happened to be the mothers, watching. Concern registered on their faces as they watched their babies, then nature took its course and into the river they plunged, mooing and bellowing to their little calves not to worry, Mum was coming too. The other cows followed and they all had their first swim. Finally all the babies and gear were carried across the river and loaded onto the Toyota on the other side, the mothers right behind, their noses over the tray, with the other cows right on their heels enquiring if the babies were okay. They all watched the ute swaying dangerously as the wheels lurched from boulder to boulder up the steep riverbank.

The Toyota finally emerged on the top of the bank, with the little calves sitting safely in the back watching the procession across the river. In their concern for the young calves the cows forgot the strange rushing river, and waded in. Eyes wide and sniffing and snorting regularly at the turbulent water, strangely different to the only water they had ever seen, in drinking troughs.

Marlee and Danielle thought they had solved the water problem—after crossing the Bullo River the smaller creek crossings should be no bother. There were a few wider creeks, but the girls knew that if the cows showed any hesitation they would just drive the calves across first. With the worst behind them, the herd settled down for the rest of their journey. Marlee kept them moving, because of the late start, and the fact that they had a lot of ground to cover to reach Turtle Creek yard, their first night's rest.

Then it rained. As soon as the storm started, the cattle baulked, frightened by the thunder and lightning, never having witnessed it before. They were still coming through the mountains and the thunder seemed louder than it did down on the flats. The cattle started milling and would not walk, instead they became very restless. Then the rain started to pour. Well, the thunder and lightning upset them, but the rain thoroughly confused them. They were a funny sight—a whole herd of cattle just standing, looking at the sky. They blinked their eyes and shook their heads as the rain wet their faces, and put their tongues out to lick the water from their cheeks. Again it was decided this strange new thing was not going to hurt them, and with the utility voom, vooming its engine, and moving down the road, they took off at a fast clip to catch up with the mobile nursery.

They reached Turtle after dark. It is usually very difficult to yard cattle in the dark, but the cows walked quietly into the yard, too tired to sniff and perform, just grateful they didn't have to walk any more. Marlee had pushed them hard, but with more rain she was worried some of the creeks would've become too deep for the utility to cross, then the herd would have had to walk so slowly for the babies to keep up that they would have been on the road for weeks. They scraped through the major creek before dark. They had one more deep crossing in the morning and then they should be right. After yarding the cattle they unrolled their swags and settled down to what promised to be a very wet night.

The next morning it took a while catching the calves to put in the utility but eventually, with the babies snugly settled in the back, and the mothers' sniffs of approval, Stumpy started the engine and they were off. They arrived at Lloyd Creek, the last big creek, at mid morning, but the crossing wasn't the main event. Everyone had to stop while one of the cows gave birth, the first baby to be born on the Bullo road. Marlee called him Lloyd, after the creek, and before he knew what was what, she had assisted him with his first drink then put him with the other babies. Stumpy moved off down the road with the new mother worriedly following.

The end of the day found them at the last camp before home. After first handing out the babies for the night the girls crawled into an uncomfortable swag and dreamed of home, a hot shower, a hot meal and a soft dry bed, with the rain on the roof, not in bed with them.

I met them at the gate the next day, a very wet and bedraggled group—even the cows looked sick of the rain. They had all been wet for more hours than they cared to remember. But with the enthusiasm that undeniably belongs to youth, the girls said, 'Oh Mummy, watch this!' They then turned to Stumpy and said, 'Hand out the babies so Mummy can watch.'

By this stage there were cows lined up at the back of the Toyota, waiting. Stumpy ceremoniously walked to the back of the ute and dropped the tray. He looked at the first cow in line and greeted her by the name he had given her and picked her baby out of his little wards. When the baby was carefully placed on the ground next to her, she sniffed it all over, just to check Stumpy had not made a mistake. When satisfied it was her baby she then proceeded to check it over to see it was in good order; then with a 'thank you' glance at Stumpy she moved away and the next cow stepped up, whereupon the same scene was acted out. The newest mother was a little confused and not quite sure what was going on and whether or not she had actually had a calf. But those first few minutes together, when Marlee helped the newborn to drink and paused while Mum had a few dozen or so licks of her baby, did the trick and when Marlee brought the little calf to her she remembered Marlee's smell as much as her baby's. Marlee helped the baby again to have a drink and after a little while the new mum was settled and content, licking her baby.

The herd quietly milled around, checking out their new home, and the mother cows fell into a group of their own. Stumpy had finished handing out all the babies and the long drove was over. The cows now started munching grass.

It's scenes like these that make all the struggle seem worthwhile.

If you face challenges continuously, one of two things happens: you either collapse under the strain and lose confidence in your ability and walk away defeated, sometimes to fight again later or just to drift into a life of non-challenge; or you win a few impossibles and are so encouraged to have a go at the next impossible that before long you find the impossibles have become possible.

Marlee walked into the office. 'Kaiser has a dislocated hock,' she said.

Kaiser was one of our very, very best breeding bulls. It's funny how it is always the most expensive bulls that get injured, never one of the old scrubbers.

'If I can convince the vet to work with me, can we try and put his leg in plaster? I would like to save him, if possible. I just can't bear the thought of shooting him, without at least *trying* to save him.'

She knew my answer. 'Yes.'

She managed to convince the vet, who was just new up from the south, still crusading, saving the north—as they all try to do for the first year, until they are forced to face reality. She conned him well; he had no idea he would be performing the operation out in the middle of the paddock, on a wild bull.

I sat in the kitchen with Marlee and Uncle Dick as the vet wrote out the plan in chalk on the shopping list blackboard.

'Well, what do you think?' he said proudly, putting down the chalk.

Marlee and I just looked at each other. Uncle Dick was leaning on one elbow on the bench, smoking a cigarette. He said nothing, but the expression said it all: 'Never in a million years is this going to work.' We changed a few things in the plan and went out into the field. The vet so sure his plan would work, the three of us so sure it wouldn't. Uncle Dick went off to weld splints to reinforce the outside of the plaster, just in case it wasn't strong enough to take the 1000-plus pounds of Kaiser's weight; Marlee disappeared to fetch the tranquilliser gun, to be used in putting Kaiser to sleep. Poor Kaiser could hardly hobble, so the dose calculation was easy and administering it even easier.

The dart was delivered right on target and we watched and waited until he became wobbly and rushed in to make sure he fell on the right side. We had to move fast, every moment counted. Dick was back with the splints and helped erect a shade tent over the operating theatre. The vet went straight to the leg and Marlee and I started on our instructions. I had to keep the front part of his body in a sitting position, to keep his lungs working properly, and watch his breathing. Marlee was preparing the bandages.

The vet announced the leg was not broken, only dislocated, and was pleased the way it had snapped back into position. This increased the chances of a full recovery—if the joint had been loose and had had to be strapped into place the chances would have been slim. Over the joint he packed cotton wool and strapped that with soft bandages, and then it was time for the plaster bandages. Marlee soaked them in water and handed them to him, one at a time, as they were wrapped around Kaiser's leg. The bandage set as we watched. It was so fast, if the vet stopped to wipe the sweat from his brow the bandage would set in a long strip and he would have to cut it off before pulling out the next length.

What was most amazing, however, was the whole operation went off exactly as planned! We had finished, the cast was hard, Kaiser was sleeping like a lamb, his temperature normal, and breathing well. There was only one hurdle we hadn't considered: he had to be kept in a small enclosure for eight weeks so he wouldn't run around on the weak leg. The small yard wasn't hard to erect, the problem was moving Kaiser. He was sleeping right in the middle of the airstrip—and how do you move a massive sleeping bull with its leg in a cast?

Marlee came up with the answer, dashed off and disappeared behind the house, reappearing a few minutes later driving the front end loader. We only had to move him 500 yards—an impossible feat for mere humans, but quite easy with a front end loader.

We rolled him over on his back, with all four legs up in the air, and carefully edged the scoop under his back. The vet, Dick and I pushed, shoved and wriggled the sleeping bull until we had him snugly in the scoop, then Marlee slowly tilted the scoop backwards on command until he finished up asleep in it, this time with all four legs sticking straight out.

The procession moved off very slowly, the vet supporting the plaster leg and me carrying the front legs. The loader went at a snail's pace and pulled up under the coconut trees in the back of the garden. We carefully deposited Kaiser on the ground, after much pulling and grunting from all of us, and left him sleeping soundly out of the danger of falling coconuts. After pulling off this amazing operation we were not going to lose him to a wayward coconut.

We assembled enough portable panels around him to make a comfortable pen and after sitting him in a good position waited for him to come out of the anaesthetic. The big question was, could he get up with the cast on his leg?

He came round and stood up without much trouble and the vet pronounced the operation a total success. I don't know what the plaster was made of, but it took one hell of a beating for the next five minutes as Kaiser tried to dislodge it. Exhausted, he finally decided to accept and ignore it. We walked inside for a cup of well-earned tea, and congratulated ourselves on having just made an impossible mission possible.

Eight weeks later we repeated the procedure and took the cast off Kaiser's leg. He was now a lot quieter, having been hand-fed every day for eight weeks, but was still far from cuddly. He was put out to it again with the tranquilliser gun and the cast was cut off with a small electric saw. Then Marlee and the vet had to leave to test cattle in the yard, and I was left to babysit Kaiser. My instructions were to keep him in the sitting position and to check regularly that gas did not build up in his stomach. We dismantled his pen so that he could spend the next few weeks in the garden walking around slowly to strengthen the leg, which was now wrapped in a thick crepe bandage for support.

Every fifteen minutes I went out and sat on Kaiser and jumped up and down, pumping out the gas that had accumulated. I thought this was very funny, but it worked, and he made amazing noises both ends as enormous amounts of wind issued forth. I became complacent and this almost cost me my life. Kaiser was so dopey and wobbly I assumed it would be a while before he was his normal ferocious self and went blithely along, every fifteen minutes, jumping on his tummy. This last time he was blearily looking at me with hooded eyes; I sat down on his back and was immediately catapulted into the air. He moved so fast that by the time I had steadied myself I found I was face to face with him. I knew I was a goner—one swift movement of his horns and I was history. He snorted angrily at me for jumping on him for hours, although now he was standing he wasn't too sure of himself or of what to do next. He had gone from sleepy to alert in a second, and was now jerking the castless leg, trying to adjust to the weightlessness of it. All this was happening in a millisecond—my eyes were registering everything but the rest of me was immobilised with shock.

He snorted once, shook his head about, swung around and ran away, all in one swift movement. Thankfully the swinging of the mighty head was not in my direction, but just a gesture of frustration at all the goings on he did not approve of. He raced away to a distance of one hundred yards before the weak leg had him limping. Then he turned to face me again, a quizzical look in his eyes, still not sure of the situation.

I let out a long breath and accepted the fact I was still standing and in one piece, albeit shaking from head to toe. I think what saved me from certain death by horns was the fact that I had fed and changed his water every day for eight weeks. As mad as he was with all the treatment he had been exposed to, he remembered that.

He was now pawing the ground and tossing his head in a very indignant manner and I knew these signs well, so I took off at top speed for the safety of the house, shaky legs and all. I wasn't at all willing to test 'the hand that feeds them' theory. I collapsed inside the door, panting, and turned, thinking Kaiser would be on my heels. But he was still in the same place, watching me with that quizzical expression.

I think achieving these seemingly impossible tasks also expands your dreams and ideas. Well, it seems to be the case with Marlee. Just recently I said I thought we should build a birdbath in the corner of the garden. Since we had improved the swimming pool, it now had a smooth finished edge rather than the old uneven edge, and the birds could not get close enough to the water to drink. Marlee agreed and said she would fit it in as soon as possible. I came out of the office a few days later to see my new natural birdbath being filled by a two-inch poly pipe. The birdbath is forty feet long and twenty feet wide! Marlee explained the logic of the size. If it was small the big birds would push all the small birds out; this size, the big birds can be at one end and the little birds can have the other end.

Simple, isn't it, when you look at it that way. We now have so many cockatoos circling the house and landing at the birdbath, that at bird drinking times, people can't hear me on the phone because of the noise overhead. One radio session that was interviewing me on tape, had to call back after drinking time because of the noise. I don't notice it anymore, but the man finally had to ask what was the racket in the background.

CHAPTER 9

September 1992–*October* 1992

We had one more muster to complete the end of the season. Because of the court judgement against us, and the continuous drain on our cash reserves to meet the payments, I could see we wouldn't have enough funds to get through the rainy season to April of the following year, when our cash flow started again. We had already sold our yearly turn-off, so with regret we now had to sell some of our breeding stock. We'd known we could fall back on this plan—if the unthinkable happened and we lost the case—and sadly the unthinkable had happened and we were now at that point where we had to lose some of our hard-earned breeders. I couldn't help but do some silent cursing. With heavy hearts we moved into Six-Mile, our biggest breeding area, and started to sort the cattle. We sold just enough to get through and economised wherever possible. It was a dreadful time.

My days were still busy in the office, answering non-stop phonecalls, faxes and letters about the book. On the 10th September I had to leave on the New Zealand promotional tour. My itinerary would take me to Auckland, Christchurch, Invercargill, Gore, Wellington, Masterton,

Waipukerau, Hastings, Napier and back to Auckland.

I left the station on the 11th, overnighted in Darwin, took a 6 a.m. flight to Cairns, where I spent the night to wait for the connecting flight to New Zealand. I started the tour in New Zealand the day before my birthday.

I loved New Zealand. I thought I would freeze to death, having been told by everyone how cold it was in September. I was bracing myself, and had the suitcases full of thick, woolly clothes. The day I arrived it was declared an Indian Summer, and for the next ten days the sun shone and the weather could not have been more perfect. So I walked around the streets of Invercargill in a longsleeve, light blouse. I wore my three lightweight blouses most of the time and only put on woollen jumpers at night.

Everything about New Zealand was perfect—the land, the colour, the people. Having lived all my life listening to the rivalry between New Zealand and Australia in cricket and football, horse racing and various other fields, I was a bit worried about how I might be accepted. But I needn't have been concerned—I was welcomed with open arms and treated like visiting royalty, and the welcome was without doubt sincere and genuine. The smaller towns were so appreciative that an author had travelled this far to spend time with them that they couldn't do enough for me, or tell me how pleased they were. However, I still wasn't entirely comfortable with being referred to as an 'author' and being 'famous' and from 'overseas', and I would frequently get the urge to look around to see who they were referring to.

The daily schedule was as gruelling as the Australian tour, but it surprised me how much you can achieve in one day when everyone you meet is pleasant and complimentary. The adrenalin just keeps pumping and you keep going, enjoying and being carried along by the limelight and attention.

The sales accelerated as I moved from town to town, and by the time I made my last speech in Auckland on the last night of the tour, the book was setting sales records. So many people arrived at the Aotea Centre for my last speech that it was a sell-out. As I stepped up to the microphone people were sitting on the floor all around the walls and the back area was full of people standing. It was a great night and an exciting end to my itinerary.

Early next morning I left for Sydney. That evening, I had dinner with my publisher, James, and Jeannine. During the dinner James mentioned the possibility of another book, and by the end of the meal the format was decided upon! By the time I had listed all the further events in my life since finishing *From Strength to Strength*, listed all the questions people wanted answered and jotted down many of the things I had forgotten, I ended up with a rough estimate of 300-plus pages. So a follow-on book was given the nod.

I returned to the station on the 26th, a bit bewildered. Another book! Many times, as I came near to completing *From Strength to Strength*, having spent ten hours a day on writing it, I thought, 'What will I do with my time once I've finished?' But I needn't have worried—we still had two months of bullcatching, many more months of office work to catch up on; and I now had 300 or so pages of a book to be completed in eight months. There was no doubt how I'd be spending my time ... working.

The rest of September, Marlee and Franz and a few stockmen were out most of the day catching bulls. I reluctantly disappeared into an office which had been sadly neglected for most of the year. It faintly resembled a controlled atom bomb explosion. I sat down in the middle of the mess and started sorting into piles of urgent, very urgent, extremely urgent, and dangerously urgent. But I kept finding myself wandering off to jot down notes for the upcoming book, or answering a phonecall from someone asking if I could possibly look into why their account had not been paid. And I would have to force myself back to the urgent piles of paperwork and reality.

However, the phonecalls from readers just didn't stop. Marlee had complained that she had spent most of the time

I was away in New Zealand taking my calls, so she was now very glad to see me home—from now on I could handle them myself and she could get on with bullcatching. She did tell me about one call she'd received ... The phone rang at 2 a.m. A man on the other end was enthusiastically saying he had just finished the book and thought it was so great he had to call and tell me so. Marlee sleepily told him I was in New Zealand, so he proceeded to tell her how great my book was. When she finally got a word in and asked him did he realise it was two in the morning, he was most apologetic. He said he'd read the book in two sittings and had started the second half at six o'clock that evening and hadn't lifted his head till he'd finished. He had no idea it was so late.

So, to spare Marlee any more latenight calls I took over the phone and she went back to working outside. Old friends from thirty years back called to say hello and well done. Our accountant in Darwin in the 1960s. A woman who grew up a few blocks away when we were children. People I knew in Manila, who now lived in Australia. One woman, who attended Marlee's fourth birthday party in Manila and who now lives in Sydney ... A woman wanted to give me a message over the phone, to give to Sara Henderson. She began by saying how much she enjoyed the book and asked how Sara was and what she was doing now. I told her she was answering the phone. She was completely overcome.

'Oh gosh!' she said. 'I am so excited. Just imagine, I'm talking to Sara Henderson! I'm more excited talking to you than I would be talking to the Queen! Wait till I tell Marge about this—she won't believe me, you know.'

I don't know if Marge believed her, and I don't know why people are surprised I answer my own phone. One lady, when she asked to leave a message for Sara Henderson, and I told her she was speaking to her, came out with, 'My God! You answer your own phone?' My reply was, 'Well there's no one else to answer it.'

I do enjoy all the phonecalls from people; it is a great compliment to receive them and the least I can do is speak to the callers.

And I did, all of September. And with wonderful praises ringing in my years I battled the piles of office work with much more gusto.

October meant office work for me, while outside Marlee chased scrubber bulls. Whenever she saw me getting depressed she took me for a spin in the bullcatcher, through the breeding paddocks. The calves were being born and after watching beautiful little Brahman calves frisking and frolicking around the paddocks the depression cobwebs would blow away and I could go back to the office work with determination.

Good news about the book continued in Australia and more good news poured in from New Zealand. The results certainly justified all the hard work done by everyone during the tour. While I was rushing around and being received so warmly, I often thought, what if you did all this work and the book was a fizzer and no one wanted to meet you? I hope I never know. I was called by the committee of the Business Woman of the Year and asked to be on the judging panel for the 1993 award. I would've found this very interesting, but only needed to travel to Sydney for one day, and I just couldn't justify spending all that money for a single day, so unfortunately had to decline. I had already been invited to attend the award later on in the month and had been asked to be guest speaker ... but the really exciting news was that Marlee was coming with me. We don't get to travel together much as one of us always has to be on the station to keep it running smoothly. In fact in the last three years we have only been away together in October 1990, for my award, and then in May for my book launch in Sydney. We enjoy travelling together, and this time would be even more of a treat as she wouldn't have to shoot off immediately after the event. We could relax and take our time. I missed Danielle, but she was with Martin, pouring concrete on some big job in one of the mines in the outback of Queensland.

The award lunch went well. Afterwards we saw friends and caught up with events in each others' lives over the past year. In the evening we went to a Japanese restaurant, an old favourite of Charlie's. The same man was behind the sushi bar. He remembered me—or should I say he remembered Charlie and me being with him, on occasions! He was very diplomatic, it was ten years since I had been there.

The next day Marlee headed back to the station to continue chasing bulls until the rain set in. Franz had been holding the fort while we were gone. It certainly was a relief for both of us to know that the station was in good hands and work was progressing while we were away, instead of the usual drunken sit-ins of the past.

I headed up the coast to Caloundra to stay with Sue and Ralph for a few days. I was speaking in Melbourne at a luncheon in four days' time. If I went back to the station I would only have to turn around and travel all the way back again. When I arrived in Caloundra I was given a royal welcome by Troubles, who remembered me immediately, and I was quickly brought up to date by Sue on Troubles' latest antics.

She had started dancing for her food. Instead of begging or doing tricks like normal dogs, she would do a funny dance routine all around the kitchen as she waited for her food to be prepared. She still had a few skin problems. The vet had told Sue the dog was very highly strung and needed extra attention to give her a feeling of security. I had to smile at this diagnosis—I have never seen a dog get the attention Troubles gets. I have never seen a lot of children get the attention Troubles gets.

However, Troubles did have a major hang-up about rain. Sue noticed that if it was raining at night Troubles would not go out to the toilet before bed. Of course Sue goes with her to make sure she obliges, otherwise she finds herself being woken at 2 a.m. by a desperate dog. One rainy night

Sue was standing under the umbrella waiting, only to be joined by Troubles, keeping out of the rain. Sue now has to take two umbrellas—one for herself and one to hold over Troubles while she goes about her business. And she asks me, do I think people consider her eccentric?!

I had four lovely days' rest in Caloundra. For me, sitting on the verandah at Sue and Ralph's house, looking out to sea down the creek and eating fresh crab and fresh bread, chatting, with soft music in the background, Troubles curled up on her lambswool rug, sighing deep sighs regularly, just about summed it up … perfection.

It was over too soon and I was off to Melbourne. But I wasn't sad because I would be straight back.

There were about 500 people at the luncheon in Melbourne and I sat next to Sir Edmund Hillary's son. We chatted about children's books—he had just written one and I told him I was writing one about some of the animals we have had on the property over the years. The lunch looked very appetising, but as usual the nerves had the better of me and I could only pick and push the food around the plate and look like I was eating. I always thought nerves were worse when you're tired—but I had just had four relaxing days and yet here I was, as nervous as ever. I think it was because this was the first time I was to deliver a slideshow while I spoke.

I was given a control panel and told to aim it at the back of the room every time I wanted the next slide. I was sure I'd do something wrong and I did; either that or the guy who fed the slides into the machine couldn't count. About halfway through the sequence the slides slipped out of order. So now, as I confidently opened with, '… and the next slide shows you the cattle improvement over the years', a ripple of laughter went through the audience as a picture of the living room of the homestead flashed up on the screen. I had to forget the notes I was following and ad lib with each slide until I was back on track and the slides were once again corresponding with my notes.

It called for some really fast footwork but I managed to

get through and instead of it being a catastrophe the audience laughed and seemed to thoroughly enjoy it. Ironic really—I know exactly what to do with wild cattle but am hopelessly lost when it comes to pressing coloured buttons on a slide projector.

The Melbourne speech over, it was then off to Brisbane to speak at a luncheon to launch the National Party's Women's Policy. Lady Flo Bjelke-Petersen was announcing her retirement, and the lunch was to introduce the new candidate running for the seat.

Since I was a little behind on my speech writing I found myself finishing it late at night, after dinner with friends. I switched on the television for the latenight news, and there was some religious character saying the world was going to end at 2 a.m.! I was strongly tempted to put the pen down, order Black Forest gateau and a bottle of champagne and eat and drink the world out. But the practical side of me told me to go on writing the speech.

I finished it a little ahead of the end of the world, had a glass of water and an apple, and went to sleep.

The world didn't appear to have ended when I woke up and my head and stomach were very glad I chose an apple and water because of the day ahead.

I turned on the television and the same man was there, now saying that he had made a mistake in his calculations and would rework his figures and give us another date! I switched off the television and headed for the shower, thankful that I could think for myself and didn't worry too much about people like that.

At the lunch I sat with Lady Flo and Senator Bill O'Chee. I was having a bad trot and did what I always dreaded I would do—trip when walking up the stairs onto the stage. Luckily I didn't fall flat on my face and was able to save myself at the last minute. There were cries of concern among the audience, but when I told everyone I had trouble controlling high-heeled shoes they all laughed and we got off to a good start.

CHAPTER 10

November 1992

I arrived in Caloundra that night and had only three days before flying again to Melbourne; but with the pace of my life lately, three days was a long time. Then I was off to the Melbourne Cup. And what a wonderful week that was! I was guest speaker at the Oaks Day Luncheon, but had been invited by the Victorian Race Club to spend the Cup week as their guest.

The visit started with cocktails at Parliament House—I had forgotten what a crush those parliament and embassy do's were. I found myself shouting to be heard or finally ending up just smiling, nodding or shaking my head and raising my eyebrows for a bit of variety. The racing I enjoyed thoroughly. All the horses were such perfect creatures; watching them in the parading ring I found myself thinking, 'Oh, I must back that one', only to think the same thing as the very next horse came into view. By the time I had looked at fifteen horses, I wanted to back the lot. How different they were from our hard-working mustering horses of the Outback. As beautiful as they appeared they would be useless on the station. But who would put such a creature in the Outback … Or our hard workers in the parading ring?

Nevertheless, despite my limited knowledge about racing, I picked first and second for the Cup. So that made my day extra exciting.

The luncheon was a success and I enjoyed my speech because I spoke about our horses on the station, our retired racehorse stallion and the antics he gets up to, and about the first Outback race meeting I went to in 1965, and the difference between then and now. A lot of people enjoyed the story about the Outback race meeting—of course it was so far removed from the glamour of the Melbourne Cup and I hadn't even given them all the facts. They wouldn't have believed me if I had. Most people could not in their wildest dreams imagine what it was like.

I did enjoy myself that week. There was something new to gawk at daily … well, new for me. I suppose the fashions were the real eye-opener. Being in the bush, I don't see the constant change in the styles, so it was a bit of a shock to see some of the outfits parading around. I think I spent most of the first few days with my mouth open, but after the initial shock wore off I just watched and enjoyed the show.

After being wined and dined for a week it was back to my little office and the piles of emergencies. There were still too many 'urgents' to be handled for me to settle down to writing, although every day I would jot down ideas and stories for the second book. Marlee and Franz were building, repairing fences, and bullcatching. Uncle Dick was quietly working through the endless line of machines that needed attention, when he felt well enough to tackle a job. His lungs were getting noticeably worse, and as each month passed his health was deteriorating.

Rain was falling regularly now, and as much as we needed rain I was praying it would be light and short storms until after Danielle and Martin's engagement party. I couldn't believe how fast the time had passed. Danielle had told me at the beginning of the year that she wanted to have her engagement party in November and I remember thinking I had eleven months to get myself ready! But here it was a week away and I was anything but ready. We were driving to Mt Isa on the 18th, so any heavy rain would really wash our plans out. I kept remembering when Marlee was bull-catching at 22-Mile a few years back. It rained eight inches in one night, and back at the homestead there hadn't been a drop. Marlee had bogged trucks, a bogged bulldozer, the only thing moving was the Toyota. She had been bullcatching and road building, doing two operations in one. As she'd cut the new road into the wilderness she would come across scrubber bulls hiding in the hills and give chase. She had trucks carting bulls back to the yard and men repairing and building fences. And in the middle of this hive of activity the heavens dumped eight inches of rain and it was suddenly a catastrophe. Suddenly the dry, dusty riverbed, which the trucks were getting dry-bogged in, was a raging torrent of water that cut straight through the operation. Marlee had workers isolated on the wrong side of the river, a bulldozer bogged and in danger of falling into the water, and a truck full of bulls bogged to the axles. Everyone needed instant attention. The sudden rush of water was only the first surge—Marlee knew there would be more as the river and the water up in the mountains joined. The show was spectacular, if you had time just to sit and watch. Sheets of water cascaded down from the faces of the mountains and raced across the flat, making movement across the ground impossible. The only way around was on foot and even that was dangerous, as sections of the riverbanks were just collapsing into the wall of water rushing by.

The people had to be rescued first, before more water came down the river. She got a rope across the torrent, to get the fencers back. All the fencing gear had to be left on high ground, possibly until the end of the rainy season. The bulldozer was then rescued with towing chains and a winch. Then it was only the truck. All in all it was an exhausting day and the rain started again just as they got the bulls into the yard right on dusk. The rain did not let up and turned the road home into a river, so everyone had a very uncomfortable night sleeping in the front of the Toyota and truck to escape the mosquitos and waiting for the road to become passable.

As for me, I spent another night pacing the floor, worrying about what might have happened, not knowing why they hadn't come home. I could see the storm sitting over the mountains out at 22-Mile, and knew it was raining there, but had no idea how much rain there had been. I decided rain had delayed Marlee, but this decision didn't stop me worrying and pacing. I remember how relieved I was when I saw the Toyota come into view at the bend of the road around lunchtime.

So this was the type of storm I wanted to hold off until after the party.

The 'Holiday' show was on television the night before we left. It came up very well and we enjoyed watching it. Soon after, the ABC sent us a long list of the people who'd called for information about the station after the show had gone to air, and we also had lots of phonecalls from people saying they had read the book and how much they enjoyed seeing Bullo after reading so much about it.

The next day Franz, in the truck, and Marlee and I in the stationwagon, left on the long journey to the party, over a thousand miles. How things change—if twenty years ago someone had told me I would travel that distance to a party I would have told them they were mad.

We drove the first leg to Katherine and made arrangements to have the truck packed while we were gone. Our plan was to pick it up on the way back and take a full load back into the station with us. We went to bed early, left in the early hours of the morning, all in the stationwagon, and took turns driving straight through to Mt Isa. We arrived late and went straight to bed again. The next day was taken up with buying spare parts to take home. Everything was so much cheaper in Queensland so we took the opportunity to buy. We had arrived a day early, keeping a day up our sleeve in case we had a breakdown. But luckily we had come through without even a flat tyre, so we could now enjoy a sightseeing tour of Mt Isa before Danielle and Martin arrived that night from Cloncurry.

We met them at breakfast and asked if we could do anything to help with the day's arrangements. The party was to be a picnic lunch and afternoon at Lake Mandara, just outside of the town. It was a great day and very family oriented. Most couples had children and so the park setting was a good idea. We found the children had plenty of room to run and scream and exhaust themselves and the parents had a relaxing time. Rain threatened when we first arrived, but quickly moved away and left us a lovely afternoon on the lawn, under shady trees, looking over the waters of the lake.

We had dinner together that night. Martin had to leave early the next morning, back to his job out at one of the mines. Sunday was his birthday so it became his birthday dinner and we gave him his present early.

However, Marlee and I were not totally relaxed. Marlee had called the station a few times and could get no answer. This was worrying us! There was a girl in the house whose job it was to answer the phone, take messages, care for the pets, and, most importantly, hand out Uncle Dick's daily ration. And there was also another mechanic, who was staying for a few weeks. He was between jobs and was helping Dick before he moved on to his next position. They both seemed reliable people—the girl had been with us for months and we were sure that as long as Dick didn't get his hands on any extra grog things would be all right. Two caretakers seemed more than adequate ... nothing could possibly go wrong. Famous last words!

Finally we decided that if we couldn't get an answer early Sunday morning we would have to drive straight back. Marlee started calling at 6 a.m. Nothing. We started the long drive back, imagining all the terrible things that would await us.

Before leaving, I had left a long and clear list of where I could be contacted or where a message could be left twenty-four hours a day. The police at Timber Creek knew we were away and the number was on the phone pad, so there was no excuse for no messages—if something was amiss. But I had no idea just how amiss things were.

We drove straight through to Katherine and arrived in the early hours, had a few hours' sleep and called the station again at 5.30 a.m. Marlee finally got an answer, but it wasn't good. Franz's beautiful, six-month-old German shepherd puppy was dead! Marlee didn't wait to hear the rest of the complicated mess, she said we were on our way. We jumped into the stationwagon, left the loaded truck, and headed west at breakneck speed.

We turned onto the Bullo road at twelve noon and arrived at the homestead a fast, rough, interrupted ride later. The road resembled a war zone. We came across one of the station Toyotas halfway in the road, leaning to the side with one wheel missing. We then met a Toyota on the way out, driven by the station manager from across the highway, and were told more of the jumbled story. Continuing on, we found the 'temporary' mechanic changing a tyre on his vehicle. He added to the amazing story by saying he had been broken down on the road for two days. And, yes, he had taken a drunken Dick out the road, but had lost him somewhere near the front gate and not seen him since. Franz helped him get his car going and he came back to the homestead.

When we arrived, I sat down with the girl first, to hear her side of the story. What she said didn't make any sense whatsoever and was hard to believe, but from what I could gather from her version, and we were to get many versions, the trouble started when she went to drive out our road 48 miles to pick up her friend at the gate of the next station, about thirty miles down the highway. This had all been arranged between them weeks before, unbeknown to us. She just took one of the unregistered station vehicles and went on a 160-mile round trip to pick up her friend. Of course, while she was away Dick wiped out the grog supply. According to her story she returned to find both the mechanics drunk. And five and a half cases of beer gone and heaven knows what spirits. She said the two men left to go to town to bring back more beer, the mechanic's parting words to her being, if he was not back by Sunday, she should come looking for him!

She said he had not returned by Sunday morning, so she set out to rescue him, and lost the wheel off the Toyota. Leaving the girlfriend and Franz's puppy under a tree in the shade with the water bag, she started to walk back to the homestead to call for help! She walked twenty-eight miles back to the homestead without a rest and called the manager of the neighbouring station, where her friend worked. He drove the one hundred miles to pick the girl up. She was still sitting under the tree, since ten o'clock in the morning. We never found out how the puppy died, again there were different versions.

I said I did not believe her story. For a start she couldn't walk twenty-eight miles in the heat of the day with no water. When she made the ridiculous statement that she chewed gum leaves for liquid, I almost laughed in her face. At that time of the year two people working on fencing go through a four-gallon container of water. You have to drink every fifteen minutes to replace lost body fluids. While she walked that distance in the heat of the day, without water, the puppy sitting in the shade, *with* water, died. There was obviously something she was covering up and I told her that. But she wouldn't budge from this story.

The next version was the mechanic's. No, he was not drunk, as the girl had stated, it was only Dick who was drunk. This was the first believable statement. Dick was the problem—again, believable—and had demanded to be driven to town. He said Dick was completely unmanageable and so he had consented to drive him. I might add at this point that Dick weighed eight stone, while this chap weighed in at about sixteen. Nevertheless, he had to take Dick to town. The story became very confusing at this point. He said the car broke down a few miles from the highway on Friday night, he went to sleep, and when he woke the next morning, Saturday, Dick was gone.

We had driven in the road on Monday at lunchtime and found him changing a flat, but I got no answer as to what he had done from the Saturday morning to the Monday lunchtime, when we saw him. Oh yes, and during this time his dog also died!

The third version came from the manager of the station who came to collect his employee—our girl's girlfriend. When he was twenty miles in the road on Sunday night he came across the broken down mechanic's car. He stopped, looked around and called, but could find no one. There was a note under the windscreen wiper saying, in effect, everything was a mess.

Confused? Well, join the mob! After three very different and conflicting versions of the three days' happenings, there was only one thing that was clear, and that was that there was a massive cover-up. A cover-up of what, we never found out; but at first we thought it was connected with Dick. There were conflicting statements about the mechanic's car breaking down, one story was a few miles off the main highway and the other version twenty miles off the highway. Dick could still be out there, wandering around in the bush, or even dead! There were just too many parts of these stories that were unbelievable. It was time to call the police.

After I made it clear I didn't accept their stories, the only thing left for them to do was leave. As the two of them—the mechanic and the girl—headed off for Cairns the police waited for them to pass through Timber Creek and then took them in for questioning. In the meantime we were calling all Dick's favourite pubs with no luck. But then Camille Fogarty from Timber Creek called to say her son had just returned from Kununurra and had picked Dick up at our turn-off at 4 a.m. MONDAY morning! He said Dick looked very much the worse for wear, but he was alive, and was now happily drinking his fill in the pub. I called the police and told them Uncle Dick was in Kununurra and they let the mechanic and girl continue on their way to Cairns. We meanwhile mourned the death of a beautiful puppy, dead because of someone's incompetence, and set about cleaning up the mess. The only bit of luck in the whole sordid episode was that we just managed to save the big generator from seizing through lack of oil. It had been running since, heaven knows when, Wednesday or Thursday right up to Monday without an oil or water check. When Marlee and Franz shut it down, there was no reading on the oil dipstick. The engine did have a safety cut-out, but Dick for some reason had it disconnected!

The fourth version of this garbled mess was told by Dick to his driving companion (Camille's son) on the way to Kununurra. Dick should have been sober at the time of the telling—but who knows! According to Dick's story everyone at the station was drunk and they were all heading for a night on the town. Which night this was, we're still not sure.

So, to this day it is still a mystery to us what exactly happened. And no one is letting on. I would certainly like to know the truth. We finally found the puppy's body, with a bra wrapped around his neck! We leave five days before for a pleasant drive to Danielle and Martin's party, leaving three staff to caretake. We arrive back to broken-down vehicles all along the road, two dead dogs, a general mess and the power plant a hair's breadth from blowing up, having run non-stop for five days. We went from two mechanics to no mechanics. Some five day outing!

I had a definite feeling I would never see Dick again. But I should have known this would happen. If I had taken the time to think about it over the past year, when he was sick and couldn't keep up with the job, I would have realised this was the only way he could leave, in a drunken stupor.

November 1992

How can I describe Dick? He was a Jekyll and Hyde—sober he was the nicest person you could wish to meet; but under the influence of grog ... well, words fail me.

He worked on Bullo, off and on, since the early 1970s. I say 'off and on' because in the early years he had to 'break out', as he termed it, at least every six weeks. He could sometimes last eight or ten weeks, but the timespan never improved much. Sometimes Charles would convince him to go off somewhere in the bush, on the station, to drink his fill and get it out of his system. But along with the desperate need for drink he also had a need to yarn with his mates.

If I look back over the years of interrupted wage records, a pattern emerges. November, for some reason, was by far his worst month. In all the years with us he could never make it through November, someone would always appear at the door and tell us he was missing. Of course, we would already know that because as 5.30 a.m. came and went, and Bertha the generator hadn't broken her silence, it would be obvious to us that something was wrong. Dick loved his generators; he always kept meticulous logbooks for them. All the other machinery could survive as best it could, with only intermittent attention, but not so the generators. They received the very best of attention.

It is impossible to mention Uncle Dick without mentioning Bertha, our most famous generator. No rooster or bell heralded in the day on Bullo, in the early days; Bertha, a Southern Cross generator, was our alarm clock. Even the birds were still asleep when she would give her wake-up call. Bertha had a soul and personality all of her own. As the station developed, she took on more and more of a load. I know it sounds silly or hard to believe, but that machine carried loads far in excess of her capacity.

I suppose because I found Bertha in Sydney—Charles had sent me there to buy a generator, a tractor, a plough and many other things—and trucked her all the way to the station, I developed a special attachment to her.

When I first saw her, she was reserve power for the Trocadero Ballroom in Sydney. She was built in 1936, so we were the same age. I found her in the basement, still wired and ready to go, but forgotten, no longer needed. It seemed no one in Sydney needed a thirty-five year-old generator anymore, because I bought her for a few hundred dollars.

During her lifetime Bertha did a remarkable job. When she was first installed, there was power to spare. But slowly, as the station developed, the electricity demand became heavier and heavier. There were times when the load was just too much for her, especially when the big freezer and chiller would both cut in at the same time. If it happened around dinner time, it would cause an amusing scene. People would be eating and talking, discussing the events of the day and the freezer would cut in. Bertha would start to labour, trying to meet the load. All conversation stopped, forks paused on their way to mouths, as everyone concentrated on Bertha's struggle. Dick would be particularly alert. Guests stared at the scene wondering why everyone had suddenly fallen silent.

Bertha would groan with each turn of the fly-wheel; lights would dim to a pin point and the overhead fans would shudder and slow down as the power dipped.

We would all hold our breath, waiting for her to give up the ghost and stall, while silently willing her on. She would cough and backfire. Then the lights would suddenly glow a little brighter and the fan start to groan as the blades increased their speed. Bertha would laboriously start to climb back up to her correct speed.

'Go girl, go!' we'd all shout aloud as she raced back up the rev counter. Her correct speed reached, the lights and fans would return to normal.

The conversation would then continue on as if nothing had happened and forks would finish their journey to mouths. Charlie would remark we needed a new generator; Dick's response would be a shake of his head.

Most mornings, I awoke at 5.30 a.m. to Bertha, announcing the beginning of the day. Some days, when I was a few beats ahead of her, I would lie in silence, waiting, and listen for her to slowly wind up to revs. When she was ready, Uncle Dick would throw the power switches one by one, giving her time in between each load to adjust and move back to revs, something akin to a person taking an extra load on their back. Between each pull of a switch, Dick waited patiently for her to take the load and adjust before he brought in the next switch.

At our end of the power line, lights would be first, followed by the fan winding up. The cassette player started up mid song and continued where it had stopped the night before. The water rattled the pipes as it surged through to crash into the tap washers. When the pressure had built to the correct pressure a pipe rattled where it entered the hot water system. When you heard this, you knew the shower was ready: the day had begun.

So if in November, or any other day of the year, the day wasn't heralded in by Bertha, we knew without a doubt that Dick had absconded during the night. Bertha would eventually be started and life would go on, with all of us hoping there were no major breakdowns before we found Dick again. Charlie would then usually track him down to one of his favourite pubs and somehow persuade him to come home, convincing him it was better for him back on the station.

One particular November he disappeared and was gone for six months. We tracked him down in the first few weeks, via the bush telegraph, to another cattle station. This was a bit of a tricky situation because we knew the owners, but Charles wasn't in the least worried—the nearest pub was only fifteen miles away, and he predicted that Dick would be sacked and back with us within the month. He was right about the pub being Dick's downfall, but wrong about the timeframe.

Dick was in heaven, every day after finishing work it was down to the local. The sessions became longer and longer; he started taking supplies back to the job so he didn't have to wait till the end of the day. His work suffered badly, as he was perpetually on cloud nine. The many stories that filtered through on the bush telegraph I'm sure had to be exaggerated, but when I paused and remembered some of the goings on at Bullo when Dick got his hands on the grog, I wonder.

There were stories of vehicles' wiring, where you'd turn on the ignition and the horn would blow, and if you wanted headlights you had to hold down the indicator ... and on it went. I think the best one was when he needed something in the ground for an earthing pole. So as not to waste time he used the steel pole of the front gate, which meant if anyone opened the gate with wet or sweaty hands they received quite a jolt. And if it rained, and you weren't a good hurdler, you were in trouble. The wiring in the homestead was an endless catalogue of disasters. There was no doubt about it, Dick's antics certainly made for a good story.

We met the owner at a dinner a few years later. By this time he had sufficiently calmed down to discuss Dick in a normal frame of mind. He kept repeating, more to himself than in general conversation, 'He seemed such a nice man when I met him on your property. What a difference drink makes.' I wanted to tell him it served him right—he got just what he deserved, stealing someone else's employee. But I only smiled. Dick had been punishment enough.

Eventually Dick arrived back at Bullo, cap in hand, asking for his job back. Charlie really should have sent him on his way; indeed, most people couldn't understand why we put up with him. But sober, Dick was a good mechanic, and most of the work done by his replacements during his absence was on par with Dick's work when blind drunk.

So we took him back and Charlie became quite adept at blocking most of his unscheduled trips to the nearest grog supply. Being the enterprising, or desperate, type, Dick decided that if he couldn't go to the pub, the pub would have to come to him. And he managed to arrange this with the help of one of his drinking mates who thanks to Dick was also working on the station. This character went by the name of Per, or Peter in English, and Charlie called him Peter-Per. Per was from Norway, and like Dick he was a dedicated drinker of anything alcoholic!

Not long after Per's arrival there was a major breakdown on one of the abattoir machines. Charles came back to the house with a long list of spare parts needed from Darwin. He said Dick would bring me all the parts numbers and I was to ring through and order immediately.

It was eight o'clock in the morning when Dick walked into my office, and despite his top job of acting I knew immediately he was drunk. When he spoke, my suspicions were confirmed. He always left his false teeth out when he wanted to hide his slurred speech, and would start the conversation by apologising for not having his teeth in. He would explain that he had a sore gum and was giving it a rest. The next giveaway was he would always start with the phrase 'time is of the essence'. And every sentence thereafter would have it in there somewhere. Sober, he hardly ever used it; drunk, it was boringly repetitive.

I thanked him for the list and waited until I heard the Toyota engine start and then went to Charles.

'He's drunk!' I yelled as I stormed in.

Charles looked up from his book. 'Don't be stupid. How could he have possibly got any grog?'

'I've no idea. But I'm telling you, he's drunk.'

I called Darwin and ordered the parts for Charles to pick up the following day. Charles went back to reading his book, dismissing my remarks completely.

That night, when Dick did not come to the house to collect his daily ration of beer, Charles reluctantly had to admit that things looked a bit fishy. Even more so when one of the stockmen arrived at the door and said Dick had told him to pick up his beer.

'No. Tell Dick I want to see him,' he was told by Charles.

After an hour, when Dick and Per had not put in an appearance, Charles set off down the flat. He returned with a disgusted expression on his face and a four-gallon plastic container of the most vile-looking, foul-smelling liquid I have ever seen.

'What on earth is that?' I asked.

'Hooch!' he shouted. 'Hooch! They're making their own moonshine! I'll have to find the still.'

'So that explains all the orders of copper tubing,' I said thoughtfully, to no one in particular. All my knowledge of stills came from watching old movies about prohibition, and I clearly remembered the endless coils of copper tubing.

Finding the first still, I say the 'first' because many more followed, was in retrospect a very funny affair. But we weren't laughing at the time—then, it was a matter of finding and destroying, or the contents would destroy us. We couldn't afford all the damage done by drunk mechanics. As soon as Dick was under the weather, he would head straight for the generator switchboard, to try to rebalance the phases. So a day's drinking could sometimes end up with the station down an alternator and many thousands of dollars, if we were lucky.

The next morning revealed two very delicate mechanics. Their heads were so fragile, even moving slowly they had to hold them in place with both hands. The look of agony on their faces was enough to melt any heart, but not Charles's. The entire abattoir staff was standing by, waiting for these two to get their act together to fix a breakdown. Charles had them out of bed bright and early, on their road to recovery. They were very unwilling participants.

Charles clanked and banged around the workshop, making as much noise as he could possibly manage. He couldn't stop thinking that the breakdown, which was costing thousands, was probably caused by his very drunk mechanics in the first place.

By now the two men really were suffering, and tiptoed around the workshop, trying not to move their heads.

Charles decided not to fly to Darwin for the parts—the mechanics were in no condition to use them. Their hands were shaking so much, even holding a spanner would be a major feat. Number one on the priority list now was the finding of the still. As long as Dick and Per had a supply of moonshine the abattoir was at a halt.

Dick and Per were obviously such old hands at the 'still' game that Charles knew they wouldn't leave it around close to the workshop. It had to be in the bush. So for most of the morning Charles scoured the nearby scrub. Then, after a quick lunch, he was back down to the workshop and his patients. After endless cups of strong coffee, under Charlie's watchful eye, the terrible two were a gruesome sight. They could not shave for fear of cutting their throats, and their eyes were so bloodshot there didn't seem to be any coloured part whatsoever. They were far too sick to eat, their only craving being for more hair of the dog.

Having no luck finding the still Charles finally hit upon the idea of getting the Aboriginal stockmen to track it down. They were mustering out in one of the far paddocks, so he had to wait until a dawn hunt the next day. Dick and Per's beer supply was withheld for another night, allowing them to continue on the road to recovery.

I shudder to think what the vile concoction did to their insides; their outsides were a shocking enough sight. But as bad as they looked, they were improving, and Charles needed them in reasonable condition when he returned from Kununurra with the parts, having arranged for them to be sent there.

By the next day Charles was confident his two derelict mechanics would be able to manage a spanner under his vigilant eye.

At about 1 a.m. Charles shot bolt upright in bed. 'Jesus Christ! They could have more hooch in the still, brewing!' he shouted. He dressed quickly and drove down the flat like a maniac. Not only did he find Dick and Per plastered, but they had also managed to bribe the head tracker. Charles had offered him an extra beer to find the still, Dick had offered him all he could drink *not* to find it. They did have more hooch brewing, had brought it back after Charles left and had enjoyed one hell of a party. So now Dick and Per were barely conscious, the poor old tracker was very unconscious and stayed that way well into the next day, and Charles once again had a container of foul-smelling muck to pour down the drain.

Next morning Dick and Per could hardly move. Charles asked me to see if I could do something medically for them. I went with him, opened the door of the caravan, took one look and sniff of the scene and walked away.

'Where are you going?' Charles said, puzzled, to my retreating back.

'If you want them in an improved state you get them there,' I replied, over my shoulder. 'But I can assure you, there is no way I will even set foot in that caravan. When they're clean and resemble human beings again, bring them up to the house and I'll feed them. But only when they bear no resemblance to that pile of stinking human garbage I just saw in that caravan.'

Charles said that perhaps if they were cleaned up they might recover faster, and that he was surprised at my attitude, as I was always helping some sick or injured animal. When I replied no animal I had ever seen had degraded itself to that level, he knew he wasn't going to budge me. I walked away.

As it happened, Charles didn't have to watch them that day—they were so sick they hardly stirred for most of it, just slept off the massive hangover, still lying in the vomit and mess they had created. My entire input was bowls of hot soup around the third day, and that was served in icy silence. What a sight they were, clean and smelling normal again … well, not quite. If you stood close enough you could still smell the vile mixture seeping through their pores. The three-day beards made them look pathetic, but they still didn't melt my heart. They apologised for not shaving. I just stared at them. Then they went on to explain that, in their condition, with their shaking hands, they would've slit their throats. I said nothing.

Dick barely touched his soup. Being an old hand at the drinking game he could go without food for days and days. Per, only a new hand, his appetite reasonably intact, was hungry. His problem was his hands were shaking so much that by the time he got the spoon to his mouth he had spilt the lot. He was reduced to resting his chin on the table and sucking the soup out of the bowl.

It was very clear the demon was alive and well inside Dick and Per and screaming to be fuelled with alcohol. You could see it in their eyes—they would do anything for grog. Charles had to watch them very carefully—if they got their hands on any alcohol at that stage of their recovery it would put them, and us, back weeks. If we managed to keep them drying out for another few days, they would be reasonable. But we had to find the still!

With Dick and Per under close guard, Charles gathered all the stockmen together and told them the first one to find the still got a whole case of beer. Thirty minutes later we had our still, along with another one-day-old batch of whatever it was. The dreadful substance was promptly poured out, the still dismantled and the copper tubing locked safely away in the storeroom.

From then on copper tubing became more precious than gold or diamonds on Bullo. Anyone who even mentioned it immediately came under suspicion. If copper tubing was required for any job, Charles would inspect the installation, measure the length of tubing required, hand over the required length, measured to the inch, and then remeasure after the job was completed.

Of course, despite all our intricate precautions, still-building continued for years, and we just had to keep tracking them down and confiscating them.

The next break-out happened when we started to get the abattoir ready for the yearly licence inspection. Dick told Charlie we needed clear plastic tubing for the air-conditioners. The water was dripping out of the drip tray and running down the outside wall and making it rust. So a roll of plastic tubing was bought, and since this wasn't on the 'suspect list' for building stills nothing was thought of it.

How wrong we were. When, once again, Bertha the generator did not herald in the new day, Charles went down the flat to find Dick and Per, and a similar scene as before greeted him.

'How did they build this still?' I asked in an incredulous voice, after he'd given me the grisly details. 'It's impossible! There's no way copper tubing could have been brought onto the property!' I was sure of this, because everyone and everything had to be checked when first arriving on the station.

'I suppose we'll soon know,' said Charles wearily, as he trudged off down the flat to deal with yet another unpleasant situation.

He soon discovered that Dick and Per had patiently replaced all the copper tubing on the various hot water systems in the abattoir, the staff kitchen, bathrooms and laundry and even a few places in the homestead, with plastic tubing. They'd then joined the lengths of copper together, which gave them enough for the next still. All the other parts were readily available.

Finding this still, however, was fairly simple. At first all the stockmen-cum-trackers were very reluctant—Dick and Per had obviously already done their negotiations and the men were therefore uncooperative. Their payment not to find the still, we found out later, was a daily ration of moonshine. But then Charles stopped all the beer rations to everyone, so the extra demand on the still became very heavy and the supply could not keep up with the demand. So once more their silence and their tracking skills were sold for the regular nightly supply of beer.

More copper tubing joined the pile in the locked storeroom.

The moonshine makers of Bullo River then became very cunning and sophisticated and moved indoors. It took quite a while to find the next still, but powers of deduction won through. Having had the trackers range for miles in every direction, Charlie soon realised that even Dick would not walk that far each time he wanted a drink, and therefore it had to be closer to home. We covered every inch of ground within a mile of the workshop … nothing.

'Maybe, underground?' I asked.

'Don't be silly,' was Charles's reply.

'Well I don't think it's silly. It can't be up, so it must be down, surely?'

'I have no idea. I'll just have to stay down in the workshop and watch!' Charles was truly annoyed now. The prospect of spending a day with Dick and Per recovering from another massive hangover was not attractive.

So once more Charles marched off down the flat to the workshop. It was only a matter of time before they would need another drink. Now they were drinking heavily, if they didn't have a 'belt', as Dick described it, regularly, they would go into the shakes. I've seen Dick in this state many times and it does not look at all pleasant. All Charles could do now was play the waiting game. Sooner or later Dick would have to go to the still for a top-up.

'Have to go and fix the compressor in the abattoir,' mumbled Dick, in the most businesslike tone he could muster, and he walked gingerly off across the flat, highstepping over imaginary objects as he tried vainly to appear in control of his limbs.

Charles watched him, every step of the way. Per tried to busy himself in the workshop, but spent most of the time pacing up and down or looking over at the abattoir. After about half an hour he couldn't stand it any longer.

'I have to go and help Dick,' he said, and in a rush stumbled off across the flat.

Charles watched Per disappear through the door when he realised that Per had taken off without his toolbox; at the same time it hit him with a jolt, as he sprinted across to the abattoir, that Dick was minus his toolbox as well.

Charles didn't need trackers to find this still. The moment

he entered the abattoir, all eyes of the sober workers looked in alarm towards the door of the meat chiller. Charles opened the chiller door and there in all its glory stood the still; well, it wasn't quite that easy to find—he had to walk down a row of meat quarters, and there at the very back of the chiller behind the corn beef pickling barrels sat the intoxicated group of Steven, the smallgoods man, Uncle Dick, the number one mechanic, and Per, the 2IC. Actually, by the time Charles arrived, Dick wasn't sitting any more, but was prone on the floor, almost incoherent, and not at all troubled about Charlie finding the secret still. In fact he asked Charlie to join them.

Being regularly discovered didn't appear to deter our still-builders in the least. When it became impossible to find copper tubing they just moved into other fields, and a few short cuts came into play.

The first short cut was uncovered when Charles found a very unsteady Uncle Dick weaving his way back to his house after starting the generator late. Dick hotly denied he was drunk, said he had slept in because he had a head cold; but then he breathed on Charles and nearly knocked him unconscious with the fumes he emitted. Charles went on the search. As soon as Dick barred the gate to his house, Charles knew where the next batch of grog was. He was expecting a miniature still in the shower recess, or cupboard. So he wasn't quite prepared for what greeted him in the fridge. There sat two pumpkins. When Charles opened the door the same overpowering fumes he'd just received from Dick hit him squarely in the face. The pumpkins had been hollowed out and filled with raisins, metho and heavens knows what else.

Charles immediately went on the rampage and found Per also had his own operation going. By now he was so mad he whipped his pistol out of its holster and shot the pumpkins to pieces—and put a few ventilation holes in the wall in the process.

This resulted in no whole pumpkins being sent down to

the kitchen, only after they had been cut into four. And the metho joined the copper tubing in the locked storeroom.

But they were far from beaten. The next time Bertha didn't start on time and Charles took off once more down the flat to find Dick still unconscious from the bout of drinking of the previous night, the evidence was resting by Dick's side—with more brewing in the fridge. It was a very potent drop, made with coconuts. They had drilled holes in the top and filled the coconut with sugar, plus whatever else, plugged the holes, waited a few days, and 'down the hatch!' In the Philippines this mixture is called Tuba, and people say it is so strong it could wipe out the whole weekend.

So now we had to store all coconuts in the storeroom as soon as they were anywhere near ripe. The room was becoming very crowded.

Before we found out about the coconut method Dick asked if he could have some of the coconut plants I was shooting, to plant in his garden. At the time I thought, 'How nice—he's planning a garden.' He was planning all right, but not a garden. On finding this latest 'still' Charlie wanted to go and chop down the coconut trees then and there. I told him he didn't have to hurry, it would be seven years before they had any fruit.

Poor old Dick waited patiently each year for the first crop. He was crestfallen when I told him at least five years. But the years did pass and when D-Day arrived Charles was ready, axe in hand. But he was saved the trouble because the trees were riddled with white ants and just fell over of their own accord months ahead of the expected first crop.

However, one of the funniest 'still' stories happened way back in the early days of Bullo. At that stage we had at least five alcoholics on the station, so it was a very busy period chasing stills. This particular one was controlled by Fred, our Italian gardener, with Uncle Dick as consultant. This story proves that if you want to hide something from someone, put it right under their nose.

Charles decided that if we had a fulltime gardener we

wouldn't have to buy any fresh vegetables and would therefore save a lot of money. Well, for many reasons, this plan didn't work out quite the way Charles expected. Where to start to explain!

Fred's arrival was very funny. Charles and I had a standing joke—I had read the book *The Barefoot Contessa* and I always told Charles that she and I were alike: I went around barefoot and my husband didn't pay me enough attention. She, for many reasons, employed a very tall and dashing gardener, who did more than the gardening. So I always said I too would get myself an Italian gardener. Of course, the children didn't know the dark and deep side of these remarks, and when one day Charles turned up with Fred, and they thought he had finally done something to please me, they came rushing into the kitchen saying, 'Quickly Mummy! Daddy has brought you an Italian gardener, for your very own!'

Fred was four-feet-nothing, and hardly the dream man I had in mind. But as Charles said, with a smirk on his face, you wanted an Italian gardener, you've got an Italian gardener. I thanked him very much, but said next time I'd pick my own.

So Fred started work—and only as the gardener! He was a dedicated drinker, as well as being good with plants, and soon had an impressive garden plot carved out of the nearest cow paddock. The concept was right—Fred would grow large quantities of the vegetables that grew easily at Bullo. Tomatoes, watermelons, rockmelons, eggplant, beans and bananas were top of the list. What we didn't use Charles would fly to Darwin to sell to the shops. In the early 1970s fresh fruit and vegies were always in short supply in Darwin; anything fresh came by truck all the way from Adelaide. So Charles could see no reason why we wouldn't make a lot of money selling the excess crop. There was no way we could lose. But lose we did. For one ton of beautiful, fresh tomatoes, hand-picked and delivered to Darwin, we finally, one week later, received ten dollars, and that sale was for pig food. By the end of the week Charles gave up in disgust. Our venture into market gardening had netted us a mere ten dollars: the tomatoes alone, in seeds, pesticides, Fred's wages, fertiliser, labour for picking and packing, cost of boxes, fuel to fly them to Darwin, Charles's time flying, as well as a week as a salesman, truck hire from airport to chiller, one week's chiller hire, etc, etc, conservatively would've cost us a ballpark figure of a few thousand dollars!

So Fred just grew very expensive vegetables for the staff. Because of the heavy demand on various items weekly, such as potatoes, which never made it to the table but ended up in the still, extra had to be purchased. The enormous demand for the 'dual purpose' potato was brought under control by sending instant powdered potatoes down to the kitchen. This certainly had an effect on the budget. I had been sending two, and sometimes three, fifty pound bags of potatoes down to the staff kitchen weekly! I was so naive, I didn't know alcohol could be made with potatoes.

There were other fruit and vegies, such as onions, lettuces and carrots, which couldn't be used to make alcohol, but which we couldn't grow enough of to meet the weekly demand. So even though we had a fulltime gardener, we still had to import. And by the time we flew in these extras, added Fred's wages, plus all the money spent on materials, we found ourselves eating very expensive fresh vegetables indeed!

But there were some things Charles was stubborn about and would not admit defeat, and a vegie garden was one of them, because it reminded him of home. So I was not allowed to mention that maybe it would be cheaper to buy all our fresh produce and not have a fulltime gardener—we were losing money each week by employing Fred, and he was growing far too much, we couldn't possibly eat it. But Charles was adamant—Fred was staying. And what we couldn't eat, he told me to just 'put it up', the American term for preserving food. I told him I was already working an average day from 5 a.m. to 10 p.m., *every* day, and didn't think I could fit in an extra hobby, so he bought a very large chest-type deep freeze and told me to cook and freeze everything.

In no time at all the chest freezer was full to the top with tomatoes, corn, beans, and any other vegie that could be frozen. A few weeks later I had to go to Darwin with Charles and while we were away Uncle Dick went on a drinking bender and the power was off for days. The station had recovered from this event by the time we returned, but some stark evidence still remained, namely the deep freeze. It had obviously been used for chilling cases of beer, and some bottles still remained, which had been left to freeze after the drinkers had moved on to spirits and collapsed. The glass bottles had naturally all cracked, or exploded, the generator had run out of fuel and the power stopped.

The power must have been off for days judging by the state of things. When I opened the lid of the freezer the sight was amazing. Tomatoes, beans, corn and carrots had all defrosted; the containers had been pushed around and upturned to accommodate the bottles of beer, so that when the power went off, the contents had poured out of the containers and mixed with beer and broken glass. When Uncle Dick recovered enough to start the generator again, the whole mess just froze solid. So what greeted my eyes was a solid block of coloured ice with pieces of glass and bottle tops sticking out of it, along with corn cobs, stewed tomatoes, string beans and carrots poking out all over the place. The poor guy left in charge to hand out the beer rations was a teetotaller, and said they all appeared late one night, raving drunk, and broke into the storeroom and carted off all the grog. He couldn't stop them. The fact that they were raving drunk when he had all the grog locked in the storeroom and was only handing out their rations daily was glaring evidence ... there was another still!

This one was of Italian design; we have over the years had stills of every nationality—Yugoslavian, Norwegian,

Hungarian, German and of course Australian. But this Italian one took the longest to find.

Fred had really done wonders with the garden and he was quite proud of the results. I had to take regular garden tours to admire the progress. He not only produced vegetables in great quantities, but also seemed to produce large quantities of drunks. Charles would burst into the house in a raging temper, 'They're drunk again! So drunk Dick can't even stand!' and the search would be on. The search would be long and far-reaching, but Charlie would come up with nothing. Of course Dick and associates were enjoying every minute of the whole game. Charles had the stockmen tracking out for miles, but he was working from the workshop and staff area and was on a very cold trail.

Ultimately, it was the drinking club's smugness that did them in. They had a celebration party, because Charlie couldn't find their still, and that eventually gave the game away. They were found collapsed in Fred's caravan, in his garden.

I had often wondered while inspecting Fred's garden why he had left a large area of tall, thick weeds at one end of an otherwise very neat and precisely laid-out garden. When I questioned him on this his reply was, 'Itsa to protecta da plants froma da wind!' This seemed sensible enough, so the wall of weeds stayed. He then always seemed to be burning little fires around the garden and when I asked about this I was told, 'Itsa da smoke—makes da bugs cough so they no toucha da plants.' Again, this appeared a reasonable answer, and I thought no more about it.

Charlie really twigged, however, when he was pondering why they would bring the hooch up to Fred's caravan, right next to the house, when surely they would have wanted to get as far away from us as they could.

'Unless the hooch is here!' we both chorused.

Out we went, to Fred's garden, and there it was. On closer inspection of the wall of weeds there was a well-padded path into the middle of the clump, and there in all its glory sat the still. All the fires set around the rest of the garden were decoys—to hide the smoke coming from the still, while the hooch was brewing. And the solid clump of weeds was a perfect camouflage—you couldn't see a thing from any side.

Fred's job that day was to pull out all the weeds and dismantle the still, under Charlie's supervision.

Another of Dick's mates was Stumpy, the stock camp cook. Stumpy, for many years, and on many occasions, was very much a part of the nefarious still operations, the pumpkin stills, and a few other activities besides. He was an avid gardener, but I found out after he left that he was growing a lot more than vegies. I'm amazed that any machinery on the station worked, with the staff either high on moonshine or pot!

I found out about Stump's little hobby only last year when a past employee called to see how the station was faring. He rambled on about the days he had worked here and told me the interesting story of why Charles had fired him.

It seems he had told Charlie that Stumpy was growing marijuana in the back of the vegie garden, and much to his surprise Charlie didn't sack Stumpy but sacked him. He asked Charlie why he got the sack instead of Stumpy, and the story was that Stumpy had told Charlie that he, the stockman, had brought in pot which he was planning to sell to all the staff. Stumpy's set-up on the other hand, was a co-op type arrangement, where everyone could have a bit free!

So the stockman was sent on his way, shaking his head. Stumpy's plants were destroyed, his job saved, but Charles warned him not to grow any more. Looking back now I am sure more pot was grown—this would explain Stump's vague periods, when he would disappear and could not be found. Dick would cover for him and say he was down fixing the broken waterpipe. And there were days when Dick himself never made it out of bed. The both of them probably just floated off on a cloud whenever the problems became too much.

There were many times when I thought Dick or Stumpy was acting strange but didn't seem or smell drunk, now it is all explained!

I have to admit, there were quite a few funny stories surrounding Dick's drinking. One of the funniest was when we had quite a few visiting VIPs. The army was staging a mock war, so there were 600 soldiers racing around the valley; as well as twenty girls from the Wilderness School, visiting on an Outward Bound exercise, and the American ambassador and his entourage for the weekend. His entourage comprised two CIA men, a pilot and co-pilot, and two staff.

Don't ask me where they all slept—the whole weekend was a nightmare. I ran around the day and night like a chicken with its head chopped off and Charles sat calmly with the ambassador, earbashing him on how to correct the world's problems. I think the pained expression on the ambassador's face almost equalled my own!

I had sixty-five for dinner on the Saturday. I was surprised Charles didn't invite the town of Katherine, just to round off the figures. Of course I didn't have enough of anything! Eighty potatoes filled the oven and there wasn't even room for the roast! And to add to my problems we only had the one bathroom. This meant that the ambassador's aide-de-camp would give me the times the ambassador wished to use the bathroom and I would have to clear the path! As I said, it was a nightmare.

The dinner guests consisted of twenty or so young soldiers, who were picked to leave the war and dance with the Wilderness girls; the ambassadorial party; and girls and teachers made up the balance. Plates and knives and forks were in painfully short supply, so everyone ate in relays, the soldiers, who were probably the hungriest, last. After I'd carved for sixty-five I handed over to one of the soldiers and moved on to the next problem of the evening, all the time keeping an eye on Dick and the rest of the staff, who were sitting in the corner of the room, all washed and in their best clothes and behaving as I had told them to. They had been given their beer ration and were forbidden to go near the bar, which was on the other side of the room. What surprised me was they were actually following my orders, even Dick!

The night was moving along nicely, and I was starting to relax a little, when the ambassador's aide-de-camp suddenly appeared at my elbow. I turned to smile, and saw a very worried look on his face.

'All the liquor seems to have disappeared out of the ambassador's private bar,' he said.

I was having difficulty comprehending these words and just stared at him, blankly.

He went on: 'The ambassador only drinks bourbon, so he takes a portable bar when he travels.' Obviously hoping now that this would get more response than his last statement. It did.

'Private bar?' I screamed. 'Where did you set up a private bar?'

'Over here.' And he led me to the corner of the room where Dick and all his cronies sat like angels in a swaying row, looking innocently at the ceiling. The aide-de-camp had even asked Dick to keep an eye on the bar for him! No wonder they hadn't tried to get near *my* bar. Apart from the fact that they wouldn't have been capable of walking, all Dick had to do was lean slightly and there it was, right at his fingertips! They had consumed three large bottles of bourbon in thirty minutes flat. I found a bottle of bourbon in the other bar for the ambassador's drink and then went back to deal with Dick.

I told them to stand up and file out the door quietly, and to go to bed and not show their faces again that night. There was enough venom in my voice to propel them out the door and across the lawn. I stood and watched them stagger and fall into the back of the Toyota while Dick took the longest time to make it into the driver's seat. Every time he lifted his foot to step up he went over backwards. One of the other men finally just pulled him into the cabin. Even as drunk as he was, he decided Dick was taking too long.

I should have realised of course that Dick was far too drunk to drive, but by this stage of the evening I was working on remote control. I was both upset that he had stolen the ambassador's bourbon and embarrassed by his behaviour. I just wanted the lot of them out of my sight. I watched as the Toyota moved off at a snail's pace, and thought that at least he was driving carefully. But to my horror, instead of turning right and driving along the causeway, he just kept going and drove right over the edge.

I quickly called Marlee and some of the soldiers and they ran down to the now overturned vehicle. Luckily, they reported back, everyone had been thrown clear and had staggered down the flat to bed—except for Dick, who was lying in the cabin laughing like a maniac, and resisting all attempts to get him out, telling them he was already in bed. So they left him lying in the roof of the overturned Toyota.

We all went back inside to the music, thinking it was over, but a few minutes later one of the stockmen appeared at the kitchen door and said he thought he had been hurt in the crash. He lifted his foot to show me half of his foot sliced off and hanging. He had walked up the flat like that … that had to be good bourbon!

The army had a doctor with them, out in the war zone somewhere. So Marlee and a few of the soldiers went looking for him. He operated on the foot on the kitchen bench and did a very good repair job. His assistants were the headmistress, Marlee, two CIA agents, and me … spasmodically. I was interested but my stomach wasn't.

While all this drama was taking place, one of the schoolgirls just happened to wander off with one of the soldiers. It was suddenly panic stations, when the regular head count, about every ten minutes, revealed the terrible fact. Teachers and headmistress raced around the house looking in every corner. But the panic was shortlived—the NCO in charge of the soldiers walked out onto the lawn and shouted the missing soldier's name, and then shouted, 'Front and centre, NOW!' And as if by magic the soldier appeared, saying he had gone off into the bushes to go to the bathroom. The missing girl appeared in the kitchen with the excuse she had been sitting out in the garden, under a tree, looking at the moon.

This dreadful night eventually ended around 3 a.m. For my part, I collapsed into bed beside the snoring Charles, who had retired at 10 p.m. after the poor ambassador had finally had to go to bed to stop him talking.

Where do I stop when it comes to Dick and his infamous escapades? Every time Charles and I left the station together it seemed to be the signal to 'break out', so it was not unusual to find Dick in Darwin a day or so after we arrived. I didn't go to town often, which I suppose was fortunate otherwise no mechanical work would ever have been done. This particular trip was to hand over all the papers for the yearly financial returns to our long-suffering accountant and friend, Peter Roberts.

The door to Peter's office was open and he could see across the foyer. We were sorting through the year's work, and Peter was asking questions and taking notes, when he looked out the door and paused in mid sentence.

'Oh no,' was all he said, his face draining of colour.

'What is it?' I asked as I turned around in my chair. I couldn't believe the sight that met my eyes. There, in the middle of the plush foyer of thick, blue-grey carpet, original paintings and large potted palms, stood Uncle Dick! No shoes, no shirt, only a pair of shorts. His sparse hair had not seen a comb or brush and was sticking out at all angles. He hadn't shaved for days, and his teeth were missing, along with his glasses. He had been in a fight and dried blood dotted his face and body. Peter and I were used to this apparition, but the receptionist took one look as Dick tried to approach her to explain his request, let out a bloodcurdling scream and rushed into the main office for protection.

Peter stood up and walked to the door. Dick saw him and started towards him, apologising for his appearance and telling his tale of woe and asking for a loan—and all while he was walking across the foyer. I sat in the chair and looked on in disgust. When Dick reached the office door he started then to apologise to me. He had not as yet got close enough without his glasses to see it was me.

'Please excuse me, madam,' he started, 'I just have to ask my old friend Peter here if …' Then he had me in focus. 'Jesus Christ! It's you!' He staggered backwards, as if he'd been hit, and continued backwards until he landed on one of the large tree pots.

Dick was sober. He was recovering from the bout of drinking the night before and was embarrassed by his appearance. He wanted to borrow money to go to buy some clothes, or at least that was his story. But he was upset that I had seen him, and more importantly that I had seen him trying to borrow money from one of my friends. Charles had given him very specific warnings about going to our friends in a drunken condition and asking for money. Of course, he did it all the time, he was just careful not to let us know about it. This time he was caught red-handed.

Dick has become a celebrity since the publishing of my book. Phonecalls and fan mail from old mates, or people who met him once and never forgot him, came in thick and fast—one chap saying, 'I knew a Dick Wicks, oh, about forty years ago. And after reading your chapter on Uncle Dick, it has to be the same Dick Wicks …' pause '… There can't be two of them!'

People he had worked for on other cattle stations got in contact; mates he had taught to weld; old diggers from the war. I was pleased for him because he is one of the great letter-writers of the century. I hoped all these rekindled friendships would improve his spirit, buck him up. He had

(Photo: David Hancock/Skyscans)

Me and Boots.

ABOVE: Marlee (LEFT) and Franz (RIGHT) at two.
BELOW LEFT: Marlee in Austria.
BELOW RIGHT: Franz at Bullo.

If this isn't happiness, then I don't know what is.

ABOVE: Marlee sitting down on the job, fishing.
CENTRE: A companion waiting to see if she catches any fish.
BELOW: The fish she caught – and the croc didn't get!

(Photo: David Hancock/Skyscans)

Danielle and I walking our horses to their paddock after a hose-down at the end of the day.

ABOVE: Mustering by helicopter
BELOW: Franz mustering on horseback

(Photo: David Hancock/Skyscans)

Dust is raised as cattle are driven into the yards.

ABOVE: Bullo's shorthorn herd, 1972.
CENTRE & BELOW: Bullo's improved herd now, 1993.

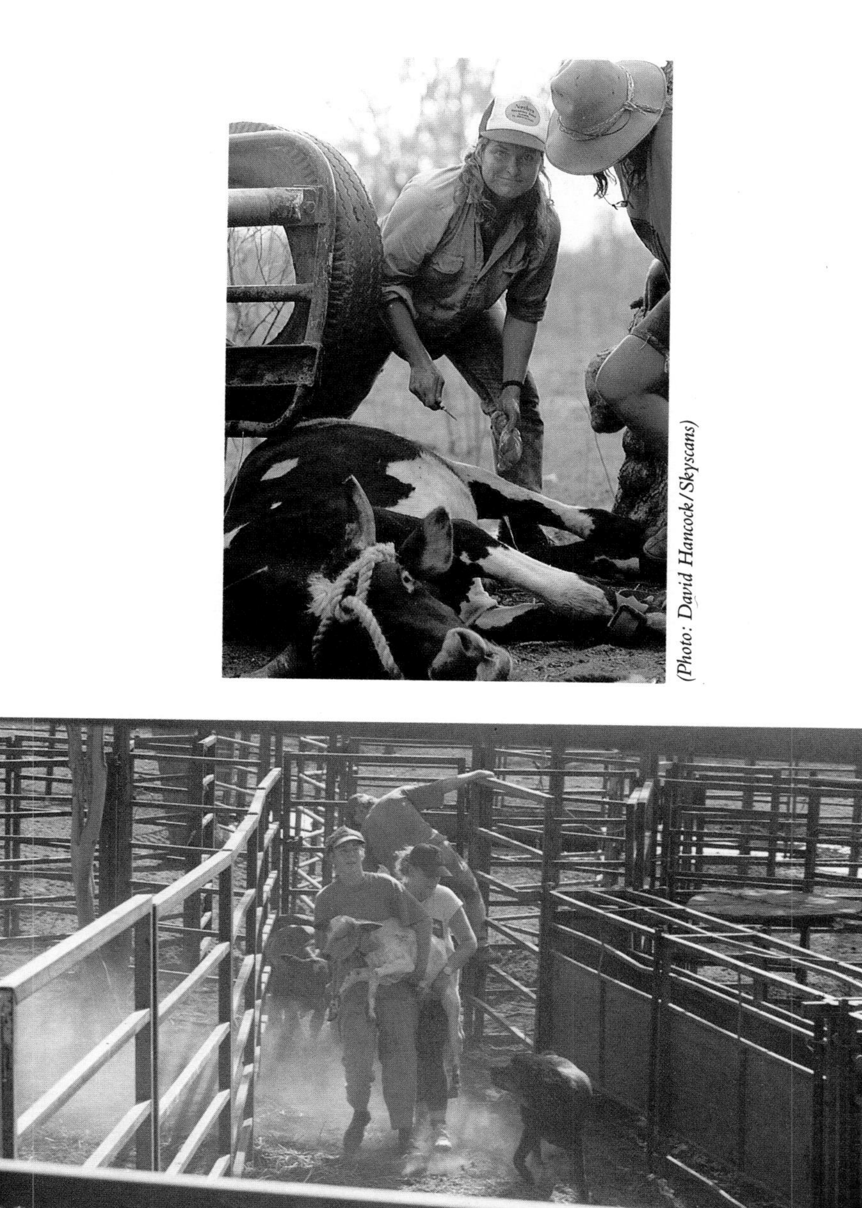

(Photo: David Hancock/Skyscans)

ABOVE: *Marlee castrating a scrubber bull that jumped into the breeder paddock.*
BELOW: *Saving a calf, newly born, out of the crowded pen (not in the picture).*

ABOVE: *The Nutwood watering point that we changed.*
BELOW: *Jedda, me and Marlee by the new troughs replacing the above set-up.*

ABOVE: Me driving the tractor.
BELOW: Building fences.

ABOVE: Marlee (making her usual face at the camera) and Jackie dressing a cut on one of the mares.
BELOW: Marlee not making a face.

The runaway trailer across the road at the bottom of the jump-up.

ABOVE: Sorghum growing – with emus on an afternoon stroll.
CENTRE: Sorghum baled.
BELOW: Meals on wheels.

(Photo: David Hancock/Skyscans)

Bullo River.

(Photo: David Hancock/Skyscans)

ABOVE: Stockmen mount up and ride out at dawn for a day's muster.
BELOW: Bullo sunsets really soothe the soul.

not been well since a holiday to Perth in December 1990, when he had ended up in hospital in Kununurra, on his way home to the station. He was very sick for weeks with double pneumonia. He came back to the station at the end of January, but did not pick up until well into March. He never really was his old self again.

He went back to the doctor again in April 1991, for more X-rays. He said the doctor told him it was emphysema. We were well acquainted with this disease so nothing much was said. It was clear, and had been for a long time, that he was not fit enough to carry his workload; so we hired another mechanic. The plan being, Uncle Dick would be on hand to direct and answer the thousand and one questions that would be asked of him in the first six months. Once the new man had the hang of things and knew the routine, Dick could just please himself and do only what he wanted. Of course, the station had enough work for four mechanics, but we couldn't afford four mechanics. Dick was told just to go along at a pace comfortable to him, and hand the bulk of the work over to the mechanic.

Being of the old school, this was not easy for Uncle Dick to do. Sometimes, when sickness makes a fair day's work impossible, it can have many different effects on one's mental attitude. Some quietly accept change, and live with it; others ignore it, pretend it hasn't happened. In my experience most people seem to conform to the latter. Dick certainly did.

He talked to me many times about it. It was familiar ground for me—I had been through it all with Charles. But Charles had been far more unrealistic and melodramatic. Dick on the other hand was, at least in the beginning, a bit more down-to-earth about his problem. But eventually he too veered off into moody unreality, unable to accept the inevitability of it. He wanted the continuous oblivion drink offered, but knew he couldn't have this while living on the station; but then he knew if he left, and went to town, he'd be letting me down. The alcohol of course always won, and he would go to town on some pretence or other. His usual excuse for the trips was to see the doctor for follow-up treatment. Most of the time he never made the surgery but ended up in the nearest watering hole, taking the medicine that quickly cured all problems. After lengthy periods he would return to the station, a little the worse for wear each time.

Around July another doctor's trip was required, and was arranged by me. This time it was another doctor in another town. After more X-rays the medico told him he would like Dick to see a lung specialist; the X-rays were not good.

The end of August I made more appointments by phone, booked the bus to Darwin and the motel, and gave Dick a lecture on the importance of keeping all his appointments. He assured me that this really was the only reason he was going to town ... but we both knew it wasn't true. As it turned out he did not keep any of the appointments. The first I knew of it was a phonecall from a very angry female, informing me that Mr Wicks had not turned up, and did I realise the specialist had come all the way from Adelaide and had so many patients to see and ... I interrupted to say I was not Mr Wicks's keeper, only his employer, and that I had no control over him once he was in town. I had apologised for Dick so many times over the years and I long ago gave up the elaborate cover-ups.

But she had to have the last word, telling me it would be a long time before he'd get another appointment as the doctor was booked out now for months. I assured her I would not be making another appointment for Mr Wicks. If Dick wanted another appointment he would have to deal with her himself.

There had been three more follow-up appointments arranged, and not wishing to face the same dressing-down I called and cancelled them.

Four days later the motel called. Dick had not been seen since the beginning of the week and hadn't used his room since then. I told them to pack his clothes and check him out of the motel. Another week passed and there was still no word. I started to worry. Usually by then the reverse charge phonecalls would start. A very under the weather Uncle Dick would wonder if I could see my way clear to help out an old friend of his that was having a spot of money trouble. In very clipped speech he would ask if I could possibly transfer some funds to the nearest bank for him to pick up. It was usually money for a square meal for the poor man's family, or money to buy spare parts to fix the car so he could get to work. All genuine heart-rending plights, to which I would say no. He would then realise I had no intention of advancing him money to continue his drinking bender. And eventually, after exhausting all avenues of supply, from acquaintances and friends, he would arrive back at the station, very much the worse for wear.

After a month had passed, during which I hadn't heard a word, either from him or via the bush telegraph, I thought it was time to call the police. The Darwin police knew him well, but called back after a few days to say he wasn't in town. I moved down the track and called Katherine police. They had played host to Uncle Dick in the slammer many a night when he was sleeping it off. After a few days they tracked him down to an Aboriginal mission just south of Katherine. Satisfied he was alive, we waited for his eventual return.

He arrived in the usual state—cuts and bruises from the many brawls; the remains of a black eye; no belongings, just the clothes he stood in: a pair of stubbie shorts, singlet and thongs.

So he was home again, although he never regained his health or state of mind after that trip. He became very silent and moody; and he hardly ate. To add to the problem, the other mechanic had left, putting the entire workload back on Dick. We still had some important work to be done on the machinery so Marlee put some of the other workers on with him to help lift, fetch and carry. But he was so abusive and unpleasant, no one wanted to go near him. In fact, you hesitated even to put a foot in the workshop for fear of getting abused.

Marlee finally asked me to speak to him; he was making it impossible to run the station. We sat down and had a heart to heart. He wanted to stay, he wanted to leave. He was lonely, he wanted companionship. He hated not being able to do a fair day's work. He couldn't stand anyone thinking he was a bludger. He didn't want to go into a home, yet he was worried that was where he'd end up. He couldn't accept that he was sick.

There was one hell of a battle going on inside him.

'It has to be your decision, Dick,' I told him. 'You know the best thing for your health is to stay here, eat regularly, work only when you feel like it, listen to your music and enjoy a few beers at sunset. But we both know you never do anything that's good for you.

'Nevertheless, you can't go on behaving as you are. You make life unpleasant for everyone around you. You just have to accept things as they are, and be as happy as you can with your lot, or go to town. But we both know what'll happen if you do go to town—you'll drink yourself into the grave.'

We finished on that sober note and he left in a very thoughtful mood.

For the next week or so he was a lot brighter and surprisingly polite to everyone who entered the workshop. He told me he'd just needed a good talking to, and I genuinely thought that for once he'd made the right decision. But I was wrong again. He disappeared in spectacular style, as only Uncle Dick could. As I write this I can feel in my bones that I will never see Dick again, and it's with a heavy heart and great sadness that I face the fact that it is the end of another unique era for Bullo and my family.

CHAPTER 11

December 1992

November the 27th was the first monsoonal storm of the season and it came at six o'clock at night, just like in the old days. It was violent and windy but so fast moving we didn't get much rain, although enough to make the soil ready for ploughing. The next day the ploughs were out and we started on the hay crop.

December started with a weather low sitting over the valley for most of the first week, but not a drop of rain. Ploughing stopped and the ground became too dry; we were still waiting for that first big rain to get the season going.

Although we were waiting and praying for rain, the truck was still travelling back and forth to Katherine, bringing in the last of the supplies before the road closed for the wet. Marlee called from Katherine saying she had the truck packed and was ready to leave for home and should arrive at eight o'clock that night. She was going to have a quick lunch and be on her way. I told her we had light rain early that morning, but it had looked heavy in the mountains. She said some big trees were down across the road from the storms when she drove out and if there was rain and the ground got too wet it might be tricky going off the road to get around the fallen trees.

There was one place on the road around 25-Mile she could get bogged.

'If I'm not home by nine-thirty, that's where I'll be—bogged,' she said cheerfully.

Franz and I watched and waited. Eight-thirty went by, then nine-thirty; still no headlights on the road. Franz started to fuel the Toyota to go in search of her. Since the rolled truck on the jump-up, I worry every time Marlee is late. Franz disappeared down the road and I was again alone, once more looking at the stars and the dark sky, in the direction of where the road bends into view.

They arrived home at midnight. The truck was well and truly bogged down to the axles. Marlee suspected that she wouldn't get through, but gave it her best, and when the truck sank to its axles she just rolled out her swag on top of the load, gazed at the stars and dozed off to sleep, waiting for Franz to come to rescue her. She has a wonderful philosophy about life—when you can't do any more with a tricky situation and wheels are in motion to solve it, don't struggle with the problem or stew over not being able to do anything. Do something else. And that something else for Marlee is sleep—something she's always lacking. That's how Franz found her, on top of the load sleeping soundly under the stars. An enormous tree blocking the road and the truck bogged.

Marlee awoke, gave him a big kiss and many hugs, climbed into the Toyota and came home.

We went Christmas shopping on the 14th, driving to Darwin in ten hours, arriving at 5 p.m. That evening we worked out the battle plan for the attack on the shops the next day. We went to bed early to recoup our energy.

I cannot remember the last time I was able to take my time Christmas shopping. Having three days to do nothing else but concentrate on buying gifts was something I was not accustomed to. Certainly not since I married Charles. Were we finally getting things under control and in order? Could we finally be eliminating panic from our lives?

While in Darwin I was interviewed by Jan Springett, of ABC Radio. Jan wanted to know about Christmas Bullo style! I told her that the first and most important step is the 1000-mile round trip to buy the presents, food and all the other goodies that make Christmas Christmas. I said we would be home by the 18th and I would have six days to prepare the cake and plum pudding and egg-nog and turkey stuffing. I mentioned how this was a rare treat because in years gone by I usually only ever had a few hours; and I told her about the time Charlie arrived mid morning Christmas Day with everything and I had to start then. I also told Jan about our Christmas tree, and how it was a large, tropical pine that the girls chopped down and hauled back to the house. This year it would have to be Marlee and Franz who would do the chopping.

I talked about the heat in December—how we would eat the Christmas meal around 5 p.m., when it's cooler. I have noticed we eat less and less of the fruit cake and plum pudding each year; desserts such as fresh fruit salad and pavlova seem to be gaining more popularity in the heat. The rest of the dinner has stayed in demand, everyone looking forward to turkey and stuffing and gravy, ham and loads of baked potatoes, no matter how hot it is. Charlie's favourite egg-nog is still going strong too, although it's not quite as potent now and we sometimes freeze it and eat it with a spoon. However, a new favourite has emerged—Marlee's iced tea, which is laced with vodka and Bundaberg rum and orange juice. It is very thirst quenching and I know Charlie would have loved it.

The interview over, I said goodbye to Jan, wished her and her listeners a very merry Christmas and Marlee and I packed the stationwagon and headed off down the track to Katherine. At Katherine we loaded the last and most important part of the Christmas shopping—the food and drink.

With every inch of space filled and the vehicle loaded to the gunwales, we turned at the Victoria Highway and headed west and home, 340 miles away.

December had seen a few mechanics come and go, and we were without one at the end of the month. Marlee and Franz were looking after the generator, which was fortunate because homestead creek was flooded and part of the road was washed away so they had to swim down to the generator to turn it on and off every day. It is said that necessity is the mother of invention, and Franz certainly proved that ... So that he didn't have to swim the creek at night he set up one of the small portable generators at the house and wired the fans and the television up to work on this machine. He could then turn the big generator off before dark and cross the flooded creek while it was still light. And of course to have fans running all night was very pleasant.

Christmas was just as I had described to Jan Springett, only it was the first year we did not have a twelve-foot-high tree. Marlee and Franz were ploughing and planting right up to Christmas Eve and were so tired that when Marlee asked if she had to go out for the tree I didn't have the heart to say yes. Besides, the paddock where the trees grew was under water and Marlee and Franz would've had to have walked all the way, which was out of the question. I said no, we could make do with something out of maybe gum tree branches. I went back to the kitchen and later Marlee called me to come see our new Christmas tree. I walked in to see half a bougainvillea bush in the living room—she had arranged long, flowered limbs of the plant in a tall vase in the middle of our very large coffee table and had streamers cascading to the table top. With all the brightly wrapped presents arranged around the table it looked beautiful, and very original.

Dear friends, Peg and Jack Cater, were in Perth to visit their daughter Susan, but sadly couldn't get up to Bullo because they had so little time and also most of the north of Western Australia was flooded, making all planes fully booked. So we were isolated for Christmas. But we could talk to everyone by phone. It was nice to be cut off by road and air for a little while, and we had our first rest for the year.

I did have one of those strange phonecalls, however, that immediately start the mind racing back over the years. The caller was an Aboriginal man from Port Keats, trying to call Bullo Community. We have got quite used to these calls over the years—whenever someone calls the operator to say they want Bullo, we get them. I patiently explained to this caller that he did not have Bullo Community, he had Bullo River Station, and asked if he had a pencil so I could give him the right number. I had been doing this for years.

My caller had been doing a bit of Christmas celebrating so our conversation was moving very slowly. When I told him again that the operator had put him through to Bullo River Station, he said, 'I know you. That Marlee?' I told him no. 'That Bonnie?' he went on. I could see us going through the whole station, so I quickly said, 'No, this is their mother.'

'Arrrr, Missus!' he cried, his voice full of emotion.

He was one of our first boys from Port Keats, way back in 1964. He was only sixteen when he first came to Bullo. He told me he was now married and introduced me to his entire family over the phone, first his wife and then all his children. We had a one-sided chat as he reminisced over his days with us, and did I remember this and did I remember that, and had I seen so-and-so lately. He filled me in on others who had worked at Bullo and where they were and what they were doing; the sad news I didn't want to hear was that my Mary had died. A few tears dropped on the desk as he went on talking, and my thoughts remained with that wonderful person whose concern and gentleness and protection in the early days made it possible for me to survive.

His wife eventually found a pencil and I gave him the

number he needed and the contact was cut after a genuine goodbye of, 'You take care, Missus.'

And then there was silence.

I sat for a long time, thinking of Mary. I had so much wanted to go and sit cross-legged on the ground with her and talk about the past. And now the chance was gone.

The Aborigines were one of the major reasons I survived the Outback in the early years. Their knowledge of the bush made life that much more bearable, while the volume of work they did by our side was staggering. The stockmen were wonderful trackers and were there many times to guide Charlie home, when he was stuck in some canyon and didn't know where he was. The children were taught how to track and to find bush tucker and clean water. Survival techniques that have stayed with them today.

As for me, the Aboriginal women took me under their wings, protected and instructed me on this very harsh land I had found myself in. Customs that went back thousands of years were taught to me; I was encouraged to understand and learn, and not to fear my surroundings. Everything in their power was done to help and please the 'missus'. They knew I was terrified and very unhappy so they set about to make me feel more comfortable with my lot and to make me smile—which they did by getting me fresh food so I wouldn't have to live on the copious amounts of dried beef and vegies. They would dig for yams and collect all the bush tucker available and show me what they did with it—endless experiments with new dishes, which I was then urged to try.

But the best smile-producer of all was fresh fish. Every afternoon all the women and children would go down to the river to catch fish, and always one extra for the missus. My girls always wanted to go, so sometimes we would all go with the group. But as the children got older I would let them go just with 'Old Mary'. In the early days on Bullo Mary was my teacher, companion and my saviour on countless occasions. I soon learned that the children were very safe with the Aboriginal women, and relaxed and let them spend hours on end roaming the bush, learning from the best.

One afternoon the children were sitting with me on the roof of the tin shed, enjoying the view and the first hint of the slightly cooler evening breeze. It was just on sunset and the sun was sinking behind the mountains, when the children pointed out the women struggling up the airstrip huddled in a group. It looked as if they were carrying someone. I immediately thought one of them had been hurt and hurriedly climbed down the ladder and rushed out to meet them.

As I approached, I could see the big grins on their faces, so knew no one was hurt, but I couldn't make out what they were carrying. They laid it at my feet with great ceremony. It was an enormous fish. The biggest barramundi I had ever seen. To this day, thirty years later, there has never been a fish of this size caught—all of five feet in length. How they landed it with only a hand line I never did find out. The descriptions were in excited pidgin English and I had trouble working out what they were telling me, especially when it was one word at a time and they were pointing to the object they were talking about! Nevertheless, the fish story was told to me in various renditions, all accompanied by much arm-waving and eye-rolling and hands thumping hearts. So although I didn't understand the words the elaborate actions gave me a very clear picture indeed.

But I think the greatest fish story happened quite a few years later, in the early 1970s. I had two lovely girls working for me from Port Keats. Their names were Sarah and Betsy. They both had a son of around four years of age whom they would bring each day to work. These little boys were very naughty and quite destructive and I had to discipline them regularly when I found them touching or breaking something. Their mothers never did try to stop them or spank them for any wrong deeds, so it was left to me to keep them in line. I did it with chocolates.

I told them if they played quietly and didn't disturb me

or annoy their mothers, then at lunchtime each day they would receive a chocolate. These chocolates proved to have great powers—I would just have to say the word and they would snap to attention. Consequently they spent most of the day thinking up things they could do to please me. Wherever I was in the house they would track me down every ten minutes to give me an update on how good they were being. Unfortunately this was a lengthy process and by mid morning it became quite wearing.

One morning when I was very busy I told them to go away and not bother me until lunchtime when it was time for their chocolate, and if I saw them before that time there would be nothing. This did the trick and they vanished and I had peace for more than two hours ... until a terrible commotion, followed by screams and howls of indignation, broke out in the kitchen. And I didn't have to go there to know who was creating the noise.

There, amid the pots and pans, were the two little boys, punching their mothers who were holding onto them to prevent them coming into the office and disturbing me. The boys had something very important to tell me and I knew I wouldn't get any peace until I heard them out.

I told them to stop crying and punching and kicking and I would listen to their story. They wanted me to come with them. This was conveyed by dragging me out the kitchen door. We were halfway across the flat, heading for the creek, when they stopped and pointed to the ground. Lying at my feet, covered in mud and dust, was a very large barramundi, still flapping.

It seems their mothers had sent the little boys down to the creek behind the house to keep them away and silent. They had been playing under the trees and running up and down the creek, when they came across a large barramundi flapping around in one of the shallow pools. During the Wet Season the creek is wide and deep and the fish come up from the Bullo River. When the rain stops, the water level drops rapidly, and sometimes catches fish in isolated pools.

The little boys had stumbled upon one such fish, trapped in a large but shallow pool. They chased the poor thing around and around for hours, until he was just plain dizzy or until they'd churned up so much mud he couldn't breathe; one way or another, the fish jumped out of the pool and they pushed and rolled and dragged it as far as they could. When they thought it could not make it back to the water, they came to get me. The fish was so big they couldn't lift it.

So they proudly presented me with this muddy lump lying, flapping, in the dirt. They were quite sure he was worth at least two chocolates, and were very proud of their morning's work. They just stood there smiling and repeating, 'Missus! Missus!', along with pointing at the fish and rolling their eyes, all of which was supposed to convey to me that this was an exceptional gift they were giving me.

When I gave them five chocolates each it set a new precedent, and I didn't see them for weeks. They spent their days combing the length and breadth of the creek looking for more stranded victims.

It was the last day of the year. And what a year! I must be getting old, or tired—or both. Usually by December the year had me feeling tired, but this year took the prize. The rainy season finally settled in and that was the signal to rest, or at least it was before we added hay-growing to our ever-expanding repertoire. Over the years I looked forward to January and February of each new year with anticipation. It always represented two months of rain and green grass breaking through. It was always a time for stopping and looking at the world. Work would continue at a steady pace, but the pressure of the previous year would be gone. I would spend time in the office catching up on the year's paperwork, which had been progressively put aside for a thousand reasons. There would always be a long list of repairs, for the homestead and the station, to be considered and acted on.

But these two months of daydreaming and rain-gazing have gradually disappeared over the last few years since we have started growing crops. Now, after the first rains set in, we start the ploughing, and that has to be done non-stop before the rain gets too heavy or the ground becomes too soft to work on. If we miss the timing then we cannot get the crop in the ground—it becomes too wet to walk on, let alone drive a tractor over. So, as in the old days of the dreaded abattoir, we were back to working twelve months of the year. This is okay for normal working hours, but when you find yourself working seven days a week, sixteen hours a day—sometimes longer—you find yourself getting a little weary around the end of the year. And as a result there have been very few New Year's Days that I've been able to stay awake to welcome in. I would always start New Year's Eve with good intentions, but come ten-thirty or eleven I knew I wouldn't make it and just gave in and went to bed.

Charles never stayed up and always retired around eight-thirty, although he did that every night anyway. However, a few times over the years he did agree to get up just before midnight to celebrate the new year, but come twelve o'clock when the alarm rang I would just sleep through, or sleepily mumble, 'Happy New Year', and fall back into a deep slumber. Charles mostly slept through everything.

The last six years, Marlee and I have been so tired we've gladly slept the old year out and the new year in. Last year Marlee ploughed it in! But not 1992! No matter how tired I was, I was determined to stay awake to see this year out. Not see it out—kick it out. Boot it out the door forever into oblivion. 1993 had to be better; no, I *demanded* it be better. I would stay awake and set the new rules for this new coming year. A few more years like 1992 and I would be finished.

It was unanimously decided therefore that 1993 deserved French champagne—leftovers from the BWOY award—and we celebrated with the smallest family New Year's Eve: just the animals and the three of us in half a million acres. I found myself being reminded of the early days on Bullo—when we were living in the caravan in the middle of the tin shed struggling to survive, with nothing of beauty in any direction. The life and landscape was hot, dusty, heartbreaking and harsh. Charles arrived home from Darwin one evening with a present for me in a box. I opened the box and there were twelve classic crystal wine goblets. Sitting in surroundings of grey cement, grey steel and tin, they looked like stars taken from heaven.

I carefully lined them up on the old Laminex table, avoiding the cracks in the surface, and sat to absorb their beauty. Many times through the terrible years that followed I would take those beautiful objects out of the safe box and just sit and look at them, to remind me that out there somewhere, beyond all the dust and struggle, beauty still existed.

Charlie had also just happened to bring with him from Darwin an esky full of ice and a bottle of French champagne. He was very good at judging when I was at breaking point, and this had been one of those times. The champagne was to get me back on track. (He was also very good at knowing how to get me back on track!) We didn't have a penny to bless ourselves with, debts and summonses were part of everyday life, yet he wasted money like this.

But that was the practical side of me talking, back then the romantic side of me won hands down, every time. So I sat there starry-eyed as Charlie casually undid the wire cap on the champagne, as if surrounded by luxury instead of a tin shed, popped the cork and poured the ice cold liquid into one of my beautiful glasses that he had carefully chilled beforehand. He proposed a toast to our wonderful future and I sat there dreamily looking at him and believing every word emphatically.

The children, on the other hand, were more excited about the whole esky of ice, high on the list of treats, just behind ice cream, milkshakes and chocolates. They had a wonderful time making large glasses of Milo and milk, crammed to the top with ice cubes, followed by orange juice and more ice cubes. The next day was spent seeing how many iced liquid drinks they could make before all the precious ice was gone. They had the day off school while teacher recovered from a hangover.

Charlie was sure he wouldn't have to 'treat' me for another month or so. He'd done his bit, even though I later found out that he'd simply put it on credit. It took me six months to pay the bill.

The glasses have hardly seen the light of day in all these years, except on very special occasions.

I brought them out to welcome in 1993.

Marlee, Franz and I, and the dogs and Boots, sat outside and looked at the stars. We talked about Charlie, mostly the outrageous things he did, but also the kind and brave things. Over the years I've mellowed towards him—I don't get as mad with him now.

I don't think Marlee has forgiven him completely, but she does reminisce with me.

Soon the night had gone and it was near to midnight. I had found a cassette tape with songs to see out the old year, and with that playing in the background we watched the countdown on the television. Franz had timed the cork-popping perfectly, so that on the stroke of midnight the champagne cork hit the roof and heralded in the new year. I raised my glass to Charlie over on the mountain where we had scattered his ashes.

'This will be our year, Charlie,' I vowed silently. 'So get off your backside and do something! Cheers.'

We sipped champagne, ate ham and mustard sandwiches and my homemade fruit cake, and talked in 1993, sitting under the stars.

I stayed out under the stars a long time after Marlee and Franz had gone to bed, holding my 'star' glass and remembering so many, oh so many things.

I finally went off to bed, sad and happy. Mostly happy, and definitely optimistic. As I drifted off to sleep I could see the glass on the bedside table twinkling at me in the moonlight. I smiled; I had a very good feeling that 1993 was going to be The Year!

CHAPTER 12

January 1993

There were clouds everywhere on the first day of January 1993. I was interviewed on talkback radio in Sydney. The topic was 'thinking positively', and I was asked to give advice to the people struggling on the land.

What a task! How can you advise someone who already works twice the normal working hours every day, and who still doesn't have enough money for a reasonable life? I could only say, 'Hang in there.' And keep repeating my plea.

The next day was Danielle's birthday, and for most of the day on Bullo we had lovely soft rain, with the sunshine peeping through the clouds. We called her very early in the morning to wish her Happy Birthday, and told her her present was late, as usual. She could see it in early February, when she visited, and she would need the utility to take it home. By now she was well and truly intrigued. I almost couldn't wait to see her reaction when she found out it was a stepping exercise machine!

We were still going through mechanics like they were going out of fashion. I was beginning to believe they were a breed of their own. I thought Uncle Dick was unique, but after so many replacements I was strongly suspecting he possibly was not out of the ordinary, but what was classed as a 'normal' mechanic. Heaven forbid!

One chap wanted half a case of beer a day. Warning bells went off in my head—no, never again. I told him it was not possible during the wet, with the road closed, to keep up such a supply. The cheeky bugger then issued his ultimatum—the beer, or he would go. I told him we were sorry to lose him. Like hell we were! One of my many New Year's resolutions was no more alcoholics on Bullo ... unless I became one, and that was highly unlikely. If I hadn't turned to drink by now, there wasn't much danger of it happening.

So Marlee and Franz kept the generators running, quite efficiently, while we searched for our next prima donna.

We still hadn't heard from Dick since his disappearance back in November. We kept track of him through friends and knew he had stayed with an old Bullo employee in Kununurra and then moved on to Katherine and out onto a station to catch up with Stumpy. He apparently also visited Jo-anne at the Katherine library. She called to let me know he was coming to her house for dinner. I heard from her after that and she said he looked reasonably well and wasn't drinking too much. She said she'd keep me posted.

The weather was now very hot and most unpleasant, making thinking and writing very trying. All doors and windows were opened to create and catch all or any breeze possible. When the storms eventually came I spent the time rushing around the house closing doors, and watching the roof, waiting for it to blow away again and cringing every time I heard a squeak. If any intelligent beings from outer space happened to be watching the Bullo homestead occupants for behavioural patterns, I am sure their regular logbook entries and analysis summaries would read: 'Rain always causes a peculiar ritual of rushing around abode with face uplifted, pausing frequently. When rain stops, ritual ceases. Further study required to ascertain whether this habit is widespread or localised to this area.'

January 1993

I could feel my stress levels rising. My diary made it clear that apart from half of January and May and June, the rest of my year would be spent away from home travelling to conferences and on the paperback tour of *From Strength to Strength.* So I had to spend every spare moment writing or I wouldn't finish the second book in time. What with Marlee and Franz acting as mechanics, and doing the ploughing and seeding, I had to handle the cooking and the house and the office and the phone, which didn't leave much peace and quiet for writing.

But then our luck changed.

I am pleased to announce that after thirty years of hiring and firing, tearing out my hair, resisting the temptation to murder, I have finally found the housekeeper of my dreams.

We have had a few good ones over the years, but mostly the record has been absolute shockers. The more qualified they stated they were, the more hopeless I found them. If they *could* cook, then they were extravagant with food and wasteful when preparing—throwing away half a lettuce, looking for the right shaped leaves! I caught one idiot grating the lemon rind into a cup for the recipe, and throwing away the lemon. Even the reasonable cooks, I found, were impossible to work with. In fact I was so disillusioned I wasn't even going to bother to try again, and had resigned myself to doing the cooking. But one look at the coming year's appointments book made me realise I wasn't going to be home much for the first nine months of the year. Something had to be done.

It was Marlee who insisted we start looking for someone; the impossible someone as far as I was concerned. Where to start? Luckily fate stepped in, in the form of a phone call from an employment agency in Perth. They were enquiring about one of our previous employees who had gone to them for employment. They wanted my rundown on the stockman. About two weeks later they called again—another of our employees had turned up there. By now I had become quite friendly with Julie, the consultant, and just in passing

I asked if she would like the challenge of the century. She politely said yes. I described my wonder woman and she said to leave it with her.

Julie came back to me with about four applicants, including Jackie. And I couldn't be happier! I have not set foot in the kitchen since she arrived. Some people may not realise the significance of this statement, but for me it is about as amazing as flying to the moon under your own power. If I had written down all the attributes of the ideal candidate, I would have come up with Jackie. The whole house has never been neater or cleaner, and she is a pleasure to have around. Jackie and Mugsie, her Jack Russell terrier, settled in from the first minute. Although I would have to admit Jackie had an expression on her face of, 'where have I landed', when she first stepped down from the truck. They had just finished a four hour drive from Kununurra with Franz, in the cattle truck. Jackie stood there a little dazed, but Mugsie cased the joint immediately, including our two massive Rottwielers, who towered over him with all hair raised. He completely ignored them except for a quiet growl, to prove he wasn't intimidated. He completed his tour of sniffing, walked right under the noses of the big dogs with all two inches of his tail stiff and quivering, sat at Jackie's feet and looked up at her as if to say, 'Well come on, what are you waiting for, unpack! We are home.' And it has been that way from the first minute.

Okay, it took thirty years, but at last we'd struck gold. Jackie could not have come at a better time. She was our first good-luck charm of 1993.

A phone call from Danielle however brought devastating news. Bonnie's 10-month-old baby Georgina was critically ill with meningitis and had been rushed to hospital. The fight to save her life was on.

Bonnie had to stay in the hospital 24 hours a day, her husband Arthur was travelling and Danielle couldn't fly to Darwin to help for a week. So Danielle asked if I could look after Bonnie's eldest daughter Amelia, and I said I would do anything to help. Marlee was in Darwin getting supplies and I suggested to Danielle if Bonnie wanted me to take Amelia, Marlee could bring her back to the station that night. Bonnie and I had not spoken since the court case. So Danielle called with my reply but was told a neighbour was caring for Amelia and Arthur was on his way home, but to thank Marlee and me for our offer of help.

What that little baby went through in the following weeks was unbelievable but against all odds Georgina pulled through. I called the hospital and spoke to Bonnie in the early days when Georgina was desperately ill, and things looked grim. She seemed to appreciate the calls but was probably too sick with worry for the conversations to have registered. There was no indication that it had been years since we had last said anything to each other. It is amazing how the sickness of a small child can sweep away anything in its path.

My heart is still broken, it has not healed ... I can't say if it ever will. So to answer the question asked of me a thousand times since my first book, yes I have spoken to Bonnie and yes I have talked to and played with my grandchildren.

Before I knew it, it was time to leave on the conference trail. I flew to Darwin on Friday 15th January for R&M (repair and maintenance). Facial, massage and hair. I hadn't yet written my speech but had the Sunday free for speech-writing while flying to Sydney and then the evening to finish it. I was speaking for the AMP first, and it was while writing the speech that I remembered I had my very first job with them, during the Christmas holidays. My exciting job was to fold premium notices by hand! That didn't capture the imagination, I can tell you.

The world of business was then very new to me. I was basically wild ... well, for those days. I was athletic, always running instead of walking, and this was not considered ladylike.

I sat next to the two 'icons' of the AMP, and these two ladies continually told me everything I did wrong. One day, after running all the way back to the office after shopping, I was told I was breathing too heavily! My chest was heaving up and down in a manner that was 'not in keeping with company policy'. I was told to go stand behind the filing cabinet until my chest was under control.

I told a few more of my extraordinary experiences and the audience seemed to enjoy the speech. However, I had been battling an ear infection most of 1992, which I'm sure was stress related—every time I had to make a court payment my ear problem came back, and flared up again as soon as I had another problem. As a result my ears in 1992 were constantly flaring up and calming down!

But now they really hit me in Sydney and I was feeling very dizzy, dangerously so. The dizziness mixed with nerves left me unbalanced, as if I were suffering something very close to vertigo. I finished the speech and was walking across the foyer when I felt myself falling. Luckily I was walking past seats and I flopped ungracefully into one. Eventually the dizziness cleared and I appeared back to normal. I had planned dinner with friends, but I thought it best to go straight back to the hotel to rest. Heavens knows what a few glasses of wine would have done to my steering gear!

I had to fly to Brisbane the next day for the second conference, but made an appointment with a doctor for early the next morning. I didn't relish falling off the stage during a dizzy spell. The doctor said the eardrum was slightly red, but thought I had an inner ear infection, and that this was causing the dizziness. He prescribed antibiotics. I also mentioned a slight sick feeling at the base of my throat and he said the tablets should clear up both.

The sickness went almost with the first tablets, but the strange feeling in my ears remained, minus the dizziness. The doctor had said he didn't think I would be able to fly. When

I told him I had to fly almost around Australia in the next three days, he told me I could be in for a very unpleasant time.

How wrong he was. The unpleasant time was at ground level. At 35,000 feet my ears felt great!

In Brisbane I got my first curtain call. When I finished speaking the audience just kept clapping after I had left the stage and one of the organisers told me to go back on.

'What will I do?' I asked, dumbfounded.

She was at a loss to give me any suggestions, so I just edged around the curtain again and smiled and gave a little bob in a thank-you motion, and scurried off the stage.

But felt pretty pleased inside. A curtain call!

The third AMP conference was in Perth; it was another enjoyable day. The ears were still a problem, but as long as I took the tablets the dizziness was kept at bay.

The pills lasted until the day after I arrived back at the station. Then the dizziness immediately returned, but it wasn't nearly as bad as when I was standing backstage waiting to speak. However, the heat now seemed to be giving me trouble, and my neck and jaw were starting to feel as bad as the ears. I was taking aspirin to get some relief.

The temperature was now in the forties and concentrating on my writing was difficult. I was not being very creative. Marlee decided I needed cooling down. She and Franz decided on an air-conditioner.

Marlee wanted to make it a surprise. Franz said there was no way they could install an air-conditioner in my room without me knowing. Marlee said she thought they could.

The first step was the doors. All the doors were louvred and much the worse for wear. Over the years they had been damaged in storms. I had ordered new ones and they had been sitting in the storeroom for many months.

Franz had them out, dusted off and installed in a few hours. Marlee told me she wanted to paint them but the smell of paint would be too strong for me, so I should move out of my room. She helped me take my writing into the office. Then they backed up the truck to the outside wall and removed an old air-conditioner that hadn't worked for years. The new machine was bigger, so Franz cut the hole bigger with a power saw. Marlee explained to me that the noise was Franz removing the old steel brackets.

Franz and Marlee disappeared back into my room after lunch and I sat in the living room, writing. There was a lot of to-ing and fro-ing but I was too hot and sick to take any notice. The weather was building up to another storm and the day was particularly oppressive. Waiting for the storm to break was unpleasant.

Around three in the afternoon Marlee came and led me to my room, all smiles. She opened the door and wonderful cool air met me. I looked about in amazement. There in the wall was a beautiful new air-conditioner. What a difference! We put a thermometer in the room and it dropped to twenty-one degrees in one hour; outside it was forty-five.

From then on I worked in blissful comfort. Of course, I was never alone. All day there was a continual stream of traffic. The dogs were the worst—Hunter spent the entire Wet Season with me in air-conditioning. Jedda wasn't far behind him. They would knock when they wanted to come in, and when they wanted to go out they'd just stand and look at the door. If I wasn't looking they gave a quiet bark to get my attention. As for Marlee, she would find excuses to spend time in the room ... and Franz would be close behind. Lunchtime everyone joined me.

The day after my air-conditioner was installed the storm broke. We had one and a half inches of rain, Homestead Creek flooded again, and Marlee and Franz were back to swimming to the generator shed and the workshop.

CHAPTER 13

February 1993– *March* 1993

The next mechanic was employed by phone again. It seemed we might be lucky with this one. Marlee and Franz would soon be leaving for Austria and I had to have someone in the workshop looking after the generators.

Marlee was going home to meet Franz's family. Franz hadn't been home for eighteen months, so they both were very excited. Naturally everyone in his family, indeed the whole village, was waiting to meet Marlee. In a tiny Austrian village, where land is used and measured by the metre, for a son to tell you he has to help run and care for half a million acres and thousands of head of cattle must be a little mind-boggling. Not to mention the fact that he's suddenly got married!

Although I was excited for them to have this wonderful holiday, I dreaded them leaving. Apart from missing them, I knew all the outside station care would fall on me, and with no mechanic there was no way I would get any writing done at all.

Over the years, many times, I have found myself a lone caretaker, looking after the animals and starting and stopping the generator. I thought I had given this up long ago. But it now looked as if I would be starting generators again, if we didn't find someone soon.

The latest mechanic was travelling up from Perth by car and it looked as if we might have him a whole week before Marlee and Franz had to leave. He called each day as he drove up the coast, then nothing. He either found another job and didn't have the manners to call to tell us he wasn't coming, or he just disappeared and his family and friends still think he is working in the Outback. But I doubt it. Someone would have called to contact him by now.

With that, my opinion of mechanics slipped even further down the scale.

True to life, everything happened at once. As the time approached for Marlee and Franz to leave, things went wrong. The hot water system broke down; Marlee bogged out in Nutwood and had to walk home; and the rain continued until the creek flooded up to the garden gate. My sister called from Caloundra and told me Ralph was not well and was going into hospital for tests. February was not looking good.

Ralph sick, mechanic disappeared off the face of the earth, floods, vehicles bogged … and then Jedda came on heat! We wanted her to have puppies by Hunter before he got too old, but not this time. There was definitely no room on the calendar for that.

So the first week of February found me trying to write, with Marlee in the room teaching herself German, Jedda on heat sitting at my feet whimpering, and Hunter just outside the door moaning. And still no mechanic!

To add to the chaos, I then had to fly to Perth for a conference for Combined Rural Traders. I would be away for three days.

While in Perth, Marlee called and said she had found our next mechanic. He would be in Kununurra and could come into the station with me. One day before they left for overseas! I flew direct to Kununurra and then boarded the small plane with the new mechanic and flew home. Franz showed the mechanic the workshop and the generators and then we discussed all the things I had to remember and watch during the next six weeks. Danielle was coming to stay for three weeks, so this took some of the pressure off me, as she could take care of the animals and the outside for half the time at least. She could also keep an eye on the mechanic. Marlee ran through the jobs she could show him to do while they were away.

I had three more conferences to go to. Since they were all on the east coast and there was only a day in between each conference I decided to stay down for the three. So that meant I would be away for six days in all. Danielle would be company for Jackie and watch over the station while I was away. She was flying in on the same plane that Marlee and Franz were flying to Darwin in.

The plane arrived on Sunday afternoon and we spent the afternoon and night discussing the details about cattle that Danielle needed to know. I went to bed worrying about what I had forgotten to ask Franz and Marlee. They took off at first light and as I watched the plane disappear over the horizon I wondered if I would get any writing done in the coming weeks.

Trouble started the very next day. Our main generator broke down, so the mechanic switched to our stand-by. I spent the day on the phone finding out what was wrong with the generator and asking about parts. The mechanic had never worked on generators; after many phonecalls it was established the exciter on the engine had blown up and it was an electrical job. The mechanic wasn't familiar with the electrical wiring of generators, so I arranged to fly an electrician in on the plane taking me to Kununurra for my trip to Sydney. The plane came at first light which meant that, if possible, the generator could be repaired and the electrician could fly back with me.

He tried to use some parts from one of our old generators, but with no luck. We had to order new ones. It was arranged for him to fly back in with me in six days' time.

I left Danielle in charge and told her if the stand-by generator stopped, she could have the electrician fly out and not wait for my plane. I said I would call each night but would leave my phone number anyway. And with that I left for the south, wondering what else could happen.

Danielle knew I was very upset and worried and not feeling well, so instead of calling me she called Marlee and Franz in Austria and together they worked out each problem as it arose.

I spoke at the National Mutual Conference in Launceston first. It certainly is a small world. I was telling the story about buying shares because they had the same name as my dog Hunter and suddenly the audience started clapping as a man in the front row stood up and bowed. I had bought shares in his company, Hunter Resources.

The next day I was speaking in Hobart for IAMA, a company that deals with products for people on the land, at the Wrestpoint Convention Centre. There were around 900 people there and it was a great day. I attended their dinner-dance that night and completely relaxed. The nerves had gone and I even forgot the problems at the station for the night.

I had one more speech in two days' time and had planned to continue up the coast to spend a few days with Sue and Ralph. A few calls from Danielle listing ever increasing problems, generator wise and more, made me realise I had to go straight home. The electrician flew into the station with me and had the generator fixed in a few hours and the plane flew out just before a big low settled over most of the top of Australia. Danielle was to leave a few days after I arrived home, but the low stayed and dumped rain on us for days. The main highways to Perth and Mt Isa were closed. If she flew to Timber Creek she wouldn't have been able to catch a bus in either direction.

For the next week the creek was flooded and the mechanic had to wade through the flood waters to get to the generator and workshop. At least, we told him, the creek didn't flood to the point that he had to swim. He was not amused, but he had to admit each day brought a new adventure.

Our mailplane made it into the station only a few times in the six weeks Marlee and Franz were in Austria. I received a letter from Marlee after about a month. It was an interesting letter, because the description of Austria was through the eyes of someone who has lived almost all her life in a vast Outback wilderness and who is then transported to the middle of densely populated Europe!

> *Dear Mummy,*
> *Franz and I have been here for three days now. It is just so beautiful. I don't know where to start. Very cold, most days are five degrees—below! But it is a very dry cold, so not too bad.*
>
> *I will start with the beginning of our trip. It has been so long since I travelled overseas, I'd forgotten just how much like cattle they treat you. You don't get branded on your skin, but in your passport, and you can't go or do much without your passport, so it is very much the same.*
>
> *Singapore was interesting. The three main professions seem to be gardeners, police or shopkeepers. So many police, you can't walk three steps without running into one of these small, stern-faced people. The people are all very tiny, this was really brought home to me when I went to the toilet, and I am only five-feet-two. Poor Franz was most uncomfortable.*
>
> *The drive into town was twenty-two kms of gardens, with a person tending every bush and tree. In town we walked down Boogie Street. They sell fake everything. I don't know how they manage with so many of them selling things, how they make a living is a mystery.*
>
> *We had dinner at a place where all the locals were eating. Ten satays for about two dollars Australian, cooked right in front of you on a little hotplate. The people were all*

very polite, but distant, like we were some sort of oddity they put up with because we were tourists and represented money.

Once again, I was fascinated with the size of these people. Franz was very conspicuous, towering over everyone.

I thought the airport in Singapore was huge until I landed in Frankfurt. Frankfurt was like a nightmare, where you are trapped in endless tunnels. When we landed it took fifteen minutes to taxi past all the other aircraft to our bay. Most of the terminal is underground—about five storeys, including the carparks.

The tunnels really go as far as you can see with people in glass offices in the wall every now and then. They sell things and exchange money and all sorts of things.

After we cleared immigration we were greeted by a huge sheet with 'Welcome to Europe' on it. Gepherdt, Franz's friend, had hired a car and driven 800 kms to pick us up, not far in the Outback but a major journey here.

Germany is very crowded, the buildings ugly and the air is awful. The cars are covered in black soot, like ours are covered in dust. The sky is grey and smoggy. I can now understand why people make such a fuss over our sun. Here they are lucky to see it at all, let alone a sunset!

The closer to Austria, the prettier the landscape became. The houses ornate in traditional style, and the air cleaner. We crossed the border into Austria without any trouble and our luggage made it all the way without being pulled to pieces at each checkpoint.

On the Austrian border the mountains started, and what mountains. I have never seen anything so huge!

The highway is amazing, miles of bridges along impossible mountains, and tunnels 6 kms long, right through the bottom of some great, huge mountain. It cost something like twenty million dollars per km to build. I don't think they wasted a cent.

All along there are little villages, small and neat, just like in the movie Heidi. *Here the sky is so clear and blue and the air perfect. That is why so many German tourists come here in the summer. Millstalt is just beautiful, the lake simply takes your breath away. In fact everything does.*

Franz's parents had another sheet with 'Welcome Dahmin', which means 'welcome home'. They are, as you said they would be, lovely people. The thing about Austrian people that has struck me so far is that they have a great respect for everything. Remember the American Indian we watched on television, who talked about respecting every living thing? It seems to work here in Austria. Everything is so organised, but not rigid.

The roads up the mountain to Obermillstatt are amazing. So steep and narrow and the bends incredibly sharp. They have those large mirrors on the bends so you can see what is coming; they are very necessary!

My German, though basic, is understood. They all think my accent is funny, but Franz said they like it, it is not grating.

Now everyone in the village stops to talk to Franz, people who never normally did before. They are all very curious about his Australian wife. People who plan to travel to Australia are calling Franz for advice. He has now become the village's authority. It is such a chuckle.

Franz is very happy his parents are proud of him. They are all such genuine people. Yesterday I fixed an old leather whip. I spliced the end back together and put on a 'fall' and cracker and cracked the whip. Franz said girls just can't do that sort of thing here and everyone was very impressed. I had to chuckle to myself, if they could see the things we do at home, normally.

Franz is playing ice hockey tomorrow. He is most excited. I am going to try to skate on the beginner's pond. Franz's sister-in-law is the same size as me and has offered all her ski and ice-skating gear to me so I don't have to hire or buy anything. They are a lovely and very thoughtful family. When we arrived there was a cupboard full of warm clothes for us to wear.

> *Skiing is next on my list of new things to try. And Franz is trying to convince me to go into the sauna, with* no clothes *on! This is apparently the norm in Europe, but you know me. It will be a losing battle for him, but he is still trying.*
>
> *If possible we will visit the Lippozaner stud, which is not far away from the village. In fact most places here are not far—by our standards, that is.*
>
> *I am having a most wonderful time. When we go on your world tour together, you will see what I mean. I just know you will love it too!*
>
> *By the time you get this letter we will not be far behind. Take care, I miss you, and home. All my love, Marlee.*

She was right—they were not far behind the letter. I was counting the days.

It was the 1st March before Danielle could go anywhere by road. The roads in the west were still out, so she flew out of the station to Kununurra and caught the jet to Darwin. One of Martin's friends was in Darwin with his truck so Danielle got a lift back to Cloncurry with him. That left Jackie and the mechanic and me. I had to go back to fulltime writing, I was in the position where I had to use every moment to meet my deadline for the second book. I left everything to Jackie and locked myself in the room and only appeared at seven o'clock each evening. I told the mechanic that I didn't have time to hear the saga of each piece of machinery on the property and what was wrong with it, and could he please just keep up the oil and water to the generators and just not touch anything.

So he had an easy time waiting for Franz to come back to hand over to him.

It was not long after Danielle left that Ralph had to go into hospital for a heart operation. This was upsetting to say the least. I wished I could be with Sue at a time like this, but with Danielle gone there was no way I could leave the station. It was another two weeks before Marlee and Franz were due back. So I gave the best support I could, by phone. My March phone bill was staggering.

Sue stayed home alone and this was unsettling for her, so I called her first thing in the morning and midday and before she went to bed. Troubles was a great help and really came into her own as a guard dog. She even gave up the comfort of her trampoline and curled up on the floor at the foot of Susan's bed.

Ralph certainly didn't sound his usual jovial self for many days after coming out of intensive care. By the end of the week a little bit of the spark was back in his voice and I think he thought that just maybe he would live. He hadn't been too sure up to that point.

He was progressing at a great clip and then the heart went out of rhythm. The doctor told him if it didn't correct itself, they would have to put him under again, stop the heart and jump-start him! This caused a sufficient surge of adrenalin in Ralph's bloodstream to put the heart back on track and he was saved.

He came home on election day, extremely weak and many pounds lighter, but on the road to recovery.

Susan was worried that Troubles would be too excited and rough when she saw Ralph for the first time. But she behaved perfectly, slowly walking up to him and being gentle in every movement. She seemed to know he was not well and that she had to be extra careful. She was very happy her family was back together.

Marlee and Franz came home the following weekend.

The mechanic was waiting to leave, having realised that he wasn't experienced in most of the work required on the station. But the lifestyle too was not to his liking—it was so different from anything he knew. The isolation is the thing that usually gets to people, and during the wet this isolation becomes very evident. Later in the year, when the road is open, you get so many visitors that by the time the rainy season arrives you welcome the seclusion. But just to step into it is a bit hard, although Jackie seemed to be handling it quite well.

However, it had been agreed weeks before that the mechanic would wait until Franz arrived to hand over in an orderly manner and give Franz an update. This he did. There wasn't much to explain or hand over.

So our quest began for yet another mechanic.

The house brightened immediately the moment Marlee and Franz arrived home. Their enthusiasm and happiness lifted our spirits and we sat for days listening to the wonderful stories of their adventure.

Then it was down to business. I had to get back to writing, Franz went down to the workshop and Marlee started looking for a mechanic. She was sure that out there somewhere was one who was not an alcoholic, was good at his trade, and was a pleasure to be around. He was definitely out there and by hook or by crook she was going to find him!

CHAPTER 14

April 1993–
May 1993

Marlee and Franz were still stand-in mechanics and I was writing from early morning to late at night, to enable me to have the first 200 pages of the new book ready to take to Sydney on the twenty-third. The paperback of *From Strength to Strength* was to be available in the bookstores on the 7th April. I started a ten-day tour for the Victorian Young Farmers, touring all around the state, then moved straight into the paperback book tour of Australia and New Zealand. Doesn't sound much when you say it, but it was far too exhausting. I enjoyed the countryside, meeting all the people, and I was lucky with the weather. It was the longest stretch of sunny days Victoria had had in many years. But it was too much driving and at the end of ten days I was on the verge of collapse. I arrived in Melbourne at 2 a.m. and had to be ready to start the next morning at six.

Luckily, however, I collapsed into professional hands. Jeannine knew I had had a gruelling time, and she had all arrangements made to allow me to relax. I was led into a beautiful suite at the hotel, greeted by wonderful flowers and fresh fruit and a 'welcome to your book tour' card. There was a note from the hotel telling me my massage was booked for 6 a.m. and a car would pick me up at 9 a.m. to take me to my hairdresser's appointment. Then I would be picked up at twelve.

I took a hot bath, ate some fruit and snuggled into a super soft bed, weary beyond words. As I drifted off into a very welcome sleep, I thought, 'You are too old, Sara, to work with anyone but professionals!'

After sleep, massage and a glamorous hairstyle, I was ready to face the world again. And it was off to the country—my book tour started with a luncheon in Hamilton. It was a fair distance out of Melbourne, but the weather was still perfect and the drive didn't seem long at all. In the last ten days I had gone by plane from Bullo to Kununurra to Darwin to Melbourne. Then by car to Shepparton, Wodonga, Shepparton, Bendigo, Ballarat, Horsham, Warrnambool, Geelong, Warragul, Sale, and back to Melbourne. So Hamilton seemed around the corner. I can't say enough about how wonderful the people in Australia and New Zealand were to me on my tours, and Hamilton was no exception.

The luncheon seemed to go well—I thoroughly enjoyed it. We drove back to Melbourne straight after and arrived late. Up to this stage I still hadn't seen a copy of the itinerary. When I did, I knew why Jeannine had kept it under wraps. It was a book in itself—and it didn't include New Zealand. Twenty-six pages and twenty-two days straight of interviews, radio, television, luncheons, dinners and book signings. It took most of the drive from Hamilton to digest it. Phil, the publisher's Victorian Sales Manager, who was driving me, saw me looking in my handbag and asked if everything was all right. I took out a pen and when he asked what I was doing, I replied I was crossing out Day One.

Phil put me on a plane to Adelaide at 8 p.m. after a full day. Adelaide was more of the same. Meeting some of the people I saw on the first tour, including Jan Springett. My interview with her was again enjoyable and the book was given away to some listeners who called in on the talkback segment to ask me questions about my life on Bullo.

It was out of Adelaide late and into Brisbane around midnight.

I met Jeannine early the next morning, just in on a plane from Sydney. Brisbane and Toowoomba took up the next two days, then it was into Sydney at ten o'clock in the evening. So far I had crossed off eight pages of the itinerary!

The next day's schedule was almost my undoing. It started at 6 a.m. with a drive to Newcastle. After radio talks and book signings all morning, we drove back to Sydney and then I boarded a plane for Bathurst.

I had fifteen minutes to change at the motel and it was off to a literary dinner. What a night and what a crowd! They were a wonderful bunch of people and the night didn't finish till 1 a.m. Well that's when I bowed out, anyway. A drive to Sydney was ahead of me; I had to be there for a twelve noon appearance at a book signing. But it was some night, a great country get together. There were 450 people there and 200 on the waiting list for cancellations. One pregnant woman told me as I signed her book that she had gone into labour that afternoon. When the pains stopped around seven o'clock in the evening and the doctor told her it could be hours before they started again or it could even be a false alarm and might be days yet, she got out of bed, dressed and came to the dinner. Now I call that a compliment!

Some wonderful things happened on the tour. One woman bought my book and was putting it in a time capsule, to give to her one week old daughter on her twenty-first birthday. Another cute story took place in Sydney. A woman was shopping and she bought a book in the local bookstore. While she was paying for her purchase her little baby leaned over and took one of my books out of the display bin at the counter. The mother didn't notice this until she went to take the baby out of the stroller at home. She called the store and told them what had happened and said she'd return the book first thing in the morning. When she rang the next day at lunchtime, she said she had started to read the book, could not put it down and would come in the next day to pay for it.

But my favourite story would have to be when I was signing books at a department store. A very sweet old lady came up to the desk, clutching my book. She gave me a polite smile and stood close to the desk, but to the side. I thought that maybe she was a bit shy so I asked her would she like me to sign her book.

'No thank you, dear, I'm waiting for the author,' she replied.

When I said I was the author, she looked at me critically, then said, 'No, I'm waiting for *this* author,' her finger pointing to my picture on the front of the book.

It took some time for Jeannine and me to convince her that I was indeed the person on the cover, and I was finally allowed to sign. But even then she walked away mumbling, 'Well you don't look like her!'

She was quite sure she had been conned.

The sales were roaring along and I appeared on the 'Midday' show on the Monday. Tuesday was the Dymocks and *Sydney Morning Herald* Literary Luncheon, at which there were 750 people and more than 200 on the waiting list.

My star could not be higher in the heaven. It is of course at these times you always have your falls. When life seems too good to be true, it usually is!

Monday night when I was having a shower I noticed a slight tenderness in my right nipple when towelling myself. I thought it was a pimple. I put my glasses on to inspect, but I could find nothing. There were no lumps or hard spots, so I left it. The next morning in the shower I was shocked to find a red line running from the nipple to under my right arm. The underarm was now tender, running down to the muscle of the forearm. I had a slight fever and an obvious infection. I also had appointments from 9 a.m. onwards and a luncheon for 750 people.

I called Jeannine and told her I had to get some antibiotics quickly, before the infection took hold. I had to leave for New Zealand the next day.

Jeannine tried to get the hotel doctor to come to the room in the next half-hour, before all my appointments, but he couldn't manage it. He arranged for Jeannine to pick up the tablets, telling her he wanted to see me early the next morning. He called me and asked a lot of questions, then went back and told Jeannine that he would prescribe the tablets, but there was a possibility I had a very rare breast cancer and that if this was the case the tablets wouldn't help. Nothing would. You were usually dead in around ten days! Naturally Jeannine didn't tell me this.

The poor thing spent the whole day watching me and asking if I felt okay. She had the tablets in her hand and at one second to tablet time, she was there with water and pills. As soon as I would swallow them, she would want to know if I was feeling any different. I said the fever was gone and the tenderness seemed to be decreasing. But she would want to know how much better! I thought she was just worried about me getting through the luncheon. But she watched me like a mother hen, all day, carefully leading me to my room that night and for the hundredth time asking me how I was feeling.

I went up in the lift, walked into the room, stripped and stepped into the shower, and she was on the phone again, from downstairs, just checking on me! I said I was in the shower, and yes the red line was a lot better and I was going straight to bed. The luncheon had been a success so I really couldn't see why she was still nervous. But then after I got the all-clear from the doctor, Jeannine told me what he had said to her. No wonder she was panicking—I have no idea how I could have faced 750 people with a possibility I could have been dead in ten days! I do not think I could have pulled it off.

So we had great reason to celebrate at lunch. We planned to have a long one, then go to the airport for my plane to New Zealand. It was a great lunch, with Jeannine and I celebrating my reprieve, and James, who didn't know about this drama, celebrating yet another reprint and wonderful sales figures. I broke my 'no drinking while working' rule and had champagne, then more at the airport.

I slept all the way to New Zealand, where I was taken over by Catriona for another great tour. And another staggering schedule. In four days I had seventeen media interviews, eleven book signing sessions, two 'off the cuff' library gathering speeches and two literary luncheon speeches. Phew!

I arrived back in Sydney on the 11th May. And the next morning it was off to Perth. As much as this glamorous life I was leading had to be envied, I was counting the days to getting home to my family, my funny little bedroom and my dogs. And Bullo. When I left Perth for Darwin, I flew right over the top of Bullo. I had the overwhelming desire to stay in Kununurra, where the plane was fuelling. Bullo was just thirty minutes over the hill ... by plane.

But no. It was on to Darwin for another two days.

And then it was over. And home.

It was so good to be home! I just wandered around for days, trying to bring myself back down to earth. I found I would wake up in the middle of the night, having a nightmare about missing some appointment or other. I was completely unable to concentrate on writing and was a total mess for days. Eventually, however, the adrenalin, which had been surging at high speed for weeks, slowly wound down, and my body started to relax.

Then I got the flu. I lay in the morning sun for days, too useless for anything.

After about ten days I started to feel normal again and took over the office work, answering the constantly ringing telephone. I even went back to writing at 4 a.m.

May drew to a close with dust rising from the office and writing room.

CHAPTER 15

June 1993

It was June, and we were starting a very late mustering season. The drought in Queensland that was making life impossible for the people on the land over there also affected us. So many of the properties were selling their stock because of not enough feed that the price of our cattle dropped dramatically. It was, without doubt, a buyer's market, no question about that. Cattle were being offered to buyers at every turn. However, we were holding off selling our cattle until the very last ditch, hoping for an improvement in the price. At the same time we were praying non-stop for rain for the drought areas, to make life more bearable for them and also to improve our market prices.

This rainy season, from September 1992 to May 1993, we had thirty-three inches of rain. And while this is not our average, we still consider ourselves very lucky.

In the thirty years I have come to know the Outback, I've slowly watched the rain pattern change. Our first rain, on 1st September 1992, was only light rain, slowly building up over October and November to good heavy rain throughout January and February. This continued on until May 1993, with four good, light storms to finish the season.

However, the storms through the season were light falls compared with those back in the 1960s. Back then, according to the station records, and my memory, we had nine months of 'dry' and three months of 'wet', if we were lucky. The storms are still as violent, if not more so, but the rain is not as torrential, or as consistent as back in the 1960s, and no longer has the true characteristics of the monsoonal season. When we first arrived it wasn't unusual for six, and sometimes even up to ten, inches of rain to fall in one storm or one night. Once the monsoonal trough moved down and settled over the top of Australia, Bullo would receive daily rain, just on sunset each night.

I will never forget the ferociousness of my first Outback storm. The first storms of the season have violent winds that move tons of soil for miles. Dry lightning cracks everywhere and strikes the sandstone mountains repeatedly; hundreds of bolts flashing in seconds, illuminating the sky to a whiter than white glow. Soon after, thin columns of smoke spiral up from trees, burning at regular intervals along the top of the mountain range. The wind intensifies as the huge black front gathers momentum and rolls towards the homestead, sucking in air at an amazing rate as it covers the hot land. Then, just when it seems nothing will survive this mass of destruction, torrents of rain burst from its midst. The thick dust storm it has whipped up is quickly beaten back to the earth by the downpour. A downpour so violent you cannot see twenty feet ahead of you …

My first Outback storm struck late in the afternoon, just on sunset. I had noticed the north-east sky slowly grow darker and blacker by the hour. A massive black curtain moving towards the valley, which prompted me to take the washing off the line.

The next thing I knew the children and I were huddled in the caravan in the middle of the equipment shed, waiting for what seemed like the end of the world. The wind was violently shaking us and I held the children close, terrified, while Charlie sat in the corner of the shed, in the lee of the storm, cool, calm and collected, watching nature's display, thoughtfully drawing on a cigar in between sips of his drink. Without the slightest difficulty he soon coaxed the children to join him and before long they all insisted I join them too to watch the show.

I sat shivering as the storm unleashed its might on the valley.

The rain came in swathes, giant curtains moving across a stage. Light rain in between the heavy downpour revealed the valley clearly for seconds, before it was blacked out as the next torrential curtain moved into place. It reminded me of slides clicking through a viewer. The wind, after being sucked into the moving storm for the past hour, now changed its course. It was howling, running before the storm, rearranging everything in its path.

Water could be seen rushing across the dry paddocks. On the road the water was making patterns, rippled by the wind, looking like the surface of a long, narrow pond. I momentarily forgot my nervousness, although it returned with every deafening clap of thunder. But I was mostly mesmerised by the scene around me ... the super-dry landscape thirstily soaking up its first drink in nine months.

Trees seemed to change before my eyes. Laden down with months of dust, you tend to forget they are green. Within a few minutes the dust was washed away, the mud slowly dripped off the end of each leaf and the trees lifted their newly washed faces to the wind and the rain. Paddocks turned into raging torrents of water, carrying along everything in their path in a headlong rush to the river and lower-lying areas.

The animals stood with their backs into the storm, their ears flattened, eyes closed and tails to the wind. Every now and then they would slightly adjust their back legs to keep them square on to the force of the wind and rain. Newborn foals and calves, seeing their first storm, were frisky and nervous. Thunder cracks would send them into a frantic bolt in any direction, then their mothers would call them back to their side with a reassuring whinny or a contrasting loud moo to a calf who was too far afield. It didn't take the babies long before they knew the score, then they stood close to their mums, mimicking their every move. Some were fast learners and stood under their mother's stomach, out of the rain.

The wind almost abated as the centre came to a halt over the valley, sending down even heavier rain. The lightning was directly overhead, striking continually, hitting the ground very close to the shed and some unfortunate trees further out in the nearby paddocks. One tree exploded into a ball of flames, only to be drenched with water a few seconds later. The whole valley was covered with a sea of water; we were cast adrift with trees and dry grass sticking up everywhere.

The storm moved across the valley, moved inland, losing its intensity as it travelled. The black curtain passed over the house and the sky immediately became lighter; the rain and wind stopped. It was as if a switch had been flipped.

The silence was the first thing I noticed; the roaring had gone, there was no wind whistling through the shed. The thunder was still booming, but the reverberating rumble was now in the distance instead of over our heads. The sound was easier, not all-engulfing. The lightning now danced on the mountain range, creating a cinema of entertainment miles away; no longer life-threatening.

The cool air that came with the storm, so refreshing after the relentless build-up of heat and humidity, was gone with surprising swiftness. With the same swiftness the oppressive heat seemed to ooze from the waterlogged ground, bringing back the unpleasant pre-storm weather.

Within a few minutes the storm had disappeared, the dry bulldust that swirled into clouds at the slightest breeze had miraculously turned into mud. The trees were alive—even the seasonal trees with no leaves looked different, and if you looked close there were tiny green shoots on the bare branches, just waiting for this first rain to get the show on the road.

The sun came out as the storm clouds dispersed, only to slip behind the mountains, signalling the end of the day, and the end of my first Outback storm.

I had thought nature's ultimate display of power was the sea. But now, witnessing this storm, I wasn't so sure. Each in their own way is the ultimate in power and intensity. However, I was much more at ease in the tin shed watching this storm than I had been in the middle of the China Sea on a sailboat.

So now with the rainy season well and truly over we were about to start yet another mustering season, with the usual assortment of wide-eyed and wonderful adventurers as crew.

The 1993 season's team included Jackie, a veteran of six months, who had the house ticking over like a well-oiled engine; James, from England, but now a permanent resident in Australia. Then there was Mike, a wandering stockbroker, again from England; and Kevin from Ireland, who had to defend the Irish against all comers when he first arrived. And then Nicki—a delightful, cheerful, first-year jillaroo with fifth-year ability. Then Bob, the only true-blue, top class, dyed in the wool Australian stockman. And last in our mustering team, but certainly not least, was Doug, our new mechanic.

Franz and Marlee were still looking after the generators. But we were starting to worry. We had a whole list of repairs to be done before the season, and the season was now with us. Franz and Marlee had started on the easy things, but there were a few engine overhauls that had to be done. And that they couldn't do. So the hunt for Miracle Number Two continued. To find the cook of our dreams was unbelievable, but to expect also to find a mechanic was pushing the odds right off the scoreboard.

After various machines left in pieces, an alternator burnt out, a generator engine unserviceable, another engine set alight, the stand-by generator damaged to the tune of thousands, a few close-shaves with electricity, I again wanted to give up the search. I told Marlee at the rate we were going we wouldn't have any machinery to take care of, and I wondered silently if everything could be done with horses.

Marlee persisted and came up with Doug, our second piece of good-luck for 1993.

Doug arrived while I was still on tour; in fact, he turned up on Bullo on Mother's Day! He drove up in his car from Brisbane, a trip that proved to be a miraculous saga of events. It took many days, and along the way he was robbed, had mechanical problems and ran out of money after his wallet was stolen. He called Marlee, because he didn't even have a credit card to buy fuel, and Marlee managed to get some money to him and he drove straight through to Bullo from the fuel stop on the Queensland border. I'm sure by this stage of the journey he was thinking, 'If I don't stop nothing can happen.'

He finally arrived, with a tiny puppy named Lucy, and it only took a few days to know there was a reasonable mechanic in our workshop!

So the team now assembled, we got to work.

Our first muster was Nutwood Paddock on the 11th June. The three helicopters came in on the Thursday night at sunset for a sunrise start. Nutwood Paddock and the main yard is only one mile from the homestead, so all morning I could hear the choppers rounding up the cattle as I sat writing in my room. The cattle were yarded by midday and everyone had lunch down at the turkey nest in Nutwood Paddock, and had a swim. All except Doug, who was working in the workshop, and me, who was busily writing.

Twelve hundred cattle were waiting in the yards to be processed, so as soon as lunch was over the team sprang into action; and the three choppers took off to fly to their next station.

Of our new team, only Bob had seen a yarding of this size, or indeed a yarding of cattle at all. So the rest of the team were at somewhat of a loss. Each animal is run through what is called the round yard. The yards are set up with a large receiving yard, the helicopters muster the cattle into this first yard, which takes up around fifty per cent of the yard area. Then some of the cattle, about fifty at a time, are moved into a smaller area called a forcing pen, which leads to a smaller yard that holds around twenty. From this pen the cattle go one at a time into the round yard.

At this point the animal is alone and it is then looked at and processed by Marlee. The cattle fall into the following categories: a weaner, a calf old enough to leave its mother and eat grass. These young calves, along with younger calves still too young to leave their mothers, are all put in one pen for branding. The youngest then go back to their mothers and the weaners are kept in a special paddock long enough for their mothers' milk to dry out. During these few weeks they have their 'kindergarten training,' as I call it. They are handled by stockmen on horses and taught to walk quietly and herd together. When they are well behaved, used to people and horses, they go back to their mothers' paddock and stay with them until the next year. Their training is usually about three weeks. By that time, as soon as they see a stockman on a horse they line up along the fence and start marching.

The breeding cows are the fastest through the yards. When they come into the round yard they are checked to see if they need any medical attention. If they are okay, and look healthy, they go straight through the yards and back out into the paddocks, or 'bush'. Having been branded when they were young calves, nothing more is required as long as they stay healthy.

Back in the early 1960s, when the cattle were wild and were caught for the first time and branded, there were some terrible sights. I will never forget one cow. She came into the yards with her horns grown down and curved in almost to the pupils of her eyes. She was fairly old and the horns were well developed. The stockmen put her in the crush (this confines and restrains the animal while you work), and with her head in the head bale (to stop her from throwing it around) the horns were cut off.

She was so funny when she was released. Had such a look of bewilderment as she took in the world around her. For years she had only seen the horn ends and a few things out of the sides of her eyes. Now suddenly there was this vast expanse before her. She was scared at first, because it was so strange. She wouldn't move and backed into the crush for security. The men got her out and she slowly sniffed each thing she came to, connecting the smells she had known for years with all the strange things she could now see clearly for the first time.

It took twenty minutes for her to walk across the yard and out the gate. She greeted every cow that came out after her for hours. She was so overwhelmed with her new vision and it was really wonderful to watch her enthusiasm with each new discovery.

For many years we had to save animals from horns growing the wrong way. One other cow had a horn grown into the side of her face, embedded at least one inch into the flesh. The horn was cut off and the hole packed with antibiotic powder. The cow was then kept in a small paddock closeby until the hole closed over. Thankfully these days we never see this type of problem because the cattle are handled regularly and any deformed horns are dealt with in the early years.

The breeding bulls go straight out the bush gate along with the cows. The cattle kept in the yards are the young steers, ready for sale; bullocks, older steers that have managed to get away in previous musters; and cull cattle, cattle we take out of the herd regularly to keep the herd improving. Our herd is at the stage in our improvement program where we are now culling cows with bad temperament, small boneframe, and any other visible faults.

Every one of the cattle is put through the yards one at a time, evaluated, and put into their required pen or put out 'bush'.

After all the cattle have been drafted, the first attended to are the tiny calves, so they can go back to their mothers without too much delay. The weaners are next. They are branded and go into training for the three weeks. The sale cattle go into a small holding paddock, to munch on grass until the buyers come to look at them. Because the Nutwood area runs so many cattle, we have to handle them in two musters, otherwise there are too many cattle in the yard at one time and the cattle suffer, especially the babies. One thousand four hundred went into the yards and Marlee had to hold the rest in the laneway because the yards were full. They waited patiently until the yards were clear and in they went. Up to 3000 cattle will go through the yards before we move to the next site, eight miles up the valley.

We had tourists visiting on the same day we were yarding the cattle in the paddock. They were flying around Australia on a holiday and were staying with us for a day. Being from the land and therefore horse people, two of them immediately offered to help on the yarding of the cattle. So we had two very able riders, which made the job much easier.

The yards were empty after many days of hard work, and then it was the 15th June, seven years to the day that I lost Charlie. And raining!

The last time it rained on Bullo in June was 1973, the year that Willeroo Station planted thousands of acres of sorghum. The company that owned the station had gone onto the American stock exchange. It was an attractive package—offering cropping, vast cattle properties and mining. The prospectus showed a 'last frontier' type adventure investment, and it soon became the glamour stock on Wall Street.

Charles naturally couldn't wait to get on the bandwagon. He immediately started all the paperwork required to float Bullo. And true to form, handed me another sheet of paper that showed me how many millions of dollars we were going to be worth in a very short period of time.

If I'd kept all those sheets of paper of the schemes, I would have a book thousands of pages long. For many reasons, each scheme failed or ran out of money … well, they all definitely ran out of money.

June 1993

While he was compiling the Bullo River prospectus, Charlie flew me over to Willeroo. It certainly was a grand scheme, the likes the north had not seen to that date. There were ploughed fields as far as the eye could see, all waiting for green crops to appear as soon as the monsoonal rains arrived. The rains were the crucial factor, because the vast cropping adventure that was estimated to return millions the first year needed no irrigation system. Not having to install an irrigation system for those thousands of acres of sorghum was a saving of millions. The prospectus told of thousands of acres of sorghum planted at miniumum cost and guaranteed free water from the heavens. A forward contract with a large Japanese company further guaranteed the investor millions of dollars to be made in the first year. Added to the cropping were cattle by the thousands and exciting mining plans. No wonder the shares sky-rocketed.

That rainy season, the monsoonal trough descended over the top of Australia, as guaranteed, and the sorghum flourished, just grew by the day. The crop was declared a resounding success and the reports of million dollar profits poured in as the tonnage estimates ticked up cash.

While all this success was happening at Willeroo, Charlie was working non-stop on the Bullo float. The US stock market was abuzz with talk of Willeroo. The shares soared and there were no sellers. Charles saw dollar signs as he worked towards the completion of the Bullo prospectus.

The rainy season finished on Bullo, and generally around the north, on the 20th April, with a rainfall of 1.45 inches. A month later, having had no further rain, the wet was declared over and the sorghum crop at Willeroo Station was declared a bumper one. They only had to wait for the harvest in a few months' time.

Everything was going as planned, everything was on track, the shares were booming in the US, Charles was about to make his next fortune ... and it rained in June. Not a light shower but heavy rain, inches of it. In June it was the worst thing that could happen to the sorghum crop, and the heads of grain went to mildew, ruining the whole lot. So instead of millions made, millions were lost. At first the investors thought they were saved, as the Japanese company had signed a forward contract, meaning the crop belonged to them. A decision was made to go ahead and harvest and deliver to the wharf, according to the contract. So the thousands of acres were harvested and trucked to Darwin to be shipped to Japan.

The contract didn't mention anything about mildew sorghum, but it did mention that only a certain percentage of foreign seed could be present in the grain. If it was over the stated amount, the crop could be refused. When the grain arrived at the ship, random tests were done and the presence of foreign seed was over the allowed percentage. The whole shipment was therefore refused. All the extra millions to harvest and transport the grain to the wharf was added to the millions already lost, and the total was staggering.

The publicity in America was tremendous. The reports had been continual since the crop had been planted and the success widely publicised. Most of Wall Street was waiting for the tons per acre so they could work out the profits. The unseasonal rain was played down, the harvest and delivery went ahead without too much of a stir in America, and the shares stayed popular. When the Japanese company refused to take delivery disaster struck. The share price tumbled, and very quickly the Australian Outback was not the glamour stock any more.

Charles was only a few weeks off floating Bullo's shares, having timed his move to ride on the wave of success of the sorghum harvest. He was riding a massive wave and he was dumped. He didn't bother to go any further with his plans; the bubble had burst. Outback cattle stations and vast cropping enterprises were no longer popular with Wall Street.

Friends and tourists were starting to arrive regularly now, in between and during cattle mustering. And as usual we had more road dramas. We had two road-trains at the yards loading cattle. The first truck loaded and left but got stuck on the first jump-up at 22-Mile. Our grader went out to give the rig a tow. Instead of hooking the grader up to the front of the prime-mover, the driver put it in between the truck and the trailer! The chain snapped between the trailer and the grader, and the trailer full of cattle went careering down the road and finished up across the bottom of the jump-up, each end of the trailer hanging out in midair. One side over a steep drop and the other over a water drain.

Marlee was back at the yards. When Franz came in from the road and told her about the trouble at the jump-up she arranged for our small truck and trailer to drive out to unload the cattle from the trailer and bring them back. When she arrived at the scene she was very upset when she found out the ridiculous way the driver had rigged the grader, but held her silence and went about the task of getting the trailer back on the road. To get in position to hook up with the towing gear Marlee had to slowly edge the grader down the cliff. It wasn't as steep as the drop on the other side, but was plenty steep enough. She pushed rocks and gravel up as she went along—virtually building a road to move along as she crept around the end of the overhanging trailer.

After hours of manoeuvring and backing up and pushing material, she finally hitched up to the towing gear. She inched the trailer around into a position where the truck could back up to its door to crossload the cattle. It took many trips in our small truck and trailer to get the cattle back to the yards. They would rest there before they left on the next trip, in a few days time.

On the last trip back to the yards *our* towing gear snapped and the poor steers once more went careering down the road, although this time into a riverbed. Again, all okay, except for being a little unnerved about travelling! Marlee just stood there shaking her head. Twice in one day!

Franz finally got them back to the yards where they were safe on the ground again, and after a feed of hay they settled down to a peaceful night. Can you imagine the conversation with the other cattle? 'Man, did I have a day! Careering backwards down a jump-up, hanging over a cliff face for hours, crossloaded onto another truck; then a runaway down into a riverbed. Jeez!'

The trailer had to be moved the next morning because we still had the second road-train back at the yard loading more cattle to go out the road. Marlee made an easy job of swinging the trailer around after the tons of cattle weight had been removed and had the grader and trailer back at the homestead bright and early. It was then back down to the yards and the next problem.

This truck was nowhere near solving the problem.

I wonder if we have not gone too far? This massive truck, nothing mechanically wrong with it, had been shut down by a computer, a faulty computer, it seemed.

The bloody thing waited until we had loaded one hundred plus cattle before it decided not to work. Then for reasons unknown it shut down the engine. Our mechanic could do nothing, the entire engine was controlled by this silly little box, which apparently keeps the engine running at the optimum running setting thereby saving fuel.

I hate to think of the cost for the three days delay at our cattle yards and the cost for an expert in the field of truck computers to drive out to Bullo from Derby W.A., a few thousand kilometres. A lot more than the few litres of fuel saved.

I think technology had gone too far this time!

To finish this terrible day there was a fax saying if I didn't pay the court costs judgement handed down that week, Trippe would start legal proceedings to recover same.

June was over at midnight, thank heavens.

In a few days it would be Charlie's and my thirty-third wedding anniversary.

CHAPTER 16

July 1993

Having established Charlie as a bounder and a cad, the general reaction has been, 'Why did you stay?'

But he did have other, outstanding qualities. I'm not sure they were good qualities, but they were certainly outstanding. Charlie was such a complex mixture, it would need a team of top pyschoanalysts to work out the whole picture. And even then you wouldn't end up with the complete Charlie. But one thing for certain, he would have them all pegged in a very short time.

I was fairly up on his dreams—he was quite sure he could run the world, and was waiting for the right people to realise this and ask him to step into the role. When I pointed out to Charlie, during many of our heated discussions, that he wasn't doing too well running half a million acres of it, I was told not to be cheeky.

I do know he was very brave, or maybe it was just foolhardy ... again, I'm not sure. He would tempt fate daily if he had the opportunity, and would tell me repeatedly that I was a coward whenever I refused one of his invitations to join him on the testing field. When I did flatly refuse his generous offers, saying if I lost, there would be no one to look after the children, this was not acceptable. And Charles would be even more convinced that I was a coward and that it was therefore his duty to change this flaw in my character. Maybe he was just trying to do away with me? I will never know. I was far too busy saving myself and the children from all the accidental, life-threatening confrontations Charles created, to accept what he considered *deliberate* challenges!

As a young man Charlie won many top sailing races on the east coast of America, mostly on and around Chesapeake Bay. This was not only because he was an exceptional sailor, but also because of his daring, his desire to win and his compulsion to behave completely differently from the normal, conventional, accepted manner. When his eccentric and outrageous plans for a race didn't work, he would be miles behind the fleet, sometimes crossing the line twenty-four hours behind the other boats. But when he won, *aaahhh* ... when his crazy scheme worked, he would fly across the line with nary a boat in sight, taking line honours, class honours, the lot! This now and then glory was obviously worth all the defeats, because this is how he lived in all the time I knew him.

In school he excelled in football and track. He would put so much of himself into the event that he would throw up before the start.

The Second World War came along and completely utilised his overabundant enthusiasm and energy. He joined the navy on the 5th July 1940, at the age of twenty. I was four years old, riding my red dinky up and down the corridor of the Union Hotel in North Sydney. He was commissioned as ensign on November 7th and assigned to the battleship *New Mexico* and served in the Pacific, around Hawaii, then in Iceland and a tour in the north Atlantic. It was the Atlantic tour that made him decide he would be more comfortable in the air, he said. One tour there was enough for him. The only time that battleship stopped rolling from side to side was when it was docked. He told me that, without a doubt, it was one of the worst experiences of his life. He immediately transferred to naval air, and had to resign his commission and start at the bottom again. As much as he loved the sea, knowing Charlie, he would have already decided that flying a fighter plane would mean he was virtually his own boss—and that was far more Charlie's style.

He was what was called a 'ninety day wonder', meaning he learned to fly in ninety days. The fighting skills and tactics had to be instinctive for him to go straight into war and survive.

He was horrified when he was assigned to a bomber squadron. How dare they! Charlie set about to have this mistake rectified. But even Charlie's considerable charm, persuasive manner and gift of the gab couldn't get him into the fighter squadron. He decided there and then to set out to compile such an outstanding record in a bomber that the command would realise their mistake and transfer him to a fighter. Along the way, however, he just happened to establish himself as an outright hero.

He never did get to be a fighter pilot, and I think for Charlie it was a bigger challenge doing what the fighter pilots did, but doing it in a bomber! His plane was the Avenger. All the years I was married to Charles I knew nothing about this plane other than its name. So I have been doing some research lately and I now realise it was as remarkable as the pilot it was teamed up with in the Pacific in the early 1940s.

The Avenger was a significant force in the Second World War. The plane was tough, rugged and honest. As a weapons carrier, it was extremely adaptable, its payload including bombs, torpedoes, rockets and depth charges, along with wing gunpower. It was a dive bomber, torpedo bomber, effective in the day and a great night fighter bomber. All this teamed with Charlie's aggressive and ambitious nature. Then add radar, air-to-air search and interception, and even dog fighting with a Zero to its already many accomplishments, and you have quite a machine. Yet it was described as 'underpowered', 'overloaded with unnecessary junk' and had the nickname of 'Turkey'!

Despite being originally designed as a torpedo bomber, the torpedoes were so unreliable and never ran true that the pilots adopted dive bombing tactics to deliver their payload. It was fortunate the plane was well put together because it was stress-tested by Charlie, repeatedly. As it was by all the other pilots.

Many Avengers made it back to the carrier or land base with unbelievable damage, it just wouldn't quit. It was outstanding in all theatres of the war—from the Atlantic, causing havoc with the U-Boats; to the Pacific, where it destroyed around sixty Japanese warships. And Charlie was right in the thick of it every chance he got, and loving every minute.

In a book written about the Avenger in 1979 Charlie contributed a chapter about his adventures and experiences during the war. The foreword was written by Charlie's commanding officer on the *Enterprise*, Vice-Admiral William I. Martin, Ret. The author sent Charles a copy of the book in thanks for his contribution. Bill also inscribed Charlie's copy. It read:

> *To Charlie Henderson,*
>
> *He excelled in aerial combat—a rare breed of pilot—so highly skilled as to get all the performance from Avenger that aeronautical engineers had designed into it—even to proving it a FIGHTER!*
>
> *With admiration, respect and affection.*
>
> *Bill Martin*

Charles often told us stories of their adventures during the war. Many nights and days the children and I would sit enthralled as Charlie relived his amazing experiences.

During his wartime flying Charlie sank ships, bombed and destroyed airstrips and land installations and shot down four enemy aircraft in air-to-air combat. After shooting down five aircraft, a fighter pilot was considered an 'ace'. Charlie shot down four in the Avenger bomber. Despite doing many wonderful things the plane was not hailed as one of the wonders of the war. In fact, it had quite a few very unnerving habits like 'settling off the bow' of the carrier on take-off. Even on a catapult launch, there were the alarming seconds when the plane lost contact with the deck and sank (or settled) into black nothingness, the propeller desperately fighting to adjust to the load that had suddenly been thrust upon it. In daylight it required a strong stomach to wait to see if you went into the drink before your plane took control of the situation. But at night the feeling of floating and then sinking slowly into the black void below created men with strong nerves.

Charlie described take-off to me many times ... and the surge of adrenalin he would feel as the plane 'settled' off the bow, for those few split seconds.

'Your engine roars as your eyes watch for the glow of the signal, in the night. Then you and the plane are catapulted down the deck towards space, the sky and sea, all enveloped in the black night. The white line down the deck, your only point of reference, suddenly disappears; the wheels break free of the friction with the deck and an eerie, floating silence pervades the roar of the engine as the propeller struggles to bite the air and laboriously lift the plane and its deadly payload into the night sky.

'The plane would painfully drop towards the water while struggling to gain control. As it drops, your stomach rises up into your throat, but at the same time you have this sinking feeling.'

How your stomach can be going in two different directions at once, I do not know. But Charles assured me it did.

'You wait for the stabilising effect of the water to sustain lift, to stop your descent; but for many seconds, stomach and nerves all suffer the terrible uncertainty.

'Coming off the deck, the water seems all too close, just feet below you. But when looking back, during those sinking seconds, the deck looks like the top of a very high mountain. You stay low over the water, to gain speed, even though the desire is to get as high as you can as quickly as possible. With a lot of confidence in yourself as a pilot and more in your plane not to miss a beat, it finally starts to climb. At all times, you are conscious of the fact that if the engine misses one beat, you will be in the water in seconds.

'You gain altitude and finally realise you've broken free. And you can relax, until the next time.'

Then all he had to do was find his target, avoid the anti-aircraft guns, drop the bombs and rockets, avoid the enemy fighters, find his way back to the carrier without being shot down, hope the carrier was not under attack, hope it was where it was supposed to be, hope the carrier escorts didn't think he was enemy planes attacking and open fire, hope he didn't run out of fuel before he could find his carrier in a fleet that covered an area of more than forty miles, hope the sea wasn't too rough to prevent landing, and hope when he did land on the deck he didn't miss the hook!

No wonder flying after the war was boring for Charlie.

There was no doubt, life on board the carrier during the war was the most exciting time of Charlie's life. He completed two tours, flying with Air Group 10, around the middle of 1944. It was about this time that the merits of night flying were becoming recognised and Charlie's commander, Bill Martin, started to form a night squadron. Charles was in like a flash. He already found the challenge exciting, but to be a night attack fighter bomber was just his cup of tea, and to be aboard the *Enterprise* again suited him just fine. So it was more training. Night flying was a whole new kettle of fish up to this point in the war, and had only been tested lightly. Bill was one of the first few to advocate its advantages. But he had problems selling his night bombing theory. It was argued that this sort of thing was supposed to be done during the day, when you could see. But Bill argued that with radar, night flying would be twice as effective as day. He was very stubborn and was finally allowed to train his squadron of eager and daring pilots. They practised long and hard. Whenever they had the chance they flew at night, using only instruments, tracking down targets by radar.

This dedicated training paid off, and when the squadron returned to the carrier it was a squadron with special skills and was ready for any mission.

Of course after Charles had tried every avenue to become a fighter pilot and failed, he applied his favourite philosophy, 'turn a problem into an asset'. He wanted a fighter plane but he had a bomber. And now at night the squadron had to do much more than just bomb. So he and some of the other enthusiastic members of the squadron set about to change their Avengers into a more manoeuvrable, faster bomber, which could put up a good fight, and have a few surprises up its sleeve as well.

Naturally all the changes and modifications requests they had in mind were turned down by Bureau of Air so Bill finally went to the top to seek help. He was in turn told that the aeronautical engineers had studied these modifications and had reported back that the plane could not fly if these changes were carried out. Bill told the admiral that in that case he would like alternative transport back to his squadron, because he had just flown there in a modified TBM Avenger and he sure as hell didn't want to fly back in it if it couldn't fly!

The changes went ahead. Because they were now flying full time at night, it was reasoned that the turret gun wasn't needed; so it was removed, along with a lot of armour plate that protected the gunner and other unused equipment. It all added up to around 1500 pounds. With the space gained and weight loss achieved they put in more fuel tanks, increasing the plane's endurance. The rearrangement of weight moved the plane's centre of gravity forward and as a result pilots found it was difficult keeping the tail down. This was a problem, as the tail hook was a very important factor in landing and staying on the deck! It was solved by putting a large lump of lead in the tail, and the plane once again behaved like a flying machine.

Navigating at night caused many problems. Getting the planes lined up, in the right position to approach the carrier, was difficult. And landing on a moving deck was not without its hazards either. To help with the approach a hooded amber light was positioned where it was only visible at a certain point in the approach pattern. When the light was visible to the pilot he would start his turn towards the flight deck. At this point on his advance he could pick up the deck signalling officer and stop flying on instruments and come in to land with the deck officer. Indirect red lighting was used in the cockpit, in the briefing room; even the pilot's flashlights were red. Everything possible was done to preserve night visibility. Cockpit instruments were regrouped to better accommodate night flying, along with a buzzer alarm installed on the radio altimeter to prevent the pilots misjudging height and flying into the water. The new .50 calibre wing guns had night sights. They were ready!

A week later they went into Truk.

It was the squadron's first night attack. It was in the eerie dark hours before sunrise ... they came in low over the harbour. Charles swooped low over the anchored ships, dropping one bomb on each run, making every one count, weaving and dodging AA fire and only flying straight and steady for the split second of the drop. After he had inflicted as much damage as possible he headed out to sea and safety to rendezvous with the squadron. He spotted a small sea plane and immediately gave chase; it was much faster than the Avenger and headed for safety, trying to lure Charles into the fire of the anti-aircraft guns. Charles let off one last burst from his guns and pulled away sharply to avoid the flak.

Now completely out of ammo, he headed once more for the rendezvous. As he approached the outer reef he saw another Avenger approaching out of the first faint shafts of light of the new day. It was trailing a lot of smoke, but what held Charles's full attention was the Japanese Zero coming up on its tail. The wounded plane was a sitting duck, although a tail shot is no easy matter. Charles knew it was just a matter of time—the Zero only had to change its angle and that would be it. So in went Charlie ... His guns were empty so he did the only thing he could—he harassed the Zero by diving on him, and the Zero got as mad as hell. He forgot the wounded Avenger and decided to teach this saucy bomber who dared to play Chicken with a *Zero* a real life or death lesson. He soon realised Charlie didn't have any ammo, so he was now sure it was a death lesson he was about to teach.

The wounded Avenger limped off into the sunrise billowing smoke but on course for home, while Charlie had one hell of a mad Zero pilot on his hands, intent on punishing him for interfering with his easy kill.

The Zero pulled up gracefully in a chandelle, in the lead and perfectly positioned for a high side run. As he climbed, Charles dived off in a forty-five-degree downward line from the Zero. As the Zero hit the top of his climb, and peeled off to start his attack run, Charles pulled up from his dive and executed a neat half-roll and ended up on the opposite course. They were now face to face, approaching each other on a collision course, playing Chicken!

Charles would describe each second of the attack, savouring it. He had the Zero in his sights, the two planes flashed towards each other at alarming speed, Charles's finger on the button to ignite his guns, even though he had no ammo the reflexes leading up to an attack centred around pushing that button.

'Come on, you bastard,' he whispered. 'Come to Daddy, you son-of-a-bitch! Nearly there! Nearly there! Come on! Wait! Don't go too soon ... wait ... NOW!' And at that split second he wrenched the control stick to the side and executed a violent snap roll, throwing the plane over until it was standing on its wing-tip. He corrected and stabilised the roll to hold the plane in that position as the two planes flashed past each other at impact point.

Playing Chicken was the only thing he could do. With

no ammo left, the Zero was too fast for him to run. So the only time they were equal was when coming at each other on a collision course, testing pilot skill. Charlie was at a disadvantage plane-wise; he had to manoeuvre into position with a plane not up to the fighter he was facing. He survived the first run—by jumping sideways at that precise moment when he knew the Zero would fire a hail of bullets at him.

He climbed sharply into a near stall, keeping his eyes on the Zero. He had gained those few precious seconds while the Zero registered shock at the agility of this bomber. But the Zero then climbed faster, and positioned himself on an opposite run—looking like he had accepted Charles's challenge to a duel. Again the two planes faced each other and repeated the action. For a second time Charles snapped his plane out of the Zero's path at the last second, to the same side. The Zero had anticipated a jump to the other side and corrected his course at the last moment to send a hail of bullets off in the direction he thought Charles would jump. He knew the bullets would rip open the underbelly of the bomber. He was wrong and Charlie had won two out of two. The hail of death sprayed off into the morning sky, eventually falling harmlessly into the depths of the sea.

Charles got the better of the Zero and started to climb. The Zero calmly lined up on an opposite course, taking his time, knowing he had the upper hand and could call all the shots.

Charles lined up in the now early morning sun, taking all and any advantage he could find. Sweat ran down his arms as he started the third run. What will he think I'll do now? were Charlie's thoughts as he raced towards death. Will he think I'll do three in a row? Charlie judged the sun perfectly and started his screaming dive in a blazing backdrop frame. The Zero lined up on an attack position. Charlie was fully aware his life depended simply on which way he jumped. At this point, screaming towards the other plane, he understood the mentality of the Kamikaze—his adrenalin pumping through his veins, his only thought was, 'I'll take him with me.' It would be so easy ... He jolted himself back to reality. What if he shoots a second earlier to catch me before I jump? Too many thoughts now scrambled his brain as the planes raced towards each other. The Zero watched and waited for one hesitation, one sign of weakness, then he would just pick off his target.

Charlie jumped for the third time, the Zero stayed straight and true and fired a split second earlier. The hail of bullets passed so close to the fuselage, Charlie could feel them whizzing by. Charles had gone to the same side again; three out of three. He wiped the sweat from his hands as best he could and looked for his enemy. The Zero recovered and moved into the sun, in the few seconds it took Charlie to gather his senses after too close a call. Charles took up battle positions as the Zero waited. And they were face to face again.

Will it be four in a row? Will he know I must jump the other way? Charlie's brain was working overtime as he desperately tried to think the thoughts of his deadly opponent.

Charlie watched the Zero grow bigger and bigger ... come closer and closer ...

He didn't consciously remember deciding to jump one way or the other, he just shouted, 'NOW!' at the precise moment he would have fired his guns, if he had had ammo. And once more he was out of the path of death.

How long will this go on? reasoned Charlie. It's all right reading about all these manoeuvres. The theoretical tactics are just fine. Seriously analysing the moves and the outcomes on a blackboard in the briefing room with a bunch of other pilots is challenging ... but doing it for real is a whole new kettle of fish.

'Sweat was running down my back, legs and arms,' Charles used to tell us, when relating the story to his spellbound audience. 'I was gripping the control so tightly I was shaking. I had to brush the sweat out of my eyes continuously. I could feel my reactions starting to slow, and I knew this was what he was waiting for. But there was nothing I could do. I had to stay and fight, as long as he wanted to. I couldn't run, he could pick me off at leisure. I had to stay in there and not crack—that's what he wanted, what he was waiting for.'

Charlie lined up in the game of Russian roulette for the fifth time, knowing his odds were getting worse, but refusing to think along these lines. The bomber and the fighter were again ready to play Chicken. Again Charlie snap rolled out of the way, again to the same side; only this time the hail of bullets did not come. The Zero was now also out of bullets. What now? thought Charlie. Surely not a Kamikaze run!

He climbed into the sun, waiting, watching the Zero for the next move, cold sweat prickling his skin. With a flood of relief he saw the Zero waggle his wings in a salute to a good fight, and just maybe, to a good pilot, and head for home.

It had been an incredible encounter. Charles couldn't believe he and his plane were in one piece. However, he still had to find his squadron and still had to find the carrier, and get back without running out of fuel! But the worst for the day was over, he hoped.

Charles's success lay in his unusually aggressive tactics, in the face of unbelievable odds. To go to the aid of a wounded plane was brave and courageous to the extreme. But to go into battle with a fighter plane, a *superior* plane, with no ammo, was extraordinary bravery. The way he fought the battle was brilliant. Not waiting for the Zero to dictate the terms, he made every move as if he were attacking. If he had watched and waited and wondered he would have lost those precious split seconds that saved him each time.

Charlie received the DFC for sinking two ships that night. But he received nothing for the amazing encounter with the Zero, except thanks from the pilot he saved.

THE SECRETARY OF THE NAVY
WASHINGTON

July 1993

The President of the United States takes pleasure in presenting the DISTINGUISHED FLYING CROSS to

LIEUTENANT CHARLES ENGLISH HENDERSON, III
UNITED STATES NAVAL RESERVE

for service as set forth in the following

CITATION:

"For heroism and extraordinary achievement in aerial flight as Pilot of a Torpedo Bomber in Torpedo Squadron TEN, during an aerial attack against enemy Japanese shipping in Truk Atoll, February 17, 1944. Pressing home a night minimum-altitude bombing attack against ships inside the lagoon, in darkness and despite intense anti-aircraft fire, Lieutenant (then Lieutenant, Junior Grade) Henderson contributed to the destruction or damage of a substantial number of ships, aiding greatly in the success of the assigned operation. His airmanship, courage and devotion to duty were in keeping with the highest traditions of the United States Naval Service."

For the President,

Secretary of the Navy

The cameras on the wing guns only work when bullets are fired, so Charlie's amazing five brushes with death were never recorded on film, only burned into the minds of the Zero pilot and Charlie, and the great plane he flew.

Charlie vowed after that incident he would forget trying to be a fighter and be content being a bomber. But Charlie being Charlie, he didn't hesitate the very next opportunity he had to be in the fray.

He was on long range patrol west of Saipan, searching for the Imperial Navy, and doing it as only Charlie could—shoes off, feet up on top of the instrument panel, cigar in hand. Suddenly there was a Japanese Jake cruising along, off and below his port wing. He was into the action before he could think. Guns charged, sweat glistening, trigger finger itchy and eager, he was side by side with his quarry—although careful to keep the cloud cover between them. He dived through the cloud and came up on the Jake on the starboard quarter, in a gentle low side run. As the prominent rising sun painted on the plane filled Charlie's gunsight, it exploded into a burning ball as a short burst of bullets hit the fuel tank. Charlie yanked back on the stick, avoiding the expanding explosion of the disintegrating plane. He flashed past, miraculously untouched by the swirling flames of the inferno that seemed to engulf his plane for that brief second.

As exciting as a hit was, his next hit lacked the excitement of the Zero encounter and the manoeuvring tactics of the Jake. He came up behind a Japanese Jill, a carrier-based torpedo bomber. The Avenger was slightly faster than the Jill and it was just a matter of Charlie moving up behind and closing the gap, sitting on his tail and lining up the plane in his sights.

And then there were two.

Charlie and his radar operator Ted Halbach were convinced that they could use radar to make an air-to-air intercept. So naturally, when the opportunity came along, they grabbed it. They practised on friendly aircraft, and soon found they could make contact fifteen miles away and close in purely on radar.

Their opportunity to engage the enemy came one night as they headed home after an attack on Kyushu. Ted picked up a blip. It was a miserable night, dark and rainy. The blip was moving in their direction, slightly above and to starboard. Charlie watched, excitement building as the blip got larger and larger on his smaller cockpit radar scope. Ted talked him closer, working on the main radar screen further back in the plane.

Charles related the experience ...

'His commands came through my headphones, "Starboard ten, climb at 150 knots, range now three miles."

'The blip grew larger. The enemy was dead ahead.

'Carefully I closed the gap. "One thousand yards," came Ted's voice. Nothing ahead. All I could see was black, and rain bouncing off the canopy. Just ahead was an enemy aircraft, crusing at 140 knots, altitude 4000 feet, flying straight down between the line of islands between Kyushu and Okinawa. We knew all about him, it was all there on the radar screen. Yet we couldn't see a thing.

'"Five hundred yards," said Ted. Still nothing! "One hundred yards." My eyes strained into the darkness. "Fifty yards!" My finger was on the trigger button—the excitement pitch was unbearable, the desire just to shoot at the darkness overwhelming. Was that an outline? Was that a shape blacker than the black night? The rain danced, blurring my view. There was an outline! Like a phantom a whole plane materialised before my eyes. I eased into firing position, my port gun behind his starboard engine. Ready for the kill ...

'Just as I was to claim my first air-to-air radar contact I saw he was one of ours!

'Mad and frustrated I located his frequency on my data sheet—he came from one of our land bases—and called over the radio in a very Japanese accent, "Look-see starbroad side mellican boy!"

'He went into a violent diving turn to port as he peeled off for the deck. A mean thing to do but I was mad as hell—he had no right to be a friendly.

'I stayed mad for days, but we now knew we could make air-to-air intercepts with radar, in the worst kind of weather.'

The score was still two.

Like a kid with a new toy Charlie hunted the sky for his first air-to-air kill. It wasn't long to wait, the task force was cruising the coast of Japan, their main object being to cover the airstrips that were launching a steady stream of Kamikazes heading south to attack and destroy our ships. One evening Charlie and several other pilots set out to make the enemy's night a misery. He was scouting alone, after delivering his payload to airstrips and shipping in the area, and was now cruising home after a job well done, when Ted's voice jackknifed him into action.

'Bandit at fifteen miles! ... Extreme angle! ... Pull up!! Closing rapidly, to port, he is on opposite course.'

Charlie turned to compensate and climbed at full throttle. He had to execute a 180-degree turn at the right moment, at exactly the right speed, or he would lose the blip on the radar screen. Charlie watched as the blip stayed on the radar screen, and waited for Ted to talk him through the turn to keep them with their bandit.

'"Execute turn!" came loudly over my earphones. I completed the turn, still climbing, and waited. Had I lost him?

'The silence was deafening. I waited for Ted to find the blip. Just when I thought I'd lost him, Ted picked up a faint movement on the outer edge of the screen. He shouted instructions to turn me towards it. We had him—range fourteen miles ... still high above us ... I climbed at full throttle and levelled out at 12,000 feet. I had to better his cruising speed while climbing. Although our stripped down TBM was more sprightly than the normal bomber, we were not as fast as our yet unknown blip.

'Again it was a dirty night, with misty cloud and misty rain. Dawn was hours away as we sat and concentrated on the radar approach. Ted brought me up to firing position, at 300 yards I couldn't see a thing, and worried about my last encounter. What if it was one of ours again?

'Then there, before my eyes, was a giant tail, and slowly

the glow of four engines filled my vision. We had hit the jackpot! An Emily. I lined my port wing guns up behind his starboard engines and fired. He reacted instantly, trying every manoeuvre possible to shake me. He went into a steep dive, I held my position, firing into the engines. Nothing happened! Still I clung to him through endless manoeuvres, all done in a steep dive …

'And still no flames! And we had dropped 12,000 feet. The sea was coming up fast! One last burst before I pulled out. As I let go with a hail of bullets, a spurt of flame leapt out of the engine, before my bullets had even reached their target. When they did hit, the spark ignited into a ball of fire and I quickly pulled up and away as an almighty explosion shook the plane and a red glow filled the night sky.'

And then there were three.

Not content with the normal mission each flight, Charlie would then start hunting for enemy aircraft on his way back to the carrier. And he seemed to bump into the enemy regularly.

On this day he was almost home, about fifty miles from the flotilla, when he saw a Tojo. It was a clear, early morning, and Charlie had spotted him visually. He was behind his target, so he eased up to perfect firing range and fired. The enemy took off, smoking but otherwise intact. Charlie didn't have much time to feel disappointed because he then picked up a blip on the radar and the chase was on. It was a Rufe and he pursued the plane for many miles, engaging in more of the manoeuvres he knew all too well from his encounter with the Zero—only this time he had ammo.

Their aerial combat covered forty miles, consisting of strafing runs, tail-chasing, face to face, Chicken runs, hide and seek, attacks out of the sun … all manner of tactics to win.

Finally, in a very steep dive, to pull up on top for the winning position for an attack, Charlie managed to turn inside of the enemy plane, having used wheels down and full flaps. The Rufe tried to turn tighter and spun into the sea.

And then there were four!

At the rate Charlie was engaging the enemy it might have only been another few days before he had his fifth kill, and could have earned his stripes as an 'Ace' in a bomber, but the same day he outmanoeuvred the Rufe and scored his fourth kill, a Kamikaze pilot did a perfectly executed split-S out of cloud cover over the 'Big E' and crashed straight into the deck just behind the main elevator deck that moved the planes from below decks to the flight deck. The elevator was blown a hundred feet into the air and the 'Big E' was out of action. The ship had to go back to the States for major repairs and so never made it back to war, because peace was declared while she was home.

According to Charlie's honourable discharge papers, his war medals were:
American Defense Service Ribbon with 'A' American Area Campaign Ribbon.
Philippine Liberation with 1 Battle Star.
Asiatic-Pacific Area Campaign Ribbon with 7 Battle Stars.
2 Silver Stars.
3 Distinguished Flying Crosses.
3 Air Medals.

And the list would have been a lot longer if his floating base had not been blown out from under him.

He finished the war as Commanding Officer Night Torpedo Squadron–90 USS *Enterprise*. An entry in his first civilian pilot's flight logbook states he flew 1430 hours during the war, from 1942 to 1945.

After the war this enthusiasm for flying continued and Charlie set about to break a few peacetime records. On the 10th September 1951 he flew 27.40 hours straight, from San Francisco to Dalton, Ohio, non-stop in a Piper Pacer NX899-A. Another sixteen-hour trip in April, then

29.10 hours from Idlewild, New York, to La Guardia Airport, New York, via Gander, Newfoundland! Again non-stop. This is some detour, considering the airports are only an hour or so apart. But it was all in preparation for an attempt to fly across the Atlantic non-stop from Newfoundland to England in a single engine plane.

He took off from Gander Airport on the 6th June 1952. The entry in his logbook reads, 'Non-stop flight—took off 12.40 local time. Crashed at end of runway—airborne (120ft) see attached report.' Unfortunately the report is missing.

From 1954 to 1964 he flew 800 hours in the Philippines. Some of those hours I nervously shared. Then in 1965, all this repressed aerial brilliance was unleashed on the poor old Outback of the Northern Territory, and the more unfortunate Department of Civil Aviation in Adelaide. Charlie took to the skies in Australia on April 29th and was a constant problem for DCA from the second the wheels left the strip! Just his record of '225s', no-nos, on file with the Department of Civil Aviation, would fill a book.

When writing this chapter on Charlie's flying I was looking through log books for the dates of the various mishaps. I soon realised that Charlie's flying records were not going to help me because he forgot to fill in the flights most of the time.

At the end of each month he would give his log book to me or one of the children and tell us to look at the meat delivery book from the abattoir. Each invoice would have the date and place of delivery so then his flights for that day could be compiled from the places he delivered to!

Of course the meat invoice didn't list the forced landings etc so I struck upon the idea of calling the Bureau of Air Safety. Charlie has been gone seven years and he stopped flying around 1983. But as soon as I mentioned his name, the man who answered the phone knew all about him. The department was very helpful and sent me a five-page letter listing forty mishaps he had to report!

One of the most memorable of Charles's forced landings was on the 20th September 1971. It was very memorable for me, because I was there!

The plane was full, it was a Cherokee Six, low wing, high speed, fast take-off and landing aircraft. After our first plane, a slow, small Tri-pacer, this plane seemed like a jet. I didn't like it. I found every excuse not to fly in it, and only did so when there was no way I could possibly get out of it. My dislike for this plane was also the reason it didn't have a name, unlike all the other machinery and vehicles on the station.

The Cherokee didn't fit its surroundings. It looked fast, sleek and racy. Totally inconsistent with the slow, rambling, majestic Brahman bulls that ambled by, or the unending, vast, harsh horizons of the Outback. It looked offended—as if it expected a tarmac instead of its rough ground strip. Basically, it expected civilisation!

The day Charles arrived with this plane I told him it didn't fit in. He told me my ideas were silly. But after a while and the many mishaps that befell the plane, he had to admit that maybe there was something in my ramblings.

However, the plane did work very hard, as did everyone and everything in those days. Charlie would pile in a cargo of meat cartons far in excess of the approved weight allowance and would overload the plane to such an extent that the tail would be scraping on the ground. There were times I saw him directing staff to hold the tail up and run along on each side of the plane while he built up enough speed to take-off. As a result, the plane soon lost its racy colt appearance and became a workhorse. But the problem was it wasn't built to be a workhorse—Charlie had the wrong plane doing the wrong job.

On this fateful day—20th September 1971—instead of an

overload cargo of meat cartons, the Cherokee was carrying a full cargo of people and luggage.

The destination was Katherine, 200 miles north-north-east of Bullo on a north-east heading. It was early morning and clear blue skies; a good day for flying. The plane slowly filled with people. Charles was the pilot; John, our manager, was going to town because I had decided he required medical attention. He had been thrown from his horse at a flat gallop while rounding up some wild cattle. Luckily he hadn't broken any bones, but he had landed face-first in a clump of pandanus. His face, arms and neck were now a mass of thorns from the plants, which John hadn't bothered to remove. He'd just got back on the horse and continued after the cattle. The only attention he paid to the thorns was if one became itchy. Then he'd rub or scratch it. By the end of the day, most of the thorns had broken off at skin level, leaving all the tips still embedded in the skin. He went on mustering and ignoring this problem, but after three days he had to come into the homestead to be looked at. The embedded thorns were now infected and swollen, and 'tough, Outback' John was feeling the effects.

Even with my limited knowledge of medicine, one look at him told me he needed to see a doctor. His face and neck were twice their normal size, he could hardly see out of his eyes, and, judging by his colour, blood-poisoning wasn't out of the question.

Of course, being the 'tough, Outback' man, he was dismissing the problem as minor and was counteracting the pain, which had to be intense, with OP rum, protesting all the time that 'it' was nothing and would soon go away.

There is a code for everything in the Outback, and it was especially strong back in those early days. Apparently, according to this code, you didn't go to hospital unless the damage was obvious, impressive and life-threatening. Something like having your leg chopped off; or a broken leg with the bone poking through the skin … or maybe even having your stomach ripped open by a wild bull and half your gut lying on the ground. These were 'tough' injuries. Something all the other 'toughy' stockmen could see. Something very graphic and visual, so they could all suck in their breath through their teeth and say, 'Arrrr, well ... yair. That looks bad. Maybe y'better get it fixed, might make it hard t'ride.' So when a mere woman was now announcing that he should go to hospital, before this tribunal had reached its verdict ... major trauma!

There stood John, as casually as possible, with arms crossed, not folded, across his chest, trying hard to look tough, bleary eyed from lack of sleep, pain and a massive hangover, swaying in the breeze, mulling over the situation—was he sick enough to go to hospital? And would he still have the respect of the stockcamp when he returned? It was a scene straight out of a spaghetti western. They all stood silently, arms crossed. Just in from two weeks out in the stockcamp, dusty, scruffy, unshaven, smelly, silent, waiting, watching the discussion their boss was having with this woman who kept telling them how to do everything. Even told them they had to wash before every meal!

The mercury was climbing fast, making flying very bumpy. The hotter the day became the more uncomfortable the flight. I could see this pow-wow going on forever and, wearying of the stupidity of it all, I said, 'Okay, don't come to town. But you'd better write a will and get your affairs in order, because you'll probably die of blood poisoning within the week.' And with that I busied myself organising the children in their seats and putting on their seatbelts.

There was much mumbling in the ranks behind me. I kept my head down, wondering what next if that little speech didn't convince John. However, the words 'dead' and 'blood poisoning' seemed to carry the required weight, and soon I was hearing instructions for the next week being discussed. There were a few added instructions from Charlie, just to remind everyone who was, in fact, in charge.

Of course Charles had remained silent throughout this whole exchange, watching to see how I handled the situation. If I'd failed to get John on the plane, he would have simply ordered him. But any pulling of rank had luckily been avoided, and John could now board the plane with the 'Yep, it's serious' stamp of approval.

He got into the co-pilot's seat.

The three children were in the back seats or third row and I was sitting in the second row with a carpenter, who was going back to Adelaide to get married, after working on Bullo for a few months. This was his first flight in a small plane, and he had been sitting patiently since first light, waiting to leave.

So, with everyone secured, we taxied out for take-off.

The flight was about two hours and it looked like being a smooth one. Despite the delay, the air was still cool and not a cloud could be seen. After we were airborne, Charles switched to auto-pilot, and his conversation with John turned to the spare parts needed and the mustering details for the coming months. The children were busy reading to each other and to Danielle and playing games and I was dreaming about shops, with mixed feelings—wanting to quietly wander around, looking at all the new products that had appeared on the market since the last time I was in town, but knowing I had to complete the shopping list in my handbag, and that I wouldn't have any time for myself. Of course in the early 1970s there wasn't much in the way of shops in Katherine to get excited about anyway. It was a case of being thrilled to see a new washing trolley with a bright, plastic basket!

Our carpenter was silent; nerves had him gripping the handle of a small case he had on his lap. The handle was in danger of being snapped in half. I chatted with him to take his mind off the flying, but the absentminded nods and lack of any other response showed he was determined to stay nervous.

We were about ten minutes out of Katherine when it happened. Everyone was lulled by the droning of the engine. The children were looking out the window for the airport.

I was also scanning the horizon for the first sign of the Katherine runway. This was necessary when flying with Charlie, because he'd either be in deep conversation with someone or reading a thriller and usually flew right past wherever he was supposed to land.

The plane was still on auto-pilot and Charles was busy drawing a diagram for John. I had my eyes peeled for the airport. At first I didn't believe my eyes, or, more correctly, didn't want to believe them. I blinked a few times, hoping the image would disappear, but when I opened them again, it was still there. With a sinking heart I tugged at Charlie's shirt sleeve. He turned, saw the look of horror on my face and followed my horrified stare to see the oil seeping out from under the cowling and slowly creeping up the windscreen.

He shot into action, called flight service and told them we had a 'slight' problem. Charles's idea of a 'slight' problem was a cam rod up through the top of the engine block. We didn't know this until later, but it was one of a few reasons for oil seeping out of the cowling.

The oil was now about a hand-span wide and moving up the windscreen fast. After telling Katherine we were in emergency mode Charles quickly switched off the auto-pilot and took over the controls. He adjusted the RPM until he had the engine at the lowest possible revs without the plane stalling and falling out of the air. This way the engine pumped less oil out the hole. Charles told John to watch the oil pressure gauge and call out the pressure as it changed. This would give him an indication of how long it would be before the engine seized.

Charles's hands never stopped moving. He was constantly tuning and adjusting the engine, getting every last ounce of performance out of it. Each time John read the oil pressure change, Charles's eyes would quickly scan the ground below and ahead, looking for a likely landing place. I noticed he was staying close to the road leading into Katherine, keeping it as a last resort, not wanting to scare some poor motorist out of their skin as they saw a plane taxiing towards them down the highway.

Our poor old carpenter had gone into deep shock. He was probably seeing himself in church, but not to get married. When I told him to tighten his safety belt because we could have a rough landing, he started to panic. I told him through clenched teeth that I was just as scared as he was, but we had children on board and to 'shut-up'! From that point on he never let out a peep.

The children were still telling stories and reading to their little sister, and keeping an occasional lookout for the airstrip, and were not aware of the drama unfolding up front. As calmly as I could, I told them to tighten their seatbelts, ready for landing. My heart was beating at treble time, but I managed to smile.

As we approached the township, my fears increased. Terrifying thoughts raced through my brain: 'What if the engine fails and we crash into houses?' It was one of the only times I wasn't glad to see civilisation.

Charles had his course set in the shortest, straightest line to touchdown but had edged as far as possible away from the town. But every second of deviation was vital. I held my breath as we passed over the outer edges of Katherine and let out a sigh as trees started to fill the landscape again, with that one black line of the highway leading south stretching out for what seemed forever. It led straight to the airport.

The oil was by now more than halfway up the front of the windscreen, and just before my view was finally blanked out I saw Katherine Airport, straight ahead! We could make it! As the oil pressure got lower, John's voice got higher, and our chances of making the airstrip seemed remote. I was holding my breath for longer periods at this stage. The oil seemed to be spreading faster—although it wasn't really. Imagination is a remarkable thing when you are in a state of anxiety. It was no longer oozing out, the level in the engine was down quite low, and the oil was now spraying out in a fine film which was forming a coating over the whole windscreen. Charles could no longer see out the front of the plane—he was flying the plane at a skewed angle so he could see out the side window, which was about six inches across and used to hand papers to the pilot because there was no door on the pilot's side. He was flying on instruments now to keep the plane level, all the time peering out the window for the airstrip.

We were about 400 yards out from the airstrip. By pressing my face against my oil-spotted window I could just see the white line down the middle of the tarmac. Relief flooded over me—'We're going to make it!' my brain screamed at me. 'We're going to ...' Charles's voice interrupted my brain's celebration ...

'Well, that's done it,' he muttered.

My hand tightened on his arm, asking the unspoken question. He understood the query.

'There's a new safety fence around the airport and it's too high to clear,' he explained. The last time we had landed at Katherine there was just the standard picket and barbed wire fence. Now, in its place, there stood a very high steel mesh one.

The plane had been continually losing height as we approached, and it was clear we were lower than the new fence with still a few hundred yards to go.

'I'll have to land in the paddock outside the fence,' Charles said as he changed course slightly to the new heading: the paddock. 'Hold on tight! This is going to be rough!'

The paddock approached at high speed, the grass was long with ant hills sticking up everywhere. Heaven knows how rough the ground was under all that. I prayed there were no rocks—at least Charlie could see the ant hills and do his best to avoid them.

The ground was whizzing past in a blur. When you're landing on a smooth tarmac, you look out the window and watch the ground flying by and think nothing of it. When you're about to touchdown on the unknown, the speed is terrifying.

Charles was still flying the plane by looking out of the small side-window opening, searching for the best part of the paddock to land in. He quickly handed me his glasses to clean, yet again. I had been doing this constantly for the last five minutes since he had been looking out the hole. I quickly wiped the lenses clean and handed them back to the impatient, flicking hand. The front of my skirt was now covered with little circles of dark oil.

My face went straight back to pressing against the window, which was now fogged over with a fine mist of sprayed oil. But I could still just see what lay ahead. There was one more visible obstacle before touchdown: a barbed-wire fence.

We were sinking fast, Charles had the engine just turning over, keeping as much pressure as possible off the now almost oilless engine, not wanting it to fail at these last few crucial seconds. The fence was approaching at an alarming speed—it now looked thirty feet tall instead of three! John was at the screaming stage as he read the oil pressure. 'It's zero! It's zero!' he shrieked.

'I know, John. You can stop now,' Charles replied quietly. But John had his head against the instrument panel, eye-ball to eye-ball with the oil gauge, and he kept repeating 'zero', over and over. Charles yanked him back into upright position and told him to brace himself for landing.

The carpenter was praying, rapidly. I was so nervous I was numb, and just watched the approaching fence as if hypnotised. Marlee's hand came up and over the back of my seat to tap me on the shoulder and a little voice came from behind the seat, 'Will we be much longer? I need to go to the bathroom.' I had my face pressed against the window, willing the plane over the fence.

'Wait!' was my only answer.

'Mummy?' It was Bonnie's turn, her sister had said something, so now she had to get in on the act. 'Mummy, you have to tell Daddy something very important.'

'Not now! Daddy is busy.' We were almost to the fence.

I watched with horror as I realised we were lower than it. My mind screamed, 'Dear God! We are not going to clear it!' We were skimming above the high grass.

Bon's voice came to me again, more urgent this time. I couldn't take my eyes from the disaster looming ahead.

'Mummy! Mummy! You have to tell Daddy he's landing in the wrong place! The airstrip is over there, out my window. Tell him I can see it!'

Charles straightened the plane for landing, and suddenly we were flying blind! He pushed in the throttle to full power, the plane gave a lurch and the wheels hit the top wire of the fence. There was enough power in the last power surge and the wheels rolled over, but snapped the wire as we whooshed by. We were over! Visions of the plane flipping over and bursting into flames faded from my mind as we continued our blind rush forward. The engine had seized on the last surge of power and for a few seconds we were suspended in midair and silent, floating blind; then there was an almighty crunch as the plane fell the last few feet to the ground. Then we were racing along the ground blind. Charles could only see by looking out of the little window, and he could only do that by crouching. Since we had hit the ground he had been fighting the controls and now had to sit bolt upright with arms braced to take the jolts as the plane hit each unknown obstacle. We continued our helter-skelter rush along the ground. He had picked out the best area he could see on the approach; now he was committed, hoping he was keeping the plane on a fairly straight course.

The wheels held and suddenly we were lurching violently in our seats as the plane careered through the long grass, veering violently as we hit pot holes and other unknowns. The screeching of ant hills hitting and scraping along the wings and fuselage has stayed clearly in my mind to this day.

'Mummy?!' the children's frightened voices came to me above the squealing metal. That one word, so full of questions.

'Hang on!' I shouted. 'Hang on! It'll all be over in a minute.' But the screeching and twisting of metal continued to drown out everything as the plane lunged and thumped blindly along.

It seemed to go on forever. I didn't know if it was good or bad, not being able to see what was ahead. I think this made the whole feeling unreal. Slowly I realised the grass was no longer passing the window in a blur, the tearing of metal had stopped, I was not being jerked violently against the seatbelt. The plane had stopped! We were safe on the ground. The silence took over.

The first sound I remember was the siren of the firetruck somewhere in the distance. Charles had his head resting on his hands on top of the instrument panel; John sat staring straight ahead at the oil-covered windscreen; the children were crying quietly; I realised I was holding my breath again, and let out a long sigh.

Charles was first to recover. 'Well that was close,' his voice still with a trace of a quiver in it. He had done a miraculous job of even getting the plane as far as he did, but the landing was nothing short of brilliant. When Charlie came through, he came through in spectacular style.

I released my seatbelt in slow motion. I seemed to be in a bubble—I was moving, but I didn't feel any part of my body.

Charles shut down all the switches on the instrument panel and leaned over to me.

'Get the children out and away from the plane as quickly as possible. There's still a danger of fire.'

I turned to see if they were all right. They sat there, the three of them in a straight line, tears streaming down their faces, their lower lips trembling slightly, not at all sure what was going on, but not liking any of it. I patted their hands and said it was okay, Daddy had landed the plane and we were all safe. But we had to get out of the plane quickly. I reached over and opened the door next to Marlee and told her to take her sisters over to a nearby tree, away from the plane, and sit there. There were no doors for the second row of seats, so I had to wait for Charles and John to get out of the plane. Our carpenter clambered over the back of his seat and followed the children to the tree and collapsed there.

I was grateful to sit and wait. Even though fire was foremost in my mind I knew my legs were jelly and there was no way I would be able to stand. Charlie's hand came in the door and helped me out of the seat and down off the wing.

I walked shakily over to the children. They had regained most of their composure and were looking at the whole event in typical, child-like, critical observation.

Marlee opened with, 'Gee, Daddy sure made a mess of that landing.' To which an almost-recovered Bon replied, 'That's because the airstrip is over there. I keep telling everyone, but no one will listen. This isn't even an airstrip!'

I smiled in spite of myself.

Suddenly there was a terrible crashing noise and I spun around to see the firetruck crashing through the new security fence, followed closely by an ambulance. They both came to an abrupt halt near the plane and people started running everywhere. We were having trouble coordinating our own movements—poor John had managed to walk to the front of the plane and was now leaning on the propeller for support, trying to roll himself a cigarette, oblivious of the fire danger. His hands were shaking so much that he kept losing all the tobacco by the time he had the paper secured. He finally succeeded and was about to light up when one of the firemen rushed over and knocked the cigarette out of his mouth.

'No naked flames at the scene of the accident!' he shouted, looking John up and down and taking in the scruffy, bleary-eyed face and the dirty clothes. 'Who are you anyway? No outsiders allowed at the scene of the accident. Go away!'

'But I'm one of the passengers,' said John, hanging off the propeller.

'Oh, sorry! Stretcher!' And before John could protest he was lying down and being bustled into the ambulance.

'Anyone else injured?' the ambulance man asked, running around to each of us. But luckily, except for our nerves being completely shot, we all seemed to be in one piece. However, the carpenter had by now gone into the shakes so was promptly given something to calm him.

We got into the airport security car and headed for the terminal.

Charles filled out the required accident reports, made arrangements for the plane to be moved and then we went straight to the hotel. Once there, he made more calls to insurance companies, but before long we were all in a deep sleep, brought on by shock. We slept most of the day, only getting up for dinner, then slept all through the night.

John got to hospital a lot faster than he thought he would, and was there a lot longer as well. It took more than a day to get all the thorn tips out of the infected lumps that had formed all over his upper body and face.

But even though still badly swollen, he looked a new man the next day when we visited him. Although very restless. He asked if he could speak to Charles in private; the children and I wandered out into the garden.

Charles joined us not long after with a smile on his face. It seemed John had asked him to smuggle a bottle of rum into the hospital. Going one day without his usual few shots per night was bringing on the DTs and he was very embarrassed.

We went and bought the rum. Of course Charlie wanted me to be the smuggler; I flatly refused and made him do the dirty deed.

We put the still shaking carpenter on the bus to Adelaide, then went back to the hotel and slept again for most of the day.

The next day we were seemingly back to normal, and it was on with life and the job.

That was one trip to town I will never forget, and

although Charles loved a challenge I have a feeling that this time it was just a little too close for comfort, with too many lives at stake.

Charles arranged to lease another aircraft for the time the Cherokee was out of action, and we flew home a few days later, everyone very nervous and not enjoying one minute of the flight. I secretly hoped the Cherokee would be out of action forever. As I'd said, I didn't like it from the first day, and the flight to Katherine merely strengthened my opinion. I renewed my efforts not to fly in it.

The 'bad luck' plane soon proved my instincts right again. This time though the engine cut out in mid flight and didn't start again, forcing Charlie to crash-land out in the middle of nowhere. He had Marlee and Bon with him. Danielle was at home with me.

He was flying a load of meat to Bathurst Island and then they were going on to Darwin. It was mid afternoon when the message came through that there had been a Mayday signal from Charlie to the control tower in Darwin. Then nothing. The Search and Rescue helicopters were out looking.

I sat at the desk for what seemed like ages, all sorts of dreadful thoughts racing in and out of my mind. Danielle, standing at my side shaking my arm, brought me back to reality. I realised I just couldn't sit around imagining the worst, I had to do something.

We had a radio telephone in those days, and to call out you first had to wait for a line to the switchboard, the outpost radio service, VJY in Darwin. To get a line to an operator you watched a red light on the front of the phone, when it blinked off you pressed a button and this rang the switchboard, that is if you were lucky enough to get through. My reflexes were so slowed by shock I took quite a while to connect, and when I did manage it the line was so bad the operator could not hear me. I could hear her, because of the powerful transmitter in Darwin, but our radio signal could not be picked up that far away in bad weather.

It was very frustrating being able to hear Darwin, knowing they could give me an answer, but not being able to talk to them, and I was in tears when I put the phone down. It rang another two times that evening but I couldn't even hear the operator, just a lot of static and whirring and whistling.

I went through the process of making dinner and talking with some of the staff that came up to the house for various reasons. For reasons I cannot explain, I did not pass on the news. I suppose I had just decided in my mind that they were all right.

I carried out the bedtime ritual with Danielle, finding comfort in the routine of it all. She was bathed and dressed in her pyjamas, and extra time was taken over the hair-brushing. I didn't want the time to end because when she was asleep I would be alone. She finally told me I was taking too long, so reluctantly I moved on to the next phase, storytelling. Which thankfully went on for hours, before she fell asleep in the middle of asking a question. I kissed her on the cheek and went out of the room to face the night.

There weren't a lot of nights where I faced this terrible uncertainty, but on these few occasions I really did feel the isolation of the Outback. If I could have called my family or friends and just talked, it would have made the night a bit more bearable. But the phone was useless. I didn't even have latenight radio to listen to. I had silent company—books, and my dogs, watching my every move, knowing by instinct that I was very upset. They were watching and alert, to see if the danger that was unsettling me was real.

I played music all night, had the lights on, read books, stroked the dogs and paced the floor. I sat and looked at the night sky for hours, wondering if Charlie and the girls were out there somewhere doing the same thing and thinking of home; or were they injured, were they … No! They were safe. I just knew it.

I dozed off a few times in the chair, but would wake with a start, out of a bad dream. There was very little sleeping done.

With the first faint suggestion of sunrise, I heard a plane

engine. It had to have taken off in the dark to have reached Bullo at that time. This still didn't indicate if it was good or bad news. I watched with bated breath as the plane landed and approached the homestead. It was not ours. Fear rose and constricted the muscles in my neck, making my breathing fast and difficult. I watched as the plane taxied into the parking area; the propeller gave a 'thunk' and stopped. I could hear my heart thumping in my ears. Then the door of the plane opened and the children exploded out and raced across the flat, followed by a smiling, slow-walking Charlie.

Relief flooded over me at the sight of them all safe. Danielle ran out to her sisters, asking if they had brought her any chocolates. The girls were shouting, 'Mummy! 'Mummy! Oh boy! Wait till you hear what happened to us!' And I sagged into a nearby chair, thinking, 'I can just imagine.' Or could I?

They both spoke at once, non-stop, so excited now the words were tumbling out, falling over each other. I sat and let it all wash over me, just so happy they were alive.

I cooked breakfast and still they continued, somehow managing to get the food down without stopping. When the story and breakfast were finished it was then outside for another day of fun and games. A school holiday was declared for many reasons, but mainly because the teacher hadn't slept all night, and was a mess.

After they had bolted out the door, with Danielle close in tow, Charles and I sat in the living room with a pot of coffee and he told me his version of events ...

They were about sixty miles from Bullo over the swamp area of Port Keats, between the Moil and the Daly rivers, when the propeller just went clunk, and that was that. Charles tried to start the engine again but it was completely dead. It was later determined that both magnetos had failed, cutting all connection with the engine and instruments.

Charles knew not to waste time on an engine with no response, the plane was going down fast. The low wing aircraft was not at all aerodynamic and was dropping like a stone. He had to find a clear area for a forced landing. The plane was over a very swampy area, which was thick with trees. Charlie's eyes frantically scanned the landscape for that lifesaving stretch of clear space. He could see the road off to his right, but it was too far to glide. He smiled when he thought of gliding—the plane was falling out of the sky, about as skyworthy as a dodo.

All these thoughts travelled at the speed of machine gun bullets through his mind as his eyes continued at the same speed to survey the scene below. But then, just when he was convinced he would have to drop into the treetops, there it was, their only chance!

Off to his left was a billabong—a large billabong, surrounded by trees—but there in the middle was blessed, clear space. It looked very narrow from where Charlie was sitting, but he would have to do the best he could, he thought, as he adjusted the plane's approach. The plane came in fast, silent and powerless. He only had one chance to get it right, there was no going around again. The little girls were strapped in as tightly as possible, watching breathlessly as their daddy manoeuvred the silent plane to a perfect water touchdown. There was an abrupt jolt when the wheels hit the water and started to sink. Charles fought with the controls to keep on a straight course. The drag of the wheels in the water and the plane's speed were pulling against him; he was locked in a battle for control. The wheel assembly, designed to shear off on impact, did so, and there was another lurch as the plane flopped onto its belly at high speed. The controls felt free of the wheel drag and Charles brought the plane in fairly level, with the tail, wheels and nose hitting the water in quick succession. The drag on the wheels before they collapsed tipped the plane forward and it lifted onto its nose, skimming along, surfing at high speed. The biggest worry was flipping over—Charles didn't know how deep the billabong was and if the plane went over on its back, and they were knocked unconscious, they could drown, even in a few feet of water. Keeping the plane upright therefore was top priority, along with keeping it on a straight course and avoiding the trees.

Perversely, however, this time Charles's habit of over-loading his planes to extreme probably now saved it from flipping over—even though the overloading no doubt was the reason for the engine failure in the first place. The very heavy load of meat cartons weighed the tail down, and the plane eventually flopped back down into the water. The rocking-horse motion continued as the plane raced towards the thick stand of trees at the end of the billabong, all the while churning up the water. Charles could do nothing to stop this forward dash, could only hope the plane would stop before they ran out of water. If they hit the trees, it would not be at the impact of the first touchdown, he re-assured himself as the trees loomed larger and larger. The plane swung around and came to rest at an angle, with one wing up in the air and the other in the water in under the trees. The crazy-shaped propeller blades were framed in the windscreen like a painting, the wheels were down at the other end of the billabong.

The silence after the crash was slowly invaded as the sounds of the new surroundings started to permeate the little world of the plane cabin. The occupants sat there, gathering their senses, adjusting to the fact that they were now in a totally new environment.

The biggest worry was the depth of the water. During the moments they had spent gathering their senses, Charles had been conscious of his wet feet! He could clearly hear the sound of water bubbling into the cabin. He quickly turned to the children, who, stunned, scared and excited, all at the same time, looked back at him in childlike amazement. He was relieved to see from all appearances that they were all right. I was always foremost in his mind when it came to the children's safety, he often told me. He would never have been able to face me if something happened to them because of something he had done. He said the image of a raging lioness always came to his mind. So whether it was fear of me, or his pure skill at flying that was responsible for the safe landing, we will never know. But somehow Charles did manage to safely land a non-gliding, powerless aircraft in a billabong with barely twelve-inch clearance on each wing-tip without even breaking the radio wire!

The realisation that water was lapping at his ankles suddenly jolted him back into action. Even though he was on the low side of the plane, he had to get the children out, just in case. He was fairly confident they were in shallow water, but he wasn't taking any chances; his day so far had not been what one could call pleasing.

He forced the door open with the heel of his shoe, then carefully eased himself onto the wing, the plane lurching with his weight. After each movement he paused, letting it settle again. The eerie sound of water bubbling into the cabin made the hair stand up on the back of his neck. He twisted around and whispered to the girls to slowly edge forward. They did so, gripping him tightly, their eyes never leaving his face, waiting for the next instruction. If Daddy was whispering, then things had to be very serious indeed.

The fear of being trapped underwater in a cockpit had lived with Charles since his carrier days during the war. He had had recurring nightmares of it happening when his plane was launched off the deck and started to 'settle'. It never had. Yet here he was, thirty years later, in the middle of Outback Australia, the driest continent on the planet, crash-landed in water—and sinking!

He moved the children out the door, eased them onto the roof of the cabin and told them to stay put. He eased himself to the edge of the wing and lowered his feet into the billabong. The plane resettled with a crunch, his feet hit the soft mud with a thump, the water made a high water mark just above his knees ... and Charles let out a deep sigh of relief. One major disaster averted. The next step was to see if the radio still worked. He saw with satisfaction that the aerial was still intact, so he got back into the cockpit and started flipping switches.

Soon the crackle of the radio filled the silence of the billabong. Charles had called in a Mayday when the engine had failed, but had had no time for further communication, and didn't know if he'd been heard anyway. As it happened, Darwin Flight Service had heard, and were still searching the airways for him. He now gave them the crash location and was told the Search and Rescue helicopter was on its way. Charles said he would call in at fifteen minute intervals and turned off the radio to save the battery. Then all they had to do was wait ... Although it wasn't going to be as easy as that. The plane was right in under trees and couldn't be seen from above. This meant the helicopter would have to land out in the swamp area on the other side of the thick trees around the billabong. Charles didn't relish sloshing around in the swamp for too long. He knew, didn't have to guess, that this was crocodile country. The crocs would be very old and very big in this remote area, and probably not too pleased to have their midday siesta disturbed by a crashing plane. He decided then and there that if, for some reason, he and the children had to spend the night there, it would be in the plane with the doors *locked*.

Charles decided to get organised. He directed the children to soak all the rags in fuel and follow him. They were going to have to signal. Under their father's watchful eye they crawled under the high wing and Marlee pushed in the valve on the outlet, while Bon held all the rags on the end of a stick under the flow of avgas until they were drenched, getting instructions from her sister not to get the fuel on her skin. And more instructions to wash thoroughly after the job just in case. A few of the towelling seat covers were also added to the bonfire material, for good measure. When they had completed this task, Charles wrapped the lot in another seat cover and had the girls climb up one of the trees to attach the rags to the branches with some of the cargo tiedown rope. They were now ready to signal. The girls stayed aloft and watched for the chopper's approach; Charles checked again on the radio for the latest on the helicopter's position.

When he finally heard the engine, the chopper was way off course to the south. He told the girls to come down out of the tree and climbed up to light the material himself. By the time he had climbed back down and was in the plane speaking on the radio, the rags were burning fiercely and sending up a good column of smoke. Charles told Darwin Flight Service to tell the chopper to head for the smoke. Flight Service passed on the message and told Charles what frequency to change to, to talk directly to the helicopter. The children climbed another tree and watched where the chopper landed in the swamp. The only spot clear enough to get the chopper into was a fair distance from the billabong. Charles and the girls had to climb through the undergrowth surrounding the billabong and then wade across the swamp to their rescuers. Charles put Bonnie on his shoulders and kept Marlee close by his side, just in case. After all the noise he'd made crash-landing the plane and then the further disturbance from the helicopter, he felt sure the crocs would stay away. He handed the little girls to the rescue team and relaxed in his seat beside them. As the helicopter lifted off the ground he saw his crash site, as it grew smaller and smaller. The rescue team had been amazed how he had landed the plane without any damage, missing trees on each side by only feet and with no power. Now, when he looked down from the helicopter and had time to analyse the situation, he had to admit it was a pretty exceptional bit of flying on his part.

And so the legend of Charlie's flying exploits grew and grew.

He organised everyone as soon as he arrived in Darwin and completed all the paperwork for yet another forced landing. He made sure the children were settled for the night and arranged another plane to fly back to the station the next day. Apparently he tried many times to get through to me, but it was impossible to hear on the radio telephone at that time of night. He knew I'd be worried—for me to be told that he and the children had crashed and then to hear nothing more! Well!

He sat and watched the sun set in the west, knowing I would be sitting looking towards Darwin, looking for that flickering light, almost out of habit. He wished he could have saved me the worry, but knew he couldn't. He told himself he would take-off, very, very early in the morning and that everything would be all right when I saw the two children safe and sound. However, he wasn't so sure how happy I'd be to see him.

But sitting here, now, he told me I had looked a little pleased to see him—and he paused to seek confirmation. I had to tell him I thought he deserved another medal. He leaned back on his chair, balancing on the back two legs, his feet on the table, with his hands clasped behind his head, a smug look on his face, and smiled. He didn't speak. He didn't have to. The expression said it all: 'Yes, I do, don't I!'

Alas, the saga wasn't completely over yet. The plane still had to be recovered from its watery grave. It had very little structural damage and was resting in fresh water, so, much to my disappointment, was repairable.

By now my aversion to the Cherokee Six was all out of proportion. First a forced landing, then engine failure. And all in only seventeen months.

Since we had had such a bad run with this particular aircraft, I was genuinely relieved when Charlie finally admitted he was expecting far too much from this plane and that because it really wasn't built for the work he was expecting it to do, it had to go. So between February and June there were a lot of different planes hired and fired, while Charlie looked for the ultimate workhorse.

At one stage he was looking at an agricultural spraying plane because it could carry a ton load. It was pointed out to him that these planes were loaded by a hopper twelve feet up in the air, and just how did he think the meat cartons were going to be loaded? He replied that he'd use a ladder and someone inside to stack them. Easy! When he was asked how *he* was going to unload at the other end, the plane was immediately struck off the list. When he had to do the work it was a different matter. Of course we didn't let him off that easy. I said he could have a bracket made and he could carry his ladder under the fuselage and use a gaff hook and rope to hook each carton of meat and haul it out. I was told not to be cheeky.

Charlie finally found his workhorse in a De Havilland Beaver which he bought from Savage Airlines, Mittagong. Her call sign was Echo-Papa-X-Ray. We called her Bertha the Second. Like Bertha the First, she was expected to do the impossible.

Bertha the Second withstood the test. She was with us from June 1974 to August 1980. It seemed much longer than that; after a while it was as if there had never been any other plane in our life. This plane had a heart and soul.

It was a while before Charlie had the time or money to have the large Savage Airlines sign on both sides of the plane painted out, so people would regularly ask Charles what route the airline flew. He got so sick of telling them the plane was private that he finally had the children paint out the sign one weekend. But this didn't help that much—the plane just seemed to attract attention; and with Charlie as the other part of the equation, you had a very unusual combination.

On one of my rare trips to town I was walking back to the plane with parcels and could see a group of women tourists clustered around the plane. As I drew nearer, there was Charlie posing, his arm casually draped over the propeller, smiling his best debonair smile, cameras clicking all around him. A little later, as I passed them on their way back to the airport terminal, I heard one say in an American drawl, 'Fancy finding the Southern Cross out here in the middle of nowhere!' To which another said, 'And still flying too. And by such a charming American, no less!'

I gave Charlie one of those, 'What have you been up to?' looks, and he replied, 'Well, they said the plane looked old and famous, so I didn't like to disappoint them.'

They were right about the old and famous—Bertha certainly was old and, in the Outback at least, very famous. But to believe it was the Southern Cross ...! So now I expect in America there are a lot of photos of Bertha being passed around as the famous Southern Cross, still being flown in the Outback of Australia, and, what's more, by an American! 'And here's the photo to prove it.'

There are so many stories about Bertha; she did some unbelievable things and carried some astounding loads ...

In one of our extremely unorganised years—most years were hopelessly unorganised but this one was a nightmare—Charles did not order the fuel for the Wet Season early enough and the heavy rains washed out the road before there was a truck available to make the delivery. The fuel on hand ran out in mid February, so from then until late April, when our road was opened, Bertha carried 195 44-gallon drums of diesel over the mountain from the Auvergne Station airstrip to Bullo.

Once, when her engine had to be replaced, Charlie talked an engineer into coming to Bullo for a fishing holiday and to change the engine at the same time. It was the beginning of the rainy season.

The stay was very memorable ... for the engineer.

Uncle Dick made a steel scaffolding the height of the engine, about seven feet from the ground. The new engine was on the platform ready to be installed and Dick was just putting a tripod in position to lift the engine into place. There was a massive canvas rigged over the front of the plane and the scaffolding for shade, when out of nowhere came one of the first storms of the season, travelling at one hundred miles an hour.

Before Uncle Dick and the engineer knew what was happening, Bertha was flying—without an engine; and the scaffolding was flying *with* an engine. The canvas was gathering so much wind that everything was about to be airborne and go down the airstrip behind it, not in an organised manner. The engineer was trying to hold on to the engine so it didn't fall off the platform, Dick was helping him; and they were both screaming for help. The canvas tiedowns were all attached to the plane and the scaffolding.

Everyone came running. Charlie instructed us all to sit on the scaffolding frame to hold it down while he untied the ropes of the canvas. He untied the back ties and the canvas immediately spilled its wind and became harmless again, except for its violent flapping.

The engine was finally installed and Charlie flew the engineer back to town in Bertha, for him to catch his flight south.

One time a DCA inspector came to the station to investigate an accident involving Bertha. Charlie was taking off one morning with a full, too full, load and at that crucial time, just before lift-off, a pig ran out onto the airstrip, in front of the plane. The load was too heavy for Charlie to pull up and he wouldn't clear the pig. He was also going too fast to swerve. So he jumped over the pig and then applied the brakes after he hit ground again. He ran out of airstrip and at the last minute, right on the fence line, he swerved sharply. The wing dipped and was ripped and damaged on the barbed-wire fence. The accident was reported and the plane went in for repair and a structural check of the wing.

A few months before this accident, there was another. An Aero Club plane hit a horse on the Bullo strip on take-off. Again the end of the wing was damaged. The DCA inspector came to Bullo to file the report before flying back to Adelaide. The Aero Club had to lift the damaged plane out by helicopter, over the hill, to the Auvergne strip, then truck it to Darwin for repair. Our road was too rough.

The wings were taken off and the helicopter lifted the

fuselage and headed for the hills. Only 500 yards from the house the load started to swing dangerously. We stood and watched as the chopper pilot struggled with his pendulum cargo. He couldn't bring it under control and had no choice but to drop the plane, or the helicopter would have crashed.

We drove out to the crash site. The plane was a great deal flatter and was surrounded by cows, all sniffing this strange thing that had interrupted their grazing. The fuselage was a write-off, so the Aero Club went home with a spare pair of wings.

The DCA inspector, who had just arrived back in Adelaide from Bullo, now had to turn around and fly back to investigate this next accident!

He went back and forth so many times checking accidents on the Bullo airstrip he made up a poem! I can't remember all of it but the last two lines were, 'But if the horses don't get you, Then the pigs certainy will!'

However, I think my most memorable event with Bertha would have to be on the Darwin jet runway.

I was going to Sydney for a well-earned holiday with my sister. Charles had gone to deliver meat to Port Keats mission and was to come back to take me to Darwin. He was late, as usual, and I was sure I'd miss the plane. So I decided to go and have a whole day in Darwin and catch the plane the next day.

Charles eventually turned up and we had a tail wind all the way to Darwin and made up time; it looked like I might just make the plane. Charles called the tower and asked for permission to land. They told him 'negative', the Singapore jet was already approaching at 5000 feet. Charles was told to go around again and 'hold'. He told them he had to get me on the jet going to Sydney, and he could duck in before the jet and be off the strip while the jet was still descending. The tower told him okay, to land short and leave the runway early.

Everything was going according to plan and Charles touched down on the piano keys, then the left brake seized.

With only one brake, the plane goes round and round in circles, and if you're not a very skilled pilot the plane can ground loop. We were now travelling in ever-increasing circles down the runway, Charlie just managing to keep the plane from ground looping by using the throttle and power. Slowly he regained control and we stopped.

We were sitting, breathing deeply to recover our composure, when the voice from the control tower penetrated the silence of the cockpit.

'Can we assume that you are landed, Mr Henderson?'

Charlie gathered himself. 'Oh yes. Sorry. But my left brake has failed, had a bit of trouble.'

'We're pleased. Thought it might be one of your new landings.' A slight touch of sarcasm in the voice.

Charles just ignored it. 'No, just brakes.'

'Do you think you could manage to get the plane off the airstrip? The Singapore jet is in danger of running out of fuel.'

'Roger, roger,' Charles told the tower, then turned to me and said, 'Quickly, get out and push!'

'What are you talking about? It's three miles to the terminal!'

'We have to get off the strip and I can't steer with only one brake! You don't have to push the plane, Sara, just push against the side to keep it straight and that will make it possible for me to steer.' Charles's idea of my not pushing the plane, just holding it straight, was for me to push against the side of the eight-seater aircraft, which is very heavy, while running alongside it as he was taxiing!

I was dressed in a tight skirt, stockings and high-heeled shoes, in temperatures of forty degrees or so. I lasted about a hundred feet before I lost a shoe, I bent down to pick it up and the tail of the plane knocked me clear over. I now had gravel rash and cuts on my hands and knees, the knees out of my stockings, the heel broken on my shoe and the plane had swung around and the propeller was chasing me. Charlie was hanging out the window, screaming over the engine noise, 'The Singapore jet wants to land! Keep pushing!' I got out of the way of the propeller and climbed up to Charlie's window and told him to call the tower and get some help, well I opened with a few unprintable phrases first. Especially one about what he could do with the Singapore jet. In the meantime I told him we could just push the plane onto the grass at the edge of the tarmac so the jet could land.

Charlie steered the plane towards the grass and I pushed to hold it straight. The airport security car arrived and we watched as the Singapore jet whooshed by to touchdown. Charlie explained I was to be on that plane to Sydney, so we got in the car and were driven over to the steps to board. One of the security men rushed my luggage through, telling me not to worry—just to go on board and they would fix everything. And then Charles led an exhausted me over to the air hostesses.

I looked a mess. My hands and knees were skinned and bleeding, the bottoms were out of my stockings which were now flapping around my ankles, the heel was missing off one shoe, my skirt had split right up to my backside, my face was beetroot red and my hair, which had been in the propeller wash, was standing on end.

'My wife is going to Sydney. She's been sick,' Charles kindly whispered to the air hostess as he handed me over.

She carefully led me up the stairs, seated me and brought a wet cloth to wash my face, hands and knees. I thanked her and just slid down in the seat to hide.

As the plane taxied out to the distant runway to take-off, we passed Bertha taxiing along with Charles shouting orders out the window at three security guards who were pushing against Bertha's fuselage to keep her straight!

I pulled the shade down and flew to Sydney.

Since Bertha was sold, the new owners have completely refurbished her, inside and out and put on floats. For a while she carried marlin fishermen out to the outer Barrier Reef and landed just inside the reef and met the marlin boats.

She was then disassembled and packed in a crate and shipped to California. She now lives the life of luxury, a rich man's toy and only goes flying around to beautiful lakes to Club meets for Amphibious enthusiasts. She flies to lakes around the border of Canada not far from where she was born, all those years ago; she has done the full circle. She worked long and hard and fully deserves her now wonderful lifestyle!

Next there was Snoopy. Snoopy was a Taylor J2 Cub. Charlie bought her in Sydney in June 1971, at the same time we had bought the Cherokee Six. She was a delightful plane, painted white with black and white checks on the tips of the wings and the tail and nose. There was a wonderful picture of Snoopy, complete with flying helmet, goggles and the red scarf, just next to the pilot's door.

Snoopy had the same self-assured, arrogant expression as Charlie.

The J2 was the original Super Cub and went back so far that you really did fly by 'the seat of your pants'. The instrument panel wouldn't confuse you: there were only four things on it and one of them was a calendar. I suppose it took so long to get anywhere, you needed a calendar to keep track of the days! The fuel gauge was a knob on the top of the wings, which went into the fuel tanks and was attached to a float. The system was simple—when the knob was resting on the top of the wing, you were out of fuel. As long as you could see a space between the knob and the top of the tank, you were okay.

Like everything and everyone on Bullo, Snoopy accomplished work far beyond the capabilities printed in the operator's manual.

She had no hangar and stood out in the weather. This wasn't good, but nowhere near as damaging as the goats that insisted on running up and down the fuselage and jumping off the tail. As a result she soon had holes where their sharp feet had cut into the fabric. This little bit of fun was carried out at night until someone woke up and heard them. Then we would rush out with sticks and chase them away. It was soon evident that we were not going to get much sleep if Snoopy was to be protected, so the goats had to go. They had made such a mess of the tail fabric that it had frayed and was so damaged that the holes made flying dangerous—the air could flow through the holes, affecting the lift and control of the plane. With his skill Charles could overcome this problem in the short-term, but the tail had to be repaired as soon as time allowed. He decided that we, meaning me, could make a new cover a lot cheaper than if he had it done in Darwin, so he gave me the honour of sewing a new tail on Snoopy, all by hand. This would have been a massive job for a dedicated seamstress. However, I hated sewing and told Charlie so in positive tones.

He tried many of the other employees and could not find anyone remotely interested, so he continued to fly with threads trailing from his tail. The plane was used mostly on the station so this '225' ('no-no') under the DCA ruling for air safety went unnoticed by the outside world.

But not for long.

One day Charlie flew over to the mustering camp at Leslie Lake. He left in the morning, saying he would be there most of the day but would be back mid afternoon to do some paperwork before going to Darwin the next morning.

As the afternoon turned into sunset and he didn't arrive, I didn't worry. I thought he had probably become involved in the muster and forgotten the time. Just on sunset he walked into the kitchen. I said hello and said I hadn't heard the plane land. He replied that was because he hadn't landed the plane. It was then I noticed he was standing in a puddle of water, his clothes soaking wet. He told me he had crashed Snoopy on the other side of the river, had swum across and walked home. The stockmen had killed a steer for meat and were packing up and coming back from the camp the next day, so Charles was bringing the whole steer back to the homestead in the plane. But the load was too heavy, the grass where he took off, too long, and the run up too short. He took off and tried to clear the top of a big dead tree. Snoopy, because of the holes in her tail, could not get the normal lift. Charles, in turn, couldn't bank to avoid the tree—he was committed to going straight ahead until he'd gained a bit of height. But Snoopy could not lift those extra few feet in time, and ploughed straight into the tree with a clunk. Snoopy's propeller, which was made of wood, just snapped off and the plane slid down the tree and hit the ground with a wallop. 'Something like hitting a brick wall in slow motion,' were Charles's words when I asked him what it was like to hit a tree. It really is only something you see in a comedy!

But the story wasn't over by a long shot. DCA would have to investigate the crash. They could not see the tail fabric in the condition it was in. Anyone could tell the holes didn't occur in the crash! Charles would lose his licence for flying the plane in the state it was in. Or that was the story he told me anyway to get me to go out there in the middle of the bush and sit and sew a new tail on to the crashed plane.

It took days, camping out at night, sewing all day. My fingers felt as if they would fall off. Then the material was painted with fabric paint, with dirt rubbed in to get rid of the 'just painted' look, and the plane was ready for the DCA accident inspector. Who, I might add, had been told of the accident a week or so after the event.

I could have saved my time and fingers. DCA knew Charles was flying the plane with a holey tail. He had been into town weeks before the crash and someone at the airport had reported him. So the cover-up was a waste of time. He still got a '225'!

My other favourite plane was WOO. She was almost as famous as Bertha. The girls and I all learned to fly in WOO. We spent hours going up and down the airstrip, learning to taxi with the tail up.

Like Snoopy, and all his planes for that matter, Charles

put loads in WOO far in excess of the limit. But she had a powerful engine and he couldn't find enough space inside to load her to the point of dangerous *over*loading. So Charles would squeeze in all the cargo he could find and WOO would still lift it.

Although there was one trip he had her to the limit …

He was bringing supplies in from Auvergne Station—it was one year when our road was still closed and Charlie wanted to start mustering early. So instead of waiting till the Department of Roads got their machinery in to fix the road, he started bringing in what we needed over the mountain by air.

He had finished a few journeys and it was taking him a lot longer than expected. WOO was a smaller plane than Bertha, so there were a number of trips to go, and Charles was not patient! He still had five stockmen left to bring over the hill, or I should say 'ringers', the brave men who caught wild scrubber bulls by jumping off a galloping horse and grabbing the bull's tail. But as brave as they were, Charlie soon had them scared silly, while flying in WOO.

WOO was a two-seater, so by rights Charlie should have made three more trips to bring the men over the hill. But Charlie decided to bring them all in in one trip!

I couldn't believe my eyes when WOO came in to land. Charlie had an Aboriginal stockman sitting on each wing strut. Their eyes were so big they could have doubled as headlights! Charlie had wedged a cushion to make seats where the struts bolted onto the fuselage. He thought it was a really comfortable seat. He turned to the two ringers, who still hadn't moved, even though the plane was now on the ground and the engine had stopped.

'Wasn't it comfortable?' he asked.

They just nodded.

'See,' continued Charlie. 'I had the window down, so we could talk about the area we were flying over, and look for cattle and work out the musters. It was a really helpful trip.' Charlie was very pleased with himself.

There were another two ringers in the seat behind Charlie and one more standing hunched over in the luggage space behind. Charlie had told him not to put his feet on the floor as it wasn't strong enough to hold him—it only had fabric under the lining and he could fall right through. The poor fellow had his feet wrapped like claws around the two steel pipes that were the fuselage frame. When he got out to walk his feet had cramped into position and he had difficulty straightening them.

Charles said he thought maybe he had overloaded the plane just a little. He admitted to having a lot of trouble climbing up to 1000 feet to clear the mountain range. At one stage the plane was so low to the top of the cliff that the ringers could've jumped off the struts and run along beside it.

Of course by the time the ringers went back to town all they could talk about was their ride on the wings of Charlie's aeroplane, and how they had a great time! For many months afterwards every stockman Charles went to pick up asked if he could sit on the struts.

We eventually sold WOO back to the makers, Piper Aircraft. They were launching their latest model in Perth and wanted an early model to sit side by side with the new plane. They found out about WOO up in the wilderness and offered Charlie a price he couldn't refuse. So she was sold.

The pilot had to fly her almost non-stop to get to Perth on time for the champagne launch party. The timing was so close that he taxied up to the party straight after touchdown and was just in time for the new plane's unveiling. Flashbulbs popped as he stopped the propeller. If WOO had had any engine trouble at all he wouldn't have made the ceremony. But she didn't miss a beat, all the way to Perth.

Near the end of Charlie's flying career, after having one of his regular flight physicals, he received a letter from the Department of Aviation telling him that his licence was to be suspended because he had failed the eye test. Charlie told them he could fly with his eyes closed, but this didn't impress them in the least. He also told them he had flown thousands of hours in the night anyway, and had always managed to get back to the ship during the war, so he didn't need to see. But they still suspended his licence. So it was war as far as Charlie was concerned and he had a wonderful time during the tribunal proving there was nothing wrong with his eyesight.

Somehow he managed to convince the panel and his licence was reinstated. I think Charlie was secretly disappointed when the tribunal was over—he had certainly enjoyed being the centre of attention and would have loved to debate for many more months.

But this victory really didn't change the fact that Charlie's eyes were bad and were continuing to deteriorate. He never actually let on just how bad they were, and I have no idea how he passed the eye tests. He must have memorised all the lines because there was no way he could have read them, even the largest of the letters.

I found out the condition of his eyes when waiting one night for him to appear in the sky. It was after last light as usual, and I sat with the torches, watching the sky and waiting to light the strip to guide him in.

I spotted the twinkling light a long way out, lower in the sky than the few evening stars that were just appearing. He was still on the other side of the Victoria River but had plenty of time to get in before dark and he didn't really need the lights to see the airstrip. As I waited for him to land I watched amazed as he flew straight over the house and strip and continued on up the valley. I watched then as he turned and flew down the valley, again past the house, and towards the Victoria River! I had no idea what he was doing but by now it was getting dark, so I went out onto the strip and put the lights in position. I also turned on the spotlights along the front of the house, which light up the pool. He came in again low, swooped down over the house, finally turned and lined up with the lights on the strip and landed.

I questioned him about his joyride around the valley for thirty minutes and he told me he was looking for the airstrip. At first I thought he was joking, but soon realised he was serious. He told me that if he was any higher than forty feet when it was cloudy or dark he couldn't see the ground features. When it was dark he could see the lights and these gave him a bearing. Just on last light or twilight was the worst time for him to see, so he flew around till the lights were put on the airstrip. This night the floodlights reflected on the water in the pool and was a good location marker for him.

I was horrified that he was flying around virtually blind; he said he was handling it well—in bright daylight he was okay, and after dark the lights on the airstrip were easy to see. It was only twilight that was difficult.

I suggested that one of the girls go with him to be his eyes. He surprised me by agreeing. At first the girls were in complete agreement—it meant that they could fly and also they thought they would get out of the hard station work and school—and going to Darwin meant all the 'goodies' like ice cream, chocolate, etc. But they soon found out there were also many drawbacks to flying with Father. He would make them fly all the time; this they loved, but on the ground he made them his gofer on a very large scale. So much so that after only a few weeks the thrill of buying ice cream and chocolate milkshakes didn't seem worth all the work of constantly running messages, shopping for parts, loading and unloading the plane. One morning I found them drawing straws, not for the winner to go to town with Daddy, but the loser.

On one occasion Charles had to fly to a station on the other side of the Territory, near the Queensland border. It was a long flight and over country he was not familiar with, so I insisted that one of the older girls go with him, to do some flying and to locate landmarks.

Bonnie drew the short straw and off she went. Charlie would read most of the time when flying and Bonnie wasn't much better, so they both climbed in to the Super Cub with a book tucked under their arm.

They left at very first light and didn't land till last, last light. At dinner they entertained us with the happenings of the day …

Charles set the course and handed the controls over to Bonnie. Then he opened his book and settled down to read. Bonnie followed suit. Every now and then they would check their heading then resume their reading. When the flying time to their destination was up they looked out the window and weren't too surprised to see that the airstrip wasn't there. They flew around for a while, Bonnie trying to identify any landmark near the airstrip, but having no luck. Charles then realised that the wind was much stronger than he had thought and that they were a fair way off course.

After flying for a while, he came across a road and they started to follow it. After many more miles Bonnie spotted a signpost ahead and told her father. He said he would swoop down past it and Bonnie was to read what it said. So he did a magnificent dive bombing run on the poor old signpost and pulled up into a steep climb, then levelled out and asked Bon, 'Okay, what did it say?'

'Toilets,' she replied drily.

Ignoring her sarcasm he said, 'Well, there must be a town around here somewhere if there are toilets. Look for it!' And he started to fly down the road.

When Bonnie told him he was going the wrong way, and that the buildings were in the other direction, he executed a sharp bank and landed on the road and taxied up to the most impressive building of the group, the pub. Charles told Bonnie to go in and buy a sixpack of beer and while she was there find out where they were. She did. They were about sixty miles off course. Charles put the book away and concentrated on flying the plane. With the aid of Bonnie's eyes he was able to locate the right strip and land.

I find it interesting that all our planes that had character, are now living nice lives. Snoopy was taken from her untimely end up against a tree, was lovingly restored to her former glory and appeared on the front cover of *Aviation* magazine a few years later.

WOO lives on a sheep station outside Geraldton, has her own hangar, is no longer tied down out on the flat, in the wind and the rain. She is doing what she loved the most, whooshing around the skies, mustering.

And of course Bertha has it made!

In July 1983 Charles bought the sailing boat, the *Mary Blair* and did very little flying after that—the main reason being his eyes had deteriorated badly. After his success at the tribunal it was stipulated he must have an eye test every six months. However, very soon his eyes were so bad the eye examiner couldn't pass him any more.

Charles had two eye operations in 1984, six months apart. They were very successful and his eyesight improved so much his licence was reinstated on the 9th May 1985.

There were no entries in his pilot's logbook after that date. It doesn't mean that Charlie didn't fly, it only means he didn't bother to log his hours. He was no longer interested in adding to the already thousands of hours he had accumulated over his lifetime.

Well, it's mid-way through the month and I must finish this book. Again, there are so many things happening in my life. Again, the door to opportunity is open.

I still have years of work in front of me, but that is nothing.

I have my health, so I can still work hard, plus look forward to a little fun soon.

I am loved by my family, so I am fortunate. I have true friends; these are rare possessions. I am working towards having a few spare dollars in the bank, so I do not have to do a budget revision every week. For once I can actually see a light at the end of this tunnel!

July 1993

Bullo continues to progress and is starting to twinkle just like the vision Charlie had all those years ago when he stood in this isolated valley and said, 'Some day you will see top quality cattle grazing on improved pastures for as far as the eye can see. Mark my words.'

We are getting there Charlie … We ARE getting there!

Epilogue

Today is my thirty-third wedding anniversary. I should find it strange to be finishing the book on this day, but over these last seven years I have come to accept the strangest of things as normal. It's as if Charlie is still making events happen at a fast clip.

He affected everyone he met—sometimes for the worst, sometimes for the better. My life he put in a blender thirty-three years ago and pressed the 'high' button. The machine was turned off seven years ago, but I'm still recovering from that whirl. When I look back over the twenty-six years with him, I realise I survived him longer than anyone else, including his mother and his first wife.

He went away to school at an early age, then to university, then to war and business in the Far East. His first thirty-nine years were divided among all this, with no one in his life for the whole time.

My record is twenty-six years straight.

There was some happiness and joy in our relationship, but mostly it was emotional upset, panic, argument and disappointment. He had such complete control over my life that even now I know he is still around, influencing things around me. I worried about this up to a few years ago, when I told him to cut the strings and let me lead my own life. And in these last few years I feel he has done this, but has also stayed around—to help. He has the advantage of knowing what is ahead, and is lighting the right paths for me, showing me the way. He is making up for all the years of misery he caused me. He is dealing with enemies, watching, protecting, and creating a charmed life for me. I could be wrong about this, but it is a good feeling to have.

So again in closing, I will say to Charlie:

'Our partnership is now perfect, *you stupid son of a bitch, Yankee bastard!* Why couldn't you get it right the first time around!'